EDUCATION IN A GLOBAL SPACE

Research and Practice in Initial Teacher Education

Editors: TLK Wisely, IM Barr, A Britton and B King

Although this volume is being published by IDEAS, the contents do not necessarily reflect the views of IDEAS members or the Editorial Group. Similarly, although this volume is funded, through the IDEAS 'Taking a Global Approach to Initial Teacher Education' project, by UKaid from the Department for International Development, the views expressed do not necessarily reflect the department's official policies. Responsibility for any errors within the text lies with the Editorial Group.

IDEAS, the International Development Education Association Scotland, is a registered Scottish charity (no. SC031583) and a Scottish company limited by guarantee (no. 265641). Contact through **ideas@ideas-forum.org.uk**

Published for IDEAS by Scotdec, 3 Stafford Street, Edinburgh EH3 7AU
A catalogue record for this book is available from The British Library
ISBN 978-1-899136-16-2

Book design: www.contextdesigns.co.uk
Printed on recycled stock using vegetable inks.

Contents

FOREWORD

THIS PUBLICATION AROSE from the 'Taking a Global Approach to Initial Teacher Education' project which was devised and managed by the IDEAS network and funded by the UK Department for International Development (DfID). The project grew from IDEAS members' work with teacher educators over many years. More information on this project can be found at **www.global-approach.org.uk**

IDEAS, the International Development Education Association of Scotland, is a network of organisations across Scotland that actively support and promote Education for Global Citizenship and Sustainable Development. Members include NGOs working in areas such as international development, global poverty, sustainable development, social justice, and citizenship, and locally based Development Education Centres (DECs). The DECs provide practical teacher support through continuing professional development and innovative learning and teaching projects. IDEAS members collaborate to work at a national level, speaking to government, universities, local authorities and other key agencies across Scotland. More information on IDEAS can be found at **www.ideas-forum.org.uk**

IDEAS sees Education for Global Citizenship and Sustainable Development (EGCSD) as an active learning process that aims to:
• enable people to understand the links between their own lives and those of people throughout the world
• increase understanding of the economic, social, political and environmental forces that shape our lives
• develop skills, attitudes and values that enable people to work together to bring about change and take control of their own lives
• contribute to the development of a more just and sustainable world, in which power and resources are more equitably shared.

Initial Teacher Education (ITE) has a critical function in helping prepare teachers for their demanding professional responsibilities. This publication offers an array of perspectives on ITE with a global outlook. IDEAS' view of EGCSD is offered here in the same spirit as the publication itself, not to provide definitive answers but to promote a continuing process of engagement, reflection, discussion and action around global learning in ITE.

Global Citizenship and Sustainable Development: Transformation in the Initial Education of Teachers

Rosalyn McKeown, Secretariat of UNESCO International Network on Teacher Education
Charles Hopkins, UNESCO Chair in Reorienting Teacher Education towards Sustainability

THE INITIAL PREPARATION OF TEACHERS is a complex proposition. In many regions of the world, state, provincial, or national governments prescribe components of pre-service teacher education programmes through teacher certification standards. These standards include a wide variety of concepts and dispositions that new teachers should master during their preparation programmes. The standards outline topics such as knowledge of subject area, physical and cognitive human development, instructional techniques, classroom management, multiculturalism, etc. Some programmes also include dispositions (e.g., respect for diversity, compassion, and fairness). The list is long – often longer than teacher educators feel they can incorporate in a one-year post-graduate programme.

Teacher education has evolved and incrementally changed over the years with regular or periodic revisions of provincial or national teacher certification standards. As the frequency of international exchange (i.e. globalisation) increases and the pace of change increases, there are those amongst the education community who foresee a major change in education systems and correspondingly in the initial preparation of teachers. This change in the initial preparation of teachers will involve paradigm as well as praxis. As a learning community of teacher educators we will have the opportunity to examine all aspects of teacher education. Such examination will lead us to deal with profound questions like the relationships among teachers and learners to the purpose of teaching.

Quality and Transformation

As we read teacher certification guidelines we have the sense that they were written to create 'quality' teachers, although quality is seldom stated as the over-arching mandate. The concept of quality is important. We know that teachers of quality help students score better on tests and to achieve more in the subsequent years in school. Quality is an important goal; however, what was considered quality at the end of the 1900s seems to fall short in the context of the new millennium as our nations face the urgency of social, economic, and environmental problems at home and abroad.

Quality teaching that maintains the status quo of a world of social and economic inequity along with too rapid use of natural resources and abuse of ecosystems is no longer acceptable. Teacher educators around the world are questioning the concept of improving the quality of teachers who are arguably teaching for the wrong outcome—that is **development** rather than **sustainable development**. When surveyed, members of the International Network of teacher education institutions addressing sustainability 'repeatedly mentioned the urgency to act and the need for profound change' (UNESCO 2005, Executive Summary). Quality teaching that supports transformation to a more sustainable world is now of paramount importance.

When we speak of a more sustainable world we mean in terms of all three spheres of sustainable development—society, economy and the environment. Unfortunately, a misconception still exists that sustainable development and environmental conservation are synonymous. United Nations documents related to sustainability make it clear that social and economic issues are also at the heart of sustainability. In the educational community this translates to incorporating into the curriculum social justice issues as well as ecological and economics topics.

The goal of transformation or making a more sustainable world is taking on greater importance in teacher-education dialogue. Because our current libraries and knowledge bases do not include the solutions for living more sustainably on this planet, we, and especially the next generation will have to learn our way to such a future. In effect the leaders of today and tomorrow will have to transform the major systems in our world to be more sustainable. In parallel, the teachers of today and tomorrow will need to impart the knowledge, skills, values, and perspectives pupils will need to live in as well as transform the world they will inherit. Personally, we talk about the theme of transformation of education in general, or in teacher education specifically, as reorienting education to address sustainability.

Education for Global Citizenship and Sustainable Development

Every educator we know hopes that what they teach and how they teach it will lead to a better future. Given a choice between educating for a more sustainable world (e.g., characterised by social, environmental, and economic well-being) or for a less sustainable world (i.e., a place of social inequity, degraded environment, and large economic disparity) teachers choose the brighter future. One of the current educational paradigms for attaining that future is education for sustainable development (ESD). ESD takes many forms depending on local environmental, social, and economic contexts. In Scotland, Education for Global Citizenship (EGC) is a leading expression of ESD. EGC is noted for emphasising the social equity aspects of sustainability.

The ESD paradigm is considered so important that the General Assembly of the United Nations declared 2005 – 2014 the Decade of Education for Sustainable Development (UNDESD). What exactly is ESD? ESD has four basic thrusts:

1. Improving access to and retention in quality basic education
2. Reorienting education to address sustainability
3. Raising public awareness of sustainable development
4. Providing training for all sectors including public and private sectors of the economy, governments, and civil society (McKeown et al, 2002).

The first two thrusts speak primarily to formal education and the third and fourth thrusts to non-formal and informal education. Let us focus on the first two thrusts from a formal education perspective. The first two thrusts include both quality and transformation. Quality is an essential part of the first thrust and transformation (i.e., reorienting) of the second. By acknowledging the importance of both quality and transformation, it positions the field of teacher education to keep the best of what we currently know and practice in addition to working to create a more positive and sustainable future. It is only through social transformation that we will also improve environmental and economic conditions.

Quality

The concept of quality education is at the heart of every ministry of education and school board's deliberations. UNESCO addressed quality education as having two levels— individual and educational system (UNESCO 2004).

At the individual level the key aspects of quality education are that it:
1. Seeks out the learner
2. Acknowledges the learner's knowledge and experience
3. Makes content relevant
4. Uses many instructional and learning processes
5. Enhances the learning environment.

At the educational systems level the key aspects of quality education are that it:
6. Creates a legislative framework
7. Implements good policies
8. Builds administrative support and leadership
9. Requires sufficient resources
10. Measures learning outcomes.

Aspects 2 to 5 are related to classroom praxis and the domain of this book. 1 as well as 6 to 10 are more the domain of school administrators, governing boards of schools, and ministries of education.

The 2009 monitoring and evaluation report of the UNDESD points out that ESD practice is more frequent and developed than educational policy. This indicates that the key aspects 2 to 5 of quality education related to ESD are ahead of the second five (i.e. 6 to10).

The good news about balancing quality and transformation is that it gives us a reason to keep the best of praxis and to build on it in new ways. We are not 'throwing the baby out with the bathwater', but are saving the best. The difficult thing about saving the best is that it is difficult to weed out and throw away things that have been traditionally successful but will not meet the needs of the future. We have a Canadian colleague who was charged with revising a provincial science curriculum. He put together a well-balanced advisory group. He said that every member came with ideas about what to add to the curriculum, but no one had a suggestion what to remove. If we do not balance subtractions with additions, we 'pack' the curriculum with more than can be reasonably taught. We as teacher educators and staff of ministries of education have to be courageous in adding to and subtracting from the teacher certification standards and curriculum.

Transformation

What does it mean to transform education to address sustainability? Stephen Sterling (2001) has some excellent answers. He compares a mechanistic view of traditional education with what he calls an ecological view of education. Sterling examines three levels of schooling – core values, organisation and management of the learning environment, as well as learning and pedagogy. We are going to highlight part of the third level here because it is germane to praxis, which pre-service teachers have both a need and a desire to learn and master.

Table 1. Sterling's view of teaching and learning

MECHANISTIC VIEW	ECOLOGICAL VIEW
Transmission	Transformation
Product oriented	Process, development and action oriented
Emphasis on teaching	Integrative view: teachers also learners, learners also teachers
Functional competence	Functional, critical and creative competencies valued

Shifting from the column on the left to the column on the right is a large challenge for pre-service teachers and for the teacher educators who supervise their practice teaching. It is difficult to be a student teacher/intern who holds an ecological view of education in a traditional school. Student teachers experience a tension between fitting in and becoming the teacher they desire to be as well as simultaneously being a teacher and a learner (Britzman, 2003). If the cooperating teacher operates from the left column, and the student teacher desires to operate from the right column, frustration usually results. Student teachers often look to their university supervisors and faculty members, who embrace the ecological paradigm, for support. While the faculty can provide academic and emotional support, their influence at the schools is often limited. Supervising teacher-educators in many primary and secondary schools are considered 'guests' and, in some cases, too far removed from the classroom to have much credibility. Under these conditions it is difficult to create a quality, future-oriented teaching experience for student teachers. Student teacher placement in schools and with cooperating teachers who accept ESD or an ecological view of education are important to the success of pre-service teachers.

As we think about transformation as a theme for teacher education, we would be wise to have dialogues with our colleagues about whether we consider transformation as a goal, transformation as a mechanism for change, or transformation as both. The resulting conversations may be wonderfully insightful.

Overarching Frameworks

One of the major tensions within faculties of education between student and faculty members is the desire of the students to focus on praxis while the faculty promote understanding theory and research-based literature, and good practices. The students plead their case stressing the urgency that they feel to rapidly improve classroom praxis, 'I have to teach on Thursday.' While faculty acknowledge the urgency, their timeline is longer, hoping to help these new educators to develop the knowledge and skills to grow as professionals throughout their entire careers.

Besides classroom praxis, teacher educators also feel it is important to discuss issues of social significance as well as discuss the profound question of 'why do we teach?' The answer to 'why do we teach what we teach?' differs with perspective. Zeichner (2009) advocates social justice, others emphasise multiculturalism. We both advocate sustainability as the major theme for teacher education.

Given that sustainable development is the current paradigm of the United Kingdom and the United Nations for discussion concerning the resolution of major world problems— poverty, environmental degradation, and social inequity, it seems obvious that education for sustainable development should be the major paradigm for the educational community. It is important that our university graduates understand sustainability so that they can join the international discourse and work cooperatively in the closely interconnected world of the new millennium.

The sustainability paradigm is used by nations around the world to envision a future in which environmental, societal, and economic considerations are balanced in the pursuit of development and quality of life. The sustainability paradigm is a large switch from the perspective that economic development with casualties in the environmental and social realms is inevitable and acceptable.

Also, in Europe and North America there is currently a great desire to live 'greener' and more sustainably on a practical day-to-day basis. Voters are encouraging legislators/ parliamentarians to develop the political will to handle major problems like climate change. Our teacher-education programmes need to keep pace with large social tends and reflect these desires. If we do not address these trends, what we offer in our teacher-preparation programmes will be seen as irrelevant. As you recall, making content relevant is a key aspect of quality education.

Recommendations for ESD and Teacher Education

The need to make teacher education programmes relevant and meet the needs of pre-service teachers is crucial. Research shows us excellent ways to reorient teacher education to include global citizenship and sustainability concerns. The International Network (IN) of teacher-education institutions associated with the UNESCO Chair on Reorienting Teacher Education to Address Sustainability carried out action research at their home institutions. Each member of the IN worked within her/his sphere of influence to change programmes, practices, and policies. After 3 years the Chair and Secretariat surveyed the IN for their experiences and asked for recommendations. The following are the seven of the ten recommendations concerning pre-service and in-service teacher-education programmes:

1. Require interdisciplinary coursework on sustainability for student teachers and make materials available for student teachers on local and global sustainability.
2. Demonstrate pedagogical techniques that foster higher-order thinking skills, support decision-making, involve participatory learning, and stimulate formulation of questions.
3. Emphasise to student teachers that citizenry in a sustainable community requires active participation and decision-making; challenge them to create ways to incorporate participation and decision making into their classroom procedure and curriculum.
4. Discuss social equity (e.g., gender, racial, ethnic, and generational) with student teachers and identify ways in which the local community exhibits social tolerance, societal intolerance, equity, and discrimination.
5. Request that student teachers analyse the mandated curriculum they will be teaching to identify topics and themes related to sustainability and those that are linked to local sustainability issues.
6. Provide student teachers with opportunities to explore their own values and attitudes towards local sustainability problems and those of the surrounding region.
7. Promote understanding of global sustainability in order to encourage critical thinking and decision making that influence personal lifestyle and economic choices. (UNESCO 2005)

While not all of these recommendations are within the grasp of teacher-educators, some of them are. We especially like number 2, 'Demonstrate pedagogical techniques that foster higher-order thinking skills, support decision-making, involve participatory learning, and stimulate formulation of questions.' For those of use who teach 'methods' courses or supervise field experiences, it is within our domain to help student teachers develop the skills to implement student-centered instructional methods that stimulate participatory learning.

Sustainability Issue Analysis

Students today come to school with broad exposure to media. This media puts them in contact with people outside of their neighbourhoods and around the world. It exposes them to excessive wealth and grinding poverty as well as many inequities in the world. They hear seemingly contradictory facts, such as the world has never been wealthier and yet more than a billion people around the world live on less than one US dollar per day. Students arrive in our classrooms with the knowledge that something is not right in their community and the communities around the world; but rarely do they have a complete picture of what is wrong. This is not surprising as the media of today delivers news in sound bites and short blogs. Students have a difficult time piecing together facts to support their opinions. Teachers with sustainability issues analysis skills and instructional strategies can help the students more clearly understand complex issues.

In previous decades, we, as teachers, were taught to smooth controversy in the classroom and not to waste valuable class time enmeshed in contentious topics that had no clear solutions. Such attitudes no longer serve our society. Our students, as they assume positions of leadership and as voters, will have to deal with complex issues that have no apparent answers. They will have to learn their way forward. We must give them the tools and frameworks for thinking that help them untangle the complexities of sustainability issues and create solutions that are locally appropriate while being mindful of global consequences (e.g., cleaning up local pollution without shipping toxic and hazardous waste to another country). Having sustainability issues analysis skills and implementing them in ways that are student-centered and highly participatory may be the hallmark of a professional who teaches for both quality and transformation.

Several good issue analysis frameworks appear in the literature. The Clark (2000) model for demystifying issues is based on four questions:
(1) What is the issue about?
(2) What are the arguments?
(3) What is assumed?
(4) How are the arguments manipulated?

The Ramsey, Hungerford, and Volk (1998) issue investigation model has four stages:
(1) Science foundation
(2) Issue awareness
(3) Issue investigation
(4) Citizenship action.

McKeown and Dendinger (2008) published a framework for teaching, learning, and assessing environmental issues:
(1) What are the main historical and current causes (i.e. physical/biotic, social/cultural, or economic) of the issue?
(2) What are the geographic scale, the spatial distribution, and the longevity of the issue?
(3) What are the major risks and consequences to the natural environment?
(4) What are the major risks and the consequences to human systems?
(5) What are the economic implications?
(6) What are the major currently implemented or proposed solutions?
(7) What are the obstacles to these solutions?
(8) What major social values (e.g. economic, ecological, political, aesthetic) are involved in or infringed on by these solutions?
(9) What group(s) of people would be adversely impacted by or bear the cost of these solutions?
(10) What is the political status of the problem and solutions?
(11) How is this environmental issue related to other issues?
(12) What is a change you can make or have made in your daily life to lessen the issue?
(13) Beyond changes in your daily life, what is the next step you could take to address the issue?

Issue analysis will help teachers and students to confront misinformation and misconceptions that silently exist in our society and go unchallenged. For example, there is a misconception that internet connectivity has united people around the world. This may be true of those who are wealthy enough to have access to internet service, yet the statement ignores the existence of a digital divide, which is very real to low income countries and people in poverty. Misinformation and misconceptions hide inequities in the world, which ideally we would work to resolve in a more sustainable society.

Issue analysis skills that adolescents learn in school will give them abilities for a lifetime, which will benefit their community, nation, and world. Such skills will act as a check and balance to governments, corporations, or other entities which 'spin' or 'green wash' information to appear better to the general population.

Teaching, the Ultimate Sustainability Profession

Victor Nolet of Western Washington University in the USA believes that teaching is the 'ultimate green profession.' We like this perception of teaching in the new millennium. We have often thought teaching is a noble profession; however, in today's society, noble needs to be combined with a sense of urgency. With the prognostication that we only have 20 to 30 years to transform our societies and our interactions with nature's ecosystems or else the Earth's natural systems will be irreparably damaged, the role of this generation of educators is pivotal. It is our job as teacher educators to create a cadre of new professionals who have the knowledge, skills, perspectives, and values to transform primary and secondary education and to create classrooms that graduate students with the knowledge, ability, and inspiration to create a better world.

The road to such teacher education is not well marked. We cannot afford to be complacent and let someone else figure out how to accomplish our goal and then follow their path at a later date. We all have the responsibility to try something new and share the results with others. We have the opportunity to join a learning community of teacher educators around the world who are struggling with the same questions in their own countries. Sharing of lessons learned will be important to our progress in changing the initial preparation of teachers and redirecting the current trajectory of the future of our planet.

References

Britzman, D.P. (2003) Practice Makes Practice: *A Critical Study of Learning to Teach*, (revised ed.). Albany: State University of New York Press.

Clark, P. (2000) 'Teaching Controversial Issues,' *Green Teacher*, Vol. 62.

Ramsey, J M., Hungerford, H.R. and Volk, T.L. (1998) 'A Technique for Analyzing Environmental Issues,' in *Essential Reading in Environmental Education*. Champaign, IL: Stipes Publishing L.L.C.

McKeown-Ice, R., & Dendinger, R. (2008) Teaching, learning, and assessing environmental issues. *Journal of Geography*, 107, 161 – 166.

McKeown, R. with Hopkins, C. Rizzi, R., and Chrystalbridge, M. (2002) *Education for Sustainable Development Toolkit, version 2*. Knoxville: University of Tennessee, Waste Management Research and Education Institute. Online at http://www.esdtoolkit. org. (accessed 14/06/10)

Sterling, S. (2001) *Sustainable education: Revisioning learning and change*. Schumacher Briefings no. 6. Devon: Green Books, Ltd.

UNESCO. (2004) *Quality Education and HIV/AIDS*. Paris: UNESCO.

UNESCO. (2005) *Guidelines and recommendation for reorienting teacher education to address sustainability. Education for Sustainable Development in Action Technical Paper*, no. 2. Paris: UNESCO. Online at http://unesdoc.unesco.org/ images/0014/001433/143370E.pdf in 6 UN languages (accessed 14/06/10).

Zeichner, K. (2009). *Teacher Education and the Struggle for Social Justice*. New York: Routledge.

Education in a Global Space: Emerging Research and Practice in Initial Teacher Education

The Editors

'The trouble with our times is that the future is not what it used to be.' Paul Valery

THE TITLE OF THIS PUBLICATION, *Education in a Global Space*, was chosen to encompass a range of perspectives on the connection between teacher education and development, citizenship, environmental and sustainable development education. Our preferred, but by no means definitive, collective formulation for these perspectives is Education for Global Citizenship and Sustainable Development. What these perspectives have in common is the belief that schooling must acquire a more outward looking view of the world, a global view. They are perspectives that apply both within and across subject disciplines. It is hoped the contribution made by this volume will be to encourage teacher educators, teachers and student teachers to become critically reflective of the ways in which the world's increasing connectedness impinges on personal behaviours, life styles and social structures, to consider how that might impact on the nature of learning and, thus, on the nature of teacher education.

The subheading, *Emerging Research and Practice in Initial Teacher Education*, is intended to underline that this is not a volume offering findings from a well-established field of inquiry, at least within a Scottish initial teacher education context, but rather the presentation of an emergent field where different lineages and approaches are presented, as research papers, as opinion pieces, as exploratory studies and initial reports. It is essentially an attempt to facilitate a two-way knowledge-transfer process across the statutory/voluntary sector interface. It brings together the understandings of a wide range of interests including those of higher education institutions, professional bodies, non-governmental organisations, international authorities and individuals in a way that we hope will help stimulate and further develop research, policy and practice on issues that are seen increasingly as central to the education of young people. The book is divided into three main sections. The first, 'Framing the Global', deals with the conceptualisation of Education for Global Citizenship and Sustainable Development (EGCSD) and the context in which it is evolving, both in Scotland and internationally. The second, 'Surveying Attitudes towards the Global', examines perceptions of EGCSD among student teachers, teacher educators and practising teachers. The third, 'Enacting the Global through Pedagogy', offers a range of perspectives on and examples of the active participatory pedagogies at the heart of EGCSD. Each section begins with a brief introduction to the overall nature of the chapters included and summary information on individual chapters. These section introductions should be used as signposts to approaching the book. As the publication editors, we have compiled this introduction, the section introductions and the final concluding chapter.

The need for change in the ways in which we represent the school curriculum, and, by implication, the ways in which Initial Teacher Education (ITE) is organised, is increasingly recognised. The nature of a world more culturally and economically connected, and one in which collaboration across traditional academic disciplines gives rise to new fusions of knowledge and understandings, requires that we equip teachers and their students to teach and learn in ways that recognise this 'connectedness'.

At the same time, the ability and commitment of this 'interconnected' world to address issues of global inequity and the impacts of biodiversity loss and climate change remains open to question. McKeown and Hopkins, state in their preface to this volume that, 'teaching that maintains the status quo of a world of social and economic inequity along with too rapid use of natural resources and abuse of ecosystems is no longer acceptable'. They argue that since 'our current libraries and knowledge bases do not include the solutions for living more sustainably on this planet, we, and especially the next generation, will have to learn our way to such a future'. Again, this will require open, collaborative work that acknowledges uncertainties.

But implementing new models of collaborative practice is challenging at the best of times. In less propitious circumstances they become even more daunting, and we live in difficult times. The emerging era of austerity will challenge all publicly funded institutions, not least teacher education institutions. The temptation to shift towards potentially lower-cost models of teacher education may be politically appealing. Such models, whether conceived as having a diminished input from higher education institutions, a corresponding increase in placement or apprenticeship models, or in greater use of technology for tutor/ student interactions, have the potential to threaten both the quality and the criticality of beginning teachers. Furthermore, by their nature, austerity measures tend to promote an inflective and insular turn within systems, including education. In the dynamic and complex global space that we now inhabit, the need is greater than ever for a globally informed criticality, although it is somewhat neglected in statements around the essential qualities of contemporary teachers.

At the same time as politicians grapple with the need for greater cost effectiveness, they make the case for a school curriculum that is better tuned to the needs of the 21st century; more relevant, futures orientated and 'joined-up'. Increasingly, these are seen as characteristics of a curriculum more likely to equip young people for the challenges of a rapidly changing society. In Scotland, the introduction of *Curriculum for Excellence* (CfE) with its overarching aims of helping all young people become successful learners, confident individuals, responsible citizens and effective contributors is a bold expression of the need to renovate thinking and practice in schools. To achieve such changes in a time of national, institutional and professional insecurity will be hard, but in a sense the circumstances that have brought us to this time merely serve to emphasise how urgent the need for change is.

In moving to these new, broader goals much emphasis has been placed on the need for teachers to think outside the traditional subject and discipline boxes. This manifests itself either in the creation of new 'subjects' or in a broad exhortation to existing subjects and disciplines to embrace cross-cutting themes and cross-disciplinary strategies. It makes it necessary for all teachers to be reflective and outward looking. The challenge for initial teacher education, in a time of change and uncertainty, is to develop programmes that prepare student teachers to operate effectively within such a curricular context, where the importance attached to education for global citizenship and sustainable development may be as great as that given to the subjects that define many teachers' perceptions of their professional competence.

In the past, development educators and environmentalists knocked on the doors of policy makers seeking the merest acknowledgement of the validity of their concerns. Usually, the political response was less than fulsome. Now we see the coming of age of these very issues, of education for citizenship, sustainability and other diversity issues. They now appear as core components of the new curricula for the 21st century. But what are governments' purposes? Do global economics provide an adequate overarching framing for education for global citizenship and sustainable development? Or is there a broader, moral imperative that gives recognition to these matters? How might they impact on the nature of teaching, on schools and pupils, and on communities? This volume hopes to play a small part in raising awareness of these issues across the community of teacher educators and teachers.

Framing a curriculum in terms that challenge the traditional subject expertise of many teachers and teacher educators, even when well founded, is a bold step. Understandable preoccupations with content coverage, intellectual legitimacy, coupled with a lack of time and resources to explore issues in depth all get in the way of devising ITE experiences that adequately address student teachers' need to deal with ideas and issues from outside subject disciplines. But it is crucial to recognise that the bodies of knowledge of all subjects and disciplines are now advanced within global parameters, whether it be chemistry or physical education, language or mathematics. It must follow that a similar impact ought to occur in teaching. Such things as information literacy, critical thinking skills, collaborative problem solving, 'connected learning', while a challenge to traditional views of teaching, also provide exciting opportunities to discover and develop new and more effective pedagogies.

The idea of curriculum is complex. It is at one and the same time a theory of content, a construction of knowledge, a mediated expression of what society 'believes' in, a set of classroom processes experienced by learners. The differences between the curriculum as espoused by government, planned by schools, enacted by teachers and experienced by learners are well recognised and significant. How might this idea find its best expression in the early 21st century? Superficially there may be attraction in a curriculum that more adequately recognises the importance of the global dimension of learning. But terms such as education for global citizenship and education for sustainable development, are not unproblematic, they can be driven by opaque political intentions and sometimes by ideological fervour rather than intellectual rigour and epistemological clarity. This book aims to provide a broad and inclusive view that gives equal weight to the theoretical, practical and moral dimensions of the craft of teaching about the global dimension.

Recognition and thanks must be given to the UK Government's Department for International Development (DFID) for providing the funding that enabled the three year project 'Taking a Global Approach to Initial Teacher Education' from which this volume emerged. The funding came through DFID's Development Awareness Fund which has played a vital role in building public understanding of the issues around the UK Government's commitment to the Millennium Development Goals (MDGs), the international targets agreed by the United Nations (UN) to halve world poverty by 2015.

The 'Taking a Global Approach to Initial Teacher Education' project was developed and managed by the IDEAS[1] network, an umbrella group of organisations working in Education for Global Citizenship and Sustainable Development across Scotland. The project fostered a unique collaboration among all seven Scottish universities with ITE responsibilities and IDEAS members. As well as broadening teacher educators' engagement with and understanding of the rationale and focus of education for global citizenship and sustainable development, this initiative has cultivated the emergent body of research and practice described in this publication. IDEAS is currently working to ensure that this field of enquiry moves forward from its emergent status to become a sustained and integral focus of initial teacher education and education research in Scotland and that the established network

[1] The International Development Education Association of Scotland

of teacher educators continues to grow. More information can be found on at the website **www.global-approach.org.uk** IDEAS has been working in the schools and community sector in Scotland for many years. The time is also ripe for links between ITE and these sectors to be developed, particularly with the renewed emphasis on partnership working.

Although this volume is being published by IDEAS, the contents do not necessarily reflect the views of IDEAS members or the Editorial Group. Similarly, although funded, through the 'Taking a Global Approach to Initial Teacher Education' project, by UKaid from the Department for International Development, the views expressed do not necessarily reflect the department's official policies. Responsibility for any errors within the text lies with the Editorial Group.

FRAMING THE GLOBAL

FRAMING THE GLOBAL

2.1 Section Introduction

THE CHAPTERS IN THIS SECTION are concerned with the ways in which Education for Global Citizenship and Sustainable Development (EGCSD) has been conceptualised, supported and implemented. It opens with a chapter in which Priestley, Biesta, Mannion and Ross consider the evolving, distinctive nature of global citizenship and the issue of how it is to be defined. Tensions between social and political understandings of citizenship are discussed and they ask whether citizenship is an educational outcome or a social process. Shah and Brown (Chapter 2.3) highlight the fact that many of the major issues that global learning concerns itself with are contested and explore how putting critical thinking at the heart of global learning practice addresses this. In Chapter 2.4, Hamilton focuses on how the values and professional knowledge on which the General Teaching Council for Scotland's Standard for Initial Teacher Education is based relate to those of EGCSD. A detailed account of how one ITE programme has been reorganised to better attend to the global perspective is offered by Frame in Chapter 2.5. Her enlightening account reveals the many challenges inherent in this endeavour. Finally, in Chapter 2.6, Brown offers some thoughts on how the forthcoming Research Excellence Framework might affect the emergent field of EGCSD research.

In attempting to 'frame the global', it is important to recognise, too, that there is an increasingly coherent policy agenda surrounding EGCSD internationally through the United Nations, and at European, UK and Scottish levels. Because this is constantly shifting, a book is not the most appropriate vehicle for its dissemination. Up-to-date information on, for example, the UNESCO work on reorienting teacher education referenced in the Preface to this volume, on European Union commitments to supporting development education, on Scotland's commitments under the UN Decade for ESD, and on work in this area undertaken by the Higher Education Academy and the Scottish Funding Council can be found on the 'Taking a Global Approach to ITE' project website at **www.global-approach.org.uk**

Throughout the rest of this volume, other authors do, of course, touch on this policy context as it relates to their themes. The new curricular framework in Scotland, too, recurs as a reference point as there is an obvious and potentially beneficial synergy between EGCSD and *Curriculum for Excellence*, with respect to both content and pedagogy. Although specific to Scotland, the curricular shift it represents is, we believe, relevant and of interest beyond Scotland. The full range of documentation relating to CfE can be accessed at: **www.ltscotland.org.uk/curriculumforexcellence/index.asp**

As a final 'framing' context, it is worth also being aware that many other nations across the world have organisations similar to IDEAS, working to advocate EGCSD in its various forms. There are also other ITE networks around global learning. For example, two of the papers in this volume were first aired at the conference of the UK ITE ESD/GC Network, based in the Centre for Cross Curricular Initiatives at London South Bank University. Again, information on these organisations and networks can be found at www.global-approach.org.uk.

2.2 Education in a Global Space: The Framing of 'Education for Citizenship'

Mark Priestley, Gert Biesta, Greg Mannion, University of Stirling
and Hamish Ross, University of Edinburgh

OVER THE PAST DECADE, in many Western industrialised countries, there have been increasing calls for educational provision to develop a more global orientation. It is said that global citizenship education will equip children and young people with the knowledge, skills and dispositions that will make them more aware of, and more engaged with, global issues and phenomena. This surge of interest in global issues is driven in part by policy initiatives from the education departments of UK countries, the UK Department for International Development (DfID) and many non-governmental organisations (NGOs), and there are similar developments in other countries around the world. Nevertheless, the roots of such policies also lie in global discourses and the publications and pronouncements of transnational organisations such as the OECD. Thus, while differences exist within the various educational jurisdictions, including amongst those that comprise the UK, we suggest that the reach of this global curricular trend has been largely homogeneous within the UK and elsewhere, with strong alliances between policy makers, politicians, independent educational centres and NGOs (for example, Oxfam). Scotland is typical of such trends.

All of the above raises the issue of how we define global citizenship, which has become a fuzzy catch-all phrase, often ill-defined and poorly conceptualised. Attempts to more clearly define global citizenship invariably pose some important questions. The first of these is 'what is global about global citizenship?' Such policy seeks to bring together different traditions, which have quite different lineages: environmental and development education, and human rights and citizenship education. In this chapter we explore this process of convergence, and in doing so explore both the global origins and the global implications of such discourses. A second question concerns the relationship between global citizenship and citizenship per se. Here we might also ask what kind of notion of citizenship is assumed in or promoted by the idea of global citizenship? In addressing these latter questions, the chapter analyses a number of key dimensions of citizenship. These include the tensions between social and political conceptions of citizenship, and the relationship between citizenship as competence and social practice, as educational outcome or as social process.

Converging lineages: the roots of global citizenship

The insertion of 'education for global citizenship' (EGC) into mainstream national curricula is both interesting and problematic, because it brings together lineages of at least three sub-fields of education, namely, environmental education (EE), development education (DE) and citizenship education (CE). These educational traditions are widely differentiated, though each has a strong common critical or transformative function. Space here does not permit a full exploration. Instead our focus is to suggest that EGC is functioning as a point of convergence or a nodal point within official educational policy discourse. As a nodal point, EGC serves as a place of arrival of several strands of thinking which hitherto have struggled for mainstream formal curricular space, often being driven from outside formal education with support from NGOs and various forms of activism. Within this node, EGC on the one hand appears to allow diverse meanings to converge while subordinating some aspects of the constituent traditions. At the same time it is also creating distinctive new agendas or points of departure.

Lineage 1 – Environmental Education

'Nature study… fieldwork… conservation education… environmental education… global education (1980s version)… education for sustainable development (ESD) / education for sustainability (EfS)… global citizenship education?'

Palmer (1998) chronicles the shifts in environmental education (EE) from nature study, through fieldwork, urban studies, conservation education and into the period in the 1980s, when environmental education sought stronger links with development education in order to take cognizance of the political dimensions of environmental issues. Gough (2002) lists a number of key education texts from the 1980s growing out of the EE field that encouraged pedagogies based on 'thinking globally, acting locally' – knowing and caring about the global dimensions and significance of environmental problems and issues. After the 1992 Rio Summit, the action report, Agenda 21, called upon education to work towards sustainability by acknowledging the interlinked nature of economic, social and environmental issues. This, it was envisaged, would be best achieved by encouraging community participation, partnership working among agencies, systems thinking, and so on.

Reid (2002) suggests that education for sustainability might be regarded as the `offspring' of environmental education and development education, although Sauve (2005) recognizes at least 15 trends in EE, representing a very large diversity of models, of which ESD is but one. Sauve and Berryman (2005) have 'witnessed a rising tide of almost purely instrumental views' within EE as it became more globalized post-Agenda 21. EE is a highly attractive concept that is likely to appeal to even opposed interest groups (Bonnett, 2002; Stables & Scott, 2002) with attendant dangers, for example the potential for taken-for-granted assumptions that development implies a Western [neo-liberal] economic view. Stables and Scott (ibid.) caution that efforts to pin down sustainable development are challenging (with already slippery terms 'sustainable' and 'development' being coupled in this way).

Within EE, terms such as 'global' and the 'eco-citizen' have already been used in an effort to bring greater coalescence between DE and EE sometimes under EfS and ESD umbrellas. Gough and Scott (2006) provide examples of what they term a technocratic approach to solving the human-environment 'problematic' through an emphasis on the 'environmentally-responsible citizen'. Critics suggest that some calls for EE to widen its scope and enter a new paradigm in the UN Decade of Education for Sustainable Development are more like efforts to 'close a circle' (Sauve & Berryman, 2005). This potentially means the loss of the diverse approaches that characterized the tradition in its earlier radical form, through a desire for consensus around pre-ordained aims and technocratically measurable progress through quantifiable indicators. All of this 'essentially presents education as an instrument for the conservation of the environment, which is reduced to the status of resource for economic development, itself seen as an essential precondition and goal for social development' (ibid., 2005, p. 230). However, some socially critical approaches within the sub-field of EE are ready to accept a form of 'education for global citizenship' as a goal (Huckle, 1999), and pressure is mounting in policy circles to embed it in initial teacher education and schools' curricula internationally. Thus for EE, the arrival of EGC may on the one hand be yet another attempt to 'close the circle', or potentially, an attempt to use the construct of sustainability more strongly to 'extend citizens rights and responsibilities across time space and generations and species' (ibid., p. 39).

Lineage 2 – Development Education

'Third-world pedagogy… development education… global education… global citizenship education?'

Scheunpflug and Asbrand (2006) trace how 'Third-world pedagogy', 'development education' and, more recently, 'global education' have a clear historical lineage, with one approach leading on to the next. They assert that global education (GE):
'has established itself as an educational field which provides a 'pedagogical reaction to the developmental state of world society' working within the normative premise of overcoming inequality by being orientated towards a model of global justice …the aim of global education is to support the learners' development in terms of acquiring adequate competencies for life in a world society, preparing for an uncertain future and acquiring competencies to deal with complexity and uncertainty. (p. 35)'

As we have seen with EE (above), DE educators and theorists have also expressed their unease with 'sustainability' and worried over the possibility that social justice in third world countries might be diminished by an overly environmental focus. Scheunpflug and Asbrand (2006) suggest EfS needs the perspective of global education to bring worldwide issues of justice alongside the concerns of environmental education, and because sustainable environmental protection needs to take on board that we live in a complex globalised world. Despite these commonalities, the two fields (DE and EE) have maintained fairly distinct fields of practice, though some advance the view that EGC may be a nexus for their convergence.

As the DE field has become more professionalised and government-funded in the UK, it has become more obviously global. Indeed, 'global education' has virtually superseded DE as a term. In contrast, Hicks (2003) suggests a more nuanced nomenclature, with 'global education', 'global dimension' and 'global citizenship' working as a triad of constructs for all forms of the DE tradition. O'Loughlin and Wegimont (2007) suggest that global and development education, and awareness-raising on development issues has recently 'come in from the cold' because there is now a recognition that a global development agenda requires an informed and educated public in the developed world. This trend, supported by transnational initiatives such as the UN Decade of Education for Sustainable Development, for example, inspires Scotland to hope that 'by 2014 people in Scotland will have developed the knowledge, understanding, skills and values to live more sustainable lives' (Scottish Executive, 2006). Within this frame, DE (now 'global education') may be one small step away from accepting EGC as a keynote idea, affording more legitimacy to the field and greater policy leverage. But this approach may render DE less political, a view supported by Marshall (2005) who found NGO-based global education activists both welcomed the opportunities to come in from the margins and link with the higher-status citizenship education, and also worried that it might ghettoise DE and/or lead to a loss of its critical edge. A more reformist and activist notion is offered by Oxfam (1997), who see the global citizen as someone (among other things) who is 'outraged by social injustice' and 'is willing to act in order to make the world a more equitable and sustainable place'. The latter emphasis on the affective and political response to issues and events is reminiscent of more traditional NGO-led 'global education'.

Lineage 3 – Citizenship Education
'Civic education (modern studies)… citizenship education… education for citizenship… international education (and perhaps entrepreneurial education)… global citizenship education?'

Citizenship education rose to the surface of educational policy debates in England with the Crick Report (Advisory Group on Citizenship,1988) and various curricular reforms in the UK more widely. Citizenship has become strongly coupled with 'global' by those who wish to harness it as a response to globalisation and for those who wish to give education for citizenship (in Scotland, where it is not a 'subject') or 'citizenship education' (in England, where it is a subject area) contemporary relevance. Davies et al. (2005)

explore the differences between citizenship and global education. They suggest that such a coming together is timely with the demise of the welfare state and current perspectives on globalisation. According to such thinking, EGC would allow us to look beyond old barriers that have separated citizenship education and global education.

Within the field, different theories of citizenship (liberal, republican, cosmopolitan) provide starting points for ways of working towards justice, democracy and sustainability (see Huckle, 2008). Huckle argues for environmental and ecological citizenship. For the latter, because citizens' actions in the private as well as public sphere (through consumption for example) are seen to affect other people in far-flung places, we therefore have non-contractual, non-reciprocal and unilateral duties to others. By this view, new forms of EGC would require the individual citizen to see the private sphere as political.

This approach entails some risks. Firstly, the approach rests on the view that it is possible for individuals, through education, to come to 'reasonable agreement' or understanding about what needs to happen and who needs to do it, if they are to fairly respond in their context by, say, reducing their carbon footprint. Secondly, the risk is that ecological citizenship focuses more on the private sphere where folk are expected to privately and voluntarily 'do the right thing', while larger structures and processes potentially continue with 'business as usual'. Lastly, even if teachers were ready to take on a values-laden approach to citizenship, coming to understand what is 'the right thing' with students may be especially problematic when we need to juxtapose all competing perspectives. On the ground, Evans et al. (2009, p. 29) comment that within citizenship education and EGC, notions of social justice are less evident in teaching and learning practices related to beliefs and values. They also recognize, while offering a more comprehensive framing themselves, that EGC is often seen as a means to build 'a competitive workforce and contribute to the economic growth of the nation' [by] 'preparing students with the knowledge, skills and competencies required to compete in the global economy' (p. 23).

Lineages converge

The construct of lineage outlined above shows how each educational sub-field has made a curricular turn towards the global. This is captured best perhaps by the rhetorical policy slogan of 'education for global citizenship' as the current nodal point where the various discourses converge. We suggest that there is clear evidence in these three lineages of such a convergence in practice, but particularly in official educational policy circles. Rhetorically, the official turn seeks to bring three educational traditions together under one umbrella, using constructs such as the global dimension and education for global citizenship. As noted, as each of the three traditions potentially arrives and accepts or resists EGC, there are concerns, losses and new points of departure.

Foremost amongst these is a potential for ECG to be used to tacitly advance particularly western perspectives over other cultures' views. In supporting the view of globalisation as an already arrived entity and attempting to educate graduates and pupils to participate in the global market economy, it could be argued that the official take on the curricular global turn is, in fact, a localised feature of modern Western countries that perhaps seeks to transcend and occlude other alternative, local ('non-global' or anti-globalisation) perspectives. Jickling and Wals (2008) have earlier worried over a similar educational initiative (education for sustainable development), seeing its expression as part and parcel of 'the powerful wave of neo-liberalism rolling over the planet, with pleas for 'market solutions' to educational problems and universal quality-assurance schemes, [which] are homogenizing the educational landscape' (p. 2). While EGC may be offering a sincere and well-intentioned set of purposes for education, we need to look closer and more critically to see if it is functioning as an ideological concept that travels well, but is working (sometimes inadvertently, but sometimes deliberately) as a tool of Western modern imperialism; to homogenize and prescribe goals, thereby reducing 'the conceptual space for self-determination, autonomy, and alternative ways of thinking' (p. 4). Buying into this homogenization could mean that 'many educators have become agents in a trend towards economic globalization' (p. 6). The curricular turn towards the global may be offering a particularly western perspective on the world. It is interesting to note that the language in policy documents largely fails to foreground how they are located in a particular part of the world. Gough (2002) suggests that failing to acknowledge the 'global dimension' in education as a 'culturally shaped' representation of a reality 'is an imperialist act – an act of attempted intellectual colonization' (p. 1228). He goes on to ask 'how can we think globally without enacting some form of epistemological imperialism?' (ibid.). This critique reminds us to check whether our ethnocentric positioning prejudices our reading of the global curricular turn.

Dimensions of citizenship

Such reflexivity also raises questions about citizenship – notably the question of what sort of citizen should be developed by education systems. There are a number of key dimensions of citizenship that may be explored in this context, and which are highly relevant to the above discussion about the directions in which ECG is travelling.

One important issue concerns the distinction between a social and a political definition of citizenship. In the context of Scotland's *Curriculum for Excellence*, Biesta (2008) has argued that through notions like the 'responsible citizen', citizenship is mainly defined in social rather than political terms (i.e. doing good work in/for the community, where community itself is predominantly understood in terms of sameness). This is significant because social relationships within a context of sameness are distinctively different from political relationships – particularly if we read politics in terms of democratic politics – in that political relationships relate to plurality and difference, not sameness. Public policy on citizenship in many countries worldwide highlights a significant distinction between reasons that concern social integration and cohesion (and thus focus on the construction of communities of sameness) and reasons that relate to the democratic quality of governance (where the emphasis is more on how to live together in/with plurality and difference). In the first conception, citizenship tends to be seen as a social identity, whereas in the second it is a political identity. Biesta (2008, 2009) argues that the notion of citizenship that is predominant in Scottish education policy is characterised by functionalism (i.e. aimed at the creation of social integration through communities of sameness), individualism (i.e. citizenship is seen as a quality of individuals, they need to have the right set of dispositions (the notion of 'civic competence') and focused on consensus. Westheimer and Kahne (2004), indicate the (potential) problems with this social definition of citizenship:

'no one wants young people to lie, cheat, or steal … the visions of obedience and patriotism that are often and increasingly associated with this agenda can be at odds with democratic goals … even the widely accepted goals – fostering honesty, good neighborliness, and so on – are not inherently about democracy' … to the extent that emphasis on these character traits detracts from other important democratic priorities, it may actually hinder rather than make possible democratic participation and change. (p. 244; emphasis in original)'

To support their point, Westheimer and Kahne report on research that found that fewer than 32% of eligible voters between the ages of 18 and 24 voted in the 1996 United States of America presidential election, but that 'a whopping 94% of those aged 15-24 believed that 'the most important thing I can do as a citizen is to help others'' (ibid.). It is easy to draw the conclusion that 'youth seems to be 'learning' that citizenship does not require democratic governments, politics, and even collective endeavours' (ibid.).

A second issue concerns the emerging understanding of citizenship as a competence (i.e., as a set of skills and dispositions that individuals can possess) rather than as an ongoing practice, as something people do (see Biesta, 2009; Lawy & Biesta, 2006). The tendency in much educational policy literature is to see citizenship first of all as a competence. This then defines the task of citizenship education as that of fostering the acquisition/development of these competences (which is, for example, what is currently being developed at European level; in UK citizenship education this approach is known in terms of the acquisition of so-called 'citizenship dimensions'). Jickling and Wals (2008) see this approach as a deficit model of transmissive education of the citizen. This separation of process and outcome is problematic. If we think of citizenship as guaranteed by individuals with particular qualities, competencies or dimensions, then, at least educationally, citizenship becomes an outcome of an educational and/or developmental trajectory. If, on the other hand, we think of citizenship as something that constantly needs to be achieved (and this can never be guaranteed) then we need to emphasise the process character of citizenship. This has implications for education. In the outcome perspective, global education becomes the producer of global citizens; in the process perspective the first question to ask is whether citizenship practices are possible within schools and society more generally, and only then can we bring in education to ask what people learn from such practices, what they might learn, and how this learning might be supported and developed (see Biesta, 2010).

With regard to the idea of education for global citizenship there are, therefore, important questions to be asked about the kind of citizenship that is being promoted – and it may well be that the particular lineages that have prominence in particular contexts bring with them particular notions of citizenship, either more political or more social, either more individual or more collective, either more focused on the acquisition of competences for future citizenship or putting more emphasis on opportunities for civic action in the here and now.

Conclusion

In this chapter, we have noted the convergences in the lineages of environmental education, development education and citizenship education under the umbrella of global citizenship education. We have pointed to the role of EGC as rhetorical policy slogans that reorient three traditions to some of their own ends and to some new ones. We have commented on the manner in which this policy nexus brings NGOs, governments and international (economic) development together within a perspective on the world that is very much of its time and place in the west. This in turn demands a form of citizenship which is predicated on critical political activism, rather than upon social compliance. If we think of citizenship as something that constantly needs to be achieved (and this can never be guaranteed), then we need to emphasis the process character of citizenship.

Our genealogical analysis of EGC, combined with our reflections on the nature of citizenship, offers a fresh perspective for educational practitioners. More critical practices of EGC may serve to counter hegemonic views of globalisation and narrow social conceptions of citizenship. In the headlong rush to 'close the circle' (Sauve & Berryman, 2005) under the global citizenship umbrella, we would warn again the erasure of the rich tapestry of eco-socially critical approaches found in the lineages of EE, DE and CE.

References

Advisory Group on Citizenship (1988) *Education for citizenship and the teaching of democracy in schools* London: Qualifications and Curriculum Authority

Biesta, G.J.J. (2008) What kind of citizen? What kind of democracy? Citizenship education and the Scottish Curriculum for Excellence. *Scottish Educational Review*, 40(2), 38-52.

Biesta, G.J.J. (2009) What kind of citizenship for European Higher Education? Beyond the competent active citizen. *European Educational Research Journal*, 8(2), 146-157.

Biesta, G.J.J. (2010) How to exist politically and learn from it: Hannah Arendt and the problem of democratic education. *Teachers College Record*, 112(2), 558-577.

Bonnett, M. (2002) Education for Sustainability as a Frame of Mind. *Environmental Education Research*, 8(1), 265-276.

Davies, I., Evans, M. & Reid, A. (2005a). Globalising Citizenship Education? A Critique of 'Global Education' and 'Citizenship Education'. *British Journal of Educational Studies*, 53(1), 66-89.

Evans, M., Ingram, L. A., MacDonald, A. & Weber, N. (2009) Mapping the 'global dimension' of citizenship education in Canada: The complex interplay of theory, practice, and context. *Citizenship, Teaching and Learning*, 5(2), 16-34.

Gough, N. (2002) Thinking/acting locally/globally: Western science and environmental education in a global knowledge economy. *International Journal of Science Education*, 24(11), 1217-1237.

Gough, S. & Scott, W. (2006) Education and Sustainable Development: a political analysis, *Educational Review*, 58(3) 273-290.

Hicks, D. (2003) Thirty years of global education: a reminder of key principles and precedents. *Educational Review*, 55(3), 131-141.

Huckle, J. (1999) Locating environmental education between modern capitalism and postmodern socialism: a reply to Lucie Sauve'. Online at: http://cjee.lakeheadu.ca/index.php/cjee/article/viewFile/318/254 (accessed on 23/02/10).

Huckle, J. (2008) Sustainable Development. In J. Arthur, I. Davies, I. & C. Hahn, (eds.) *The Sage Handbook of Education for Citizenship and Democracy* (London: Sage Publications).

Jickling, B. & Wals, A.E.J. (2008) Globalization and environmental education: Looking beyond sustainability and sustainable development. *Journal of Curriculum Studies*, 40(1), 1-21.

Lawy, R.S. & Biesta, G.J.J. (2006). Citizenship-as-practice: the educational implications of an inclusive and relational understanding of citizenship. *British Journal of Educational Studies* 54(1), 34-50.

Marshall, H. (2005) Developing The Global Gaze In Citizenship Education: Exploring The Perspectives Of Global Education NGO Workers In England. *International Journal of Citizenship and Teacher Education*. Vol 1(2), 76-92.

Oxfam (1997) A Curriculum for Global Citizenship. Online at http://www.oxfam.org.uk/education/gc/files/education_for_global_citizenship_a_guide_for_schools.pdf (accessed 23/02/10).

O'Loughlin, E. & Wegimont, L. (2007) Global Education, Public Awareness- Raising and Campaigning on Development Issues: An Overview of Evaluation Practice and Policy. OECD:Bonn, 19-20 March 2007. Online at http://www.oecd.org/dataoecd/43/59/38405962.pdf (accessed 23/02/10).

Palmer, J. A. (1998). *Environmental Education in the 21st Century: Theory, Practice, Progress and Promise* (New York: Routledge).

Reid, A. (2002) Discussing the Possibility of Education for Sustainable Development. *Environmental Education Research*, 8(1), 73-79.

Sauve, L. (2005). Currents in Environmental Education: Mapping a Complex and Evolving Pedagogical Field. *The Canadian Journal of Environmental Education*, 10, 1-4.

Sauve, L. & Berryman, T. (2005). Challenging a 'Closing Circle': Alternative Research Agendas for the ESD Decade. *Applied Environmental Education and Communication*, 4, 229-232.

Scheunpflug, A. & Asbrand, B. (2006) Global education and education for sustainability. *Environmental Education Research*, 12(1), 33-46.

Scottish Executive (2006) *Learning For Our Future: Scotland's First Action Plan for the UN Decade of Education for Sustainable Development* Edinburgh: Scottish Executive.

Stables, A. & Scott, A. (2002) The Quest for Holism in Education for Sustainable Development. *Environmental Education Research*, 8(1), 53-61.

Westheimer, J. & Kahne, J. (2004) What kind of citizen? The politics of educating for democracy. *American Educational Research Journal*, 41(2), 237-269.

2.3 Critical Thinking in the Context of Global Learning

Hetan Shah and Kate Brown, DEA

Making connections within and between systems
The grandfather of critical thinking in the Western tradition is René Descartes, the 17th Century philosopher. He was so intent on the need to think critically that legend has it that he locked himself in a stove so that he could step away from distraction to think.

Western thinking took an important turn with the work of Descartes. He believed that the best way to understand something was to break it down into its component parts. This mode of operation has dominated Western thinking and there are good reasons for this – it is very powerful. It is this way of thinking that has enabled most of our academic insights such as the discovery of the atom.

But the weakness of this model of thinking is that the interconnection between the parts in any given system is more important than the individual parts. So understanding the constituent parts is not enough. We need to know how they interact. For example, the chair of the Financial Services Authority (FSA) has admitted that the FSA's failure to fully explore the ways in which individual risks compounded each other meant that the overall risks in the financial system were underestimated. This played an important role in the recent economic crisis.

Issues such as climate change require us to think systemically, and to understand that change is not just a linear process but, in some instances, non linear due to vicious (or sometimes virtuous) circles. For example, if climate change goes beyond a rise of 2 degrees centigrade, this could lead to 'runaway climate change' through a cycle of warming.

We see this issue most of all in how we tend to think of the economic sphere as separate from the social and environmental sphere. But as research by WWF (2006) shows, if everybody consumed like we do in the UK, we would need three planets to sustain us. We can only really start to understand global challenges and issues when we make connections within and between systems.

Awareness of how much is contested
All of the major concepts that global learning is concerned with are contested. For example, the notion of 'sustainability'. What is it? Is it mainly an environmental concept, or is it about social justice as well? What makes someone a global citizen? Is global citizenship a useful concept at all? These are live debates about which there is no consensus. Similarly, what

does being a developed country mean? What are the causes of international poverty? Does aid help, or does it prop up corrupt regimes? Is the best route to resolve poverty more or less globalisation and free markets? Can we equate increased wealth with greater development?

It is easy to fall into treating abstract nouns such as 'sustainability', 'global citizenship' and 'development' as though they are the names of real, clearly defined objects. In describing why he would not want his children to be educated for sustainable development, Jickling warns against conditioning young people to believe that sustainable development constitutes a constellation of correct environmental views (Jickling, 1992). Instead, he argues, we should debate, evaluate and judge for ourselves the relative merits of contested positions.

Responding to complexity and change

Relatedly, and perhaps rather obviously, the world is complex and changing. This means that individuals need to constantly question and update their own models of the world. For example some educators talking about development use a model of the world that makes a very strong distinction between poor and rich countries. There are, however, challenges to this model of development, rooted as it is in dependency theory which emerged in the 1950s. Where does China fit in? How does it make sense of the fact that India's middle class now stands at 100 million people – bigger than Europe's? And what do we make of one in three children in the UK living in relative poverty? We need newer models to understand development which see that deprivation and wealth occur within as well as across nations.

Critical global thinkers also need to explore the very real trade-offs that we must grapple with in how we might create a more just and sustainable world. In the sustainability debate this is all the more important now that everybody is 'for' sustainability and so debates must move to the next level. What would the impacts of higher energy prices be on the very poorest in society? What does 'local food' mean in its impacts on trade with poorer countries?

By developing our abilities to explore such trade-offs and to be open-minded about our models of the world today, we will be better placed to respond effectively in the future to challenges that we cannot yet anticipate.

Understanding the significance of power relationships

All global learning, indeed all education, is political. Everything has an ideological and political underpinning and is shaped by patterns of power distribution. Following the Freirean tradition, critical reflection on the way in which reality is shaped in this way can be seen as the impetus to move individuals to change that reality. The link between awareness and action is not necessarily as clear as this, but viewing the world through a more political lens is nonetheless revealing. For example, it can move us from a benevolent charitable mentality towards other countries to considering the structural issues that shape global challenges and influence the ways we view them.

An important trap to avoid in global learning is that this is not just a set of agendas about individual change and moral refrains ('be responsible; give to charity; feel bad when you fly'). Change is political, and politics needs an analysis of the roles of all different actors – government, business, NGOs as well as individuals. A systemic analysis also seeks to try and understand the incentives within the system – why do people act as they do, and what are the systemic changes that will help create behaviour change? For example in relation to international poverty, moral exhortation and charitable giving may have a relatively small effect in comparison to changes in UK tariffs policy or in consumers' shopping habits.

The political nature of global learning also means that critical global learners need to avoid swallowing anyone's line too quickly. They need to recognise that NGOs, government, business and academics can have their own agendas. Thus they need to consider: Who has power? Who is voiceless? Who benefits?

Self-reflection

The global is not somewhere 'out there' – we are all part of it. Therefore, an important element of critical global thinking involves situating ourselves in the global. This can involve making connections between the global and the local, between global processes and systems and ourselves as individuals. For example, collectively and individually we are key contributors to the problems of environmental sustainability and climate change, and, therefore, this global issue does not sit 'out there'. Similarly, there is relative poverty in the UK and we need to consider our own 'development trajectory' as much as that of other nations.

Self-reflection also means exploring our deeper prejudices and stereotypes about poorer countries. Work done by the Reading-based Development Education Centre (RISC) shows that when children are asked to draw pictures to respond to the question 'What is in Africa?' many of the drawings are of very poor communities and mud huts (Lowe, 2008). There is no recognition that there is a lot of variety in this huge continent, and that poverty is not its only constituting factor. Critical global thinking should involve challenging ourselves to remain open-minded, and aware that change for a more just and sustainable world may well involve changing ourselves.

Values literacy

The learning outcomes of global learning are often couched in terms of knowledge, skills and attitudes. However, critical global thinkers also need to connect to their deeper narratives. All societies have understandings about what constitutes a good life, which go to the heart of our values. Global learning needs to grapple with these questions.

Well-being research suggests that increased material affluence has not necessarily made us happier: the UK economy has trebled in size over the last 50 years but happiness has remained relatively flat (Layard, 2005). The research suggests that we adapt quickly to material gains – lottery winners experience a surge of happiness and then return to their previous levels of well-being. This is not to say that well-being is the key or the only goal of society – there are many other values such as freedom, or participation. But young people should be given the space to explore what values they hold, where these values might come from, and where they might clash. How do their environmental values sit with their desire to fly and travel? There may be no easy answers, but critical thinking requires us to begin by bringing to the surface the contradictions in the values that we all have and to challenge our own deeply held values and preferences.

So often, in educational literature and elsewhere, statements about values are made as though they are statements of fact. In becoming more conversant with their own values, critical global thinkers may be better able to identify the values implicit in what they see, hear and read.

What does this understanding of critical global thinking mean for teachers?

Learning is a complex process, and it is difficult to understand the relationship between young people's exposure to global issues and their ability and inclination to respond to global challenges both now and in the future. Against this backdrop, it is challenging to assess the relationship between specific teaching interventions and learning outcomes.

Whilst acknowledging the need for a greater understanding about the relationship between teaching, learning and life patterns, we make here some pragmatic suggestions about what the elements of critical global thinking outlined above mean for educators.

Firstly, our understanding of a critical global thinker extends to teachers as much as it does to students. Modelling is crucial in teaching, and to support students to be self-reflective, and to respond to complexity and change, teachers need to be doing so themselves. Anecdotal evidence from practitioners who support educators suggests that some teachers hold views that reinforce stereotypes on global issues. Hence fostering critical thinking means teachers, as well as students, questioning their own understanding and assumptions. Like students, teachers need to be supported in this.

What's more, to navigate the wealth of resources and advice available for teaching the global dimension, teachers need to be thinking critically, considering the values and power relationships that have shaped the material. As made clear in the English National Framework for Masters in Teaching and Learning (Training and Development Agency for Schools, 2009), teachers need opportunities to develop their own skills of enquiry, allowing them to feel their way in a contested field.

However, whatever resources and activities teachers select, we see some shared approaches and underlying pedagogical principles as valuable in fostering critical global thinking. For example, helping young people think systemically could start with making links between sharply delineated curriculum subjects. Within subject areas there are also many opportunities to make links between local and global: news stories about Somalian pirates can be linked to the topic of migration in the UK; local issues about drugs can be linked up to questions about the global drugs trade.

To help students understand the contested nature of concepts in global learning, we believe that educators need to be putting forward a variety of perspectives on issues they are dealing with – including intelligent 'right wing' theory as well as views from the left. Approaches such as Philosophy for Children (P4C) and Open Spaces for Dialogue and Enquiry (OSDE) can provide useful ideas on how to encourage learners to identify how values and power relationships contribute to the formation of individual or organisational viewpoints and the 'knowledge' generated from those perspectives. The use of questioning in the classroom can be important in encouraging students to consider the epistemological claims of any teaching resource or source of information.

Young people are often extremely adept at responding flexibly to changing and complex situations. Often it is teachers who are understandably reticent in entering debate on controversial issues, where values, opinions, and priorities are conflicting and where it is not possible to know the full picture. It is a challenge to build and shift teacher/student relationships in a way that makes it possible to enter discussions on a more equal footing, with no one knowing the 'right' answer. Activities such as role play, formal debates, tiered discussion groups, and ranking can all help to structure and stimulate 'talk' in the classroom, and developing clear ground rules with students can help everyone take part constructively (Brown and Fairbrass, 2009).

Finally, whilst we believe that critical thinking is crucial to global learning, we recognise that supporting such approaches is not unproblematic. Asbrand (2008) worked with German adolescents to try to understand how they learn about globalisation and development. She found that school students who explored values and global issues critically and intellectually were less able to transfer their knowledge to action than young people who learnt through volunteering in organizations outside of schools (for example, through selling fair-trade products). It clearly cannot be presumed that critical approaches to global learning lead directly to action for a more just and sustainable world. Teachers, with their knowledge of the young people they work with, have an important role in reflecting on how to support critical global thinking whilst enabling young people to feel sufficiently optimistic and aware of their power for change to take their chosen action in a complex world.

References

Asbrand, B. (2008) How adolescents learn about globalisation and development. In Bourn, D (2008) *Development Education: Debates and dialogues.* London: Institute of Education.

Brown, K. & Fairbrass, S. (2009) *The Citizenship Teacher's Handbook.* London: Continuum.

Jickling, B. (1992) Why I don't want my children educated for sustainable development. *Journal of Environmental Education* 23(4).

Layard, R. (2005) *Happiness: Lessons from a New Science.* London: Penguin Books.

Lowe, B. (2008) Embedding Global Citizenship in Primary and Secondary Schools: developing a methodology for measuring attitudinal change. *International Journal of Development Education and Global Learning*, 1(1). WWF (2006) Living Planet Report 2006.

Training and Development Agency for Schools (2009) *The National Framework for Masters in Teaching and Learning* London: Training and Development Agency for Schools

Acknowledgment
Please note that this chapter arose from a keynote speech at the 2009 conference of the 'UK Teacher Education Network for Education for Sustainable Development/Global Citizenship'. It was published previously in Inman, S. & Rogers, M. (Eds.) (2009) *Developing Critical Perspectives on Education for Sustainable Development / Global citizenship in Initial Teacher Education. UK Conference July 2009. Conference Proceedings.* London: CCCI, Southbank University.

2.4 Planning for the Global in a Scottish Context: The Perspective from the General Teaching Council for Scotland

Tom Hamilton, General Teaching Council for Scotland

PARTNERSHIP IS AT THE HEART of how Education for Global Citizenship and Sustainable Development is becoming embedded in both Initial Teacher Education (ITE) and the early professional development of teachers in Scotland. This short chapter outlines the General Teaching Council for Scotland's (GTCS) role in fostering this partnership across Scottish Education and the nature of its own current commitment to global learning.

The GTCS was established in 1965 and is a Non Departmental Public Body (NDPB) with a significant role in Scotland's Initial Teacher Education (ITE) system. While that NDPB status will change late in 2011 when the GTCS becomes an independent body, the Scottish Government's intention is that the Council's role in ITE will not only be maintained but actually enhanced. Since the mid 1960s the GTCS has 'accredited' all programmes of Initial Teacher Education in Scotland with Scottish Ministers giving final 'approval' but from independence the GTCS will both accredit and approve all ITE programmes.

Approval is currently given by Ministers, on the recommendation of the GTCS, if ITE programmes meet the requirements set out in the Guidelines for Initial Teacher Education Courses in Scotland (Scottish Executive 2006) published by the Government, so the logic of giving the GTCS the power to approve programmes suggests that the Guidelines will also be published by the GTCS rather than the Government. While this looks a major change, in reality it may be less significant. When the Guidelines were last revised and republished (December 2006) the GTCS played a leading role in their review and worked closely with the Government in developing a set of Guidelines which encouraged flexibility and change within ITE while still maintaining overall parameters for programmes. Both the Government's and the GTCS's logos appear on the cover of the 2006 Guidelines and that partnership approach towards such important matters will continue to be a feature of the work of an 'independent' GTCS.

The same will be true in the area of the Teacher Education Standards for Scotland. De facto, the GTCS has taken the lead role in the development and review of the two Standards of most significance to beginning teachers in Scotland – the Standard for Initial Teacher Education (SITE) (GTCS 2006a) and the Standard for Full Registration (SFR) (GTCS 2006b) – but with independence will come a more formalised recognition of this with the GTCS enjoined by the Government to have 'guardianship' of the Standards while continuing to work in partnership with other stakeholders in Scottish education.

Unlike the previous (and now superseded) 1993 and 1998 versions of the Guidelines for Initial Teacher Education Courses in Scotland the 2006 publication does not explicitly spell out any content for ITE programmes stating rather that students must meet the Standard for Initial Teacher Education and be prepared to deliver *Curriculum for Excellence*. However, when SITE itself is considered it is more explicit on what is required and how it is to be achieved with the following model appearing:

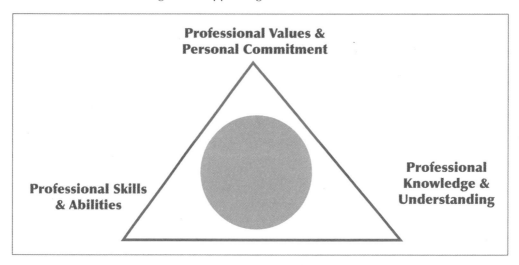

The clear placement of 'Professional Values and Personal Commitment' as one of the three significant areas of SITE is a measure of the consensual approach taken to teacher education in Scotland. These matters were discussed and debated during the original development, and later review, of both SITE and SFR but, having been agreed, have been signed up to by all parties.

Within SITE the following appears:

3.3   Value, respect and show commitment to the communities in which they work.

By the end of the programme of initial teacher education, student teachers will:

Know about environmental issues and be able to contribute to education for sustainable development.

Know about the principles of education for citizenship and be willing to encourage pupils to be active, critical and responsible citizens within a local, national, international and global context.

SITE sets a Standard to be met and part of meeting that Standard involves the inculcation of values accepted by teachers in Scotland as being part of their professional persona.

The concepts of Education for Global Citizenship and Sustainable Development are strongly underpinned by values but they also reflect more concrete 'Professional Knowledge and Understanding' and in that area SITE identifies the following:

1.1.2   Have knowledge and understanding of, for example, sustainable development, equal opportunities, additional support needs, citizenship, international education, education for work, enterprise.

Admittedly these are only 'examples' but having them included and stated within the Standard clearly gives a steer to the universities on what is expected in their programmes when it comes to GTCS accreditation and is also of significance to the individual student in identifying the profession's expectations of them.

Exactly the same triangular model is used in the SFR but, to reflect the progression from being a successful student to being a successful and fully registered teacher, while the same elements of Standard are identified the expectations are set at a higher level. So, for example in 3.3, fully registered teachers are expected to be 'active partners in the communities in which they work' and in 1.1.2 they must 'demonstrate in depth knowledge and understanding of, for example, sustainable development, equal opportunities, additional support needs, citizenship, international education, education for work, enterprise.'

These notions of deeper knowledge and understanding and of teacher activism (stemming in the latter's case at least in part from publications such as Sachs 2003) are important if the education system in Scotland is to continue to develop with professional teachers playing the leading role in system development that they should.

The GTCS is of course centrally placed to encourage such progress.

There is the ongoing GTCS relationship with the universities and ITE; there is the ongoing relationship with local authorities, schools and particularly new teachers through the Teacher Induction Scheme (TIS); and there is to be an increased relationship for the GTCS with all teachers through a proposed system of teacher reaccreditation.

The word 'steer' was used above and that was quite deliberate as the intention of the GTCS would be to continue to consult, discuss and debate with educational stakeholders and the profession as Scottish education moves forward. An independent GTCS would have no intention to begin issuing diktats but would intend to 'steer' from its central position within Scottish education.

Andy Hargreaves has written about system change coming about through the principle of steering from the top while building from the bottom (Hargreaves and Fullan (edit), 2009) and that image fits well with how the GTCS sees its role. The Council, along with various other centrally placed bodies and organisations, should give a steer to the system but real change will only come about through the active professionalism of teachers building and developing change within classrooms, schools and local authorities.

This is where organisations such as IDEAS can have effective and real influence on teachers, the central bodies and the system - bringing about results for learners and ultimately developments for society.

The following diagram has been adapted from Andy Hargreaves' opening chapter in Change Wars (op cit):

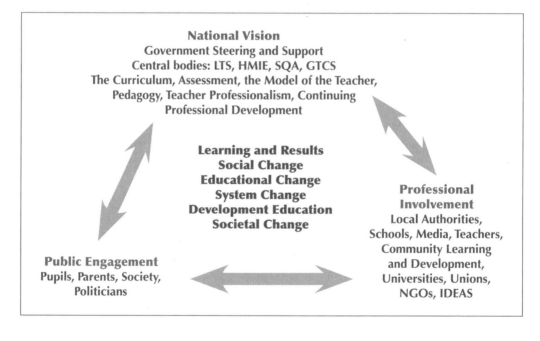

National Vision
Government Steering and Support
Central bodies: LTS, HMIE, SQA, GTCS
The Curriculum, Assessment, the Model of the Teacher,
Pedagogy, Teacher Professionalism, Continuing
Professional Development

Learning and Results
Social Change
Educational Change
System Change
Development Education
Societal Change

Professional Involvement
Local Authorities, Schools, Media, Teachers, Community Learning and Development, Universities, Unions, NGOs, IDEAS

Public Engagement
Pupils, Parents, Society, Politicians

Organisations involved in Education for Global Citizenship and Sustainable Development, such as IDEAS, need to work with, lobby and influence those doing the steering, but they also have to have direct involvement with those who are doing the building – those listed with them under Professional Involvement. Advocacy is central but the provision of teaching materials, advice and input on issues such as pedagogy by IDEAS' member organisations will also help to encourage system development. However, public engagement is also at the heart of system change (both educational and societal) and to deliver real learning and results pupils, parents and politicians all need to be actively involved in discussing the relevant issues, the values to which we should aspire and in the case of Education for Global Citizenship and Sustainable Development, quite literally, the future of humanity.

Clearly a bit of a challenge – but one we have to address!

References

General Teaching Council for Scotland (2006a) *Standard for Initial Teacher Education*. Edinburgh: GTCS

General Teaching Council for Scotland (2006b) *Standard for Full Registration*. Edinburgh: GTCS

Hargreaves, A.& Fullan, M.(Edit) (2009) *Change Wars*. Bloomington, In. USA: Solution Tree

Sachs, J.(2003) *The Activist Teaching Profession* Buckingham: Open University Press

Scottish Executive (2006) *Guidelines for Initial Teacher Education Courses in Scotland* Edinburgh: Scottish Executive

2.5 Bringing a Global Perspective to Initial Teacher Education: A B.Ed Co-ordinator's Perspective.

Barbara Frame, University of Edinburgh

Introduction

One of the main responsibilities and challenges that confront the B.Ed Co-ordinator is that of ensuring the maintenance of programme quality while introducing new priorities and obligations that do not necessarily sit comfortably with long-established practice or the prior experience of teaching staff. The policy emphasis now given to cross-cutting issues such as education for global citizenship and sustainable development represents one such challenge.

Giving students an adequate understanding of the interconnected world in which we live is increasingly recognised by educationists as an important strand of teachers' initial professional education. For different reasons national and, indeed, international policy identifies the global dimension as a development imperative. This chapter is an account of how one programme within an institution has addressed the challenge of integrating a global perspective into initial teacher education while consolidating the subject expertise of teaching staff. The chapter is very much an account of a work in progress.

The Impetus for Change

The curriculum of the B.Ed. Primary Programme in Edinburgh University's Moray House School of Education was until recently organised around five curricular areas: Environmental Studies, Expressive Arts, Languages, Mathematics and Religious Moral and Philosophical Studies. This was in line with how the curriculum has been perceived in Scottish schools since the inception of the Curriculum 5-14 Programme (SOEID, 2000) But this way of 'seeing' the curriculum is changing.

'Over the last 15 years, most primary schools have organised their curriculum through a series of curriculum areas, taking advice from '5-14 Structure and balance of the curriculum'. This approach was helpful in ensuring that pupils' learning progressed from stage to stage, building on what they had learned before. As the curriculum has developed to take fuller account of modern life, it is now beginning to include more emphasis on aspects such as health promotion, enterprise, creativity, sustainability and citizenship. In addition, curriculum design principles have placed greater emphasis on challenge and enjoyment, depth, relevance and choice in learning links between different aspects of learning, and on the quality of learning and teaching approaches. '(SEED 2007a)

The re-accreditation of the B.Ed degree provided opportunities for staff to reconsider the 'curriculum architecture' of the programme. No less powerful was the imperative to prepare students for the implementation in schools of the Scottish Government's most recent, and far-reaching innovation, Curriculum for Excellence (CfE). As has been said, the existing programme structure was based very much upon the five divisions of 5-14, but alternative architectures, including modelling new forms of integration or in-depth learning, and initiating students into the processes of curriculum design would help to prepare for them for the implementation of CfE. In considering how to plan the curriculum for the reaccredited degree it was necessary to take account of three pragmatic concerns:

- how to make stronger links between education courses, students' school placements and curriculum courses
- how to more effectively staff and resource teaching and learning
- how to use timetabling constraints more productively.

The Concept of Curriculum Architecture

In considering a redesign of curriculum it is useful to refer to the concept of 'curriculum architecture' (SEED, 2007b). Curriculum architecture is not just about structural concerns; it is also about how the aims of the curriculum are reflected in the pedagogies of the classroom. Curriculum architecture includes: pedagogy; learning environments; inclusion and diversity; how the curriculum is experienced; how it is organised; organisation for learning; organisation of assessment; opportunities for personalisation and choice; motivated students and motivated teachers; timetables and transitions. The need is to explore and discuss curriculum in a much broader sense and in contexts that are powerful, relevant and engaging.

The Programme Rationale

The twenty-first century is perceived as a period of profound social, technological, economic and cultural change. It is likely to continue to be affected by an acceleration of accessible knowledge, knowledge exchange and ease of movement, all facilitated by rapidly developing technologies. This all contributes to the notion of the 'global village' as an established reality.

The changing world will also continue to impact on childhood and society's perception of childhood. An area of multi-disciplinary scholarship is emerging incorporating education, sociology, social psychology and social policy. Initial teacher education programmes need to equip student teachers to be aware of the broad range of ideas emerging from the critical debates relating to childhood as a social construct. Examples of such ideas are 'the child as citizen' and the child as capable decision-maker, resulting, in Scotland in the creation, inter alia, of the Children's Parliament.

A further and more tangible consequence of current discourses is the CfE initiative, arguably the most radical curriculum development programme in a generation. Clearly, this was a key influence in the B.Ed. review process. CfE introduces new ways of conceptualising what is important for children to learn, and how they can best learn. This, of course, ought to have profound implications for the nature of schools and schooling, including the craft of teaching and knowledge about learning. Teacher education programmes need to play a key role in examining the new curriculum, preparing new practitioners to implement it effectively but also instilling new practitioners with the disposition to be critical, enquiring and creative curriculum designers.

Consequently, the outcome of the B.Ed. review needed to demonstrate that the process had taken account of the continuing rapid evolution of the social, political, economical and cultural contexts within which education takes place.

In the wider professional context there was a need to consider a variety of broad ideas and initiatives:
- an increased emphasis on the knowledge economy, enterprise, global citizenship, the world of work, sustainable living
- the impact of developing technologies
- new understandings about learning including research from neuroscience
- changing views about children and childhood (childhood as important in its own right – childhood as preparation for adulthood; children as vulnerable – capable; children as victims – villains)
- current issues relating to Early Years Education 0-8 (Scottish Government, 2008); Longitudinal Research in Early Years Education - 'Growing Up in Scotland Study (Scottish Government (Scottish Centre for Social Research), 2003)
- inter-professional working in educational settings and beyond
- Additional Support for Learning Act (Scottish Parliament, 2004), recent initiatives in inclusion, social justice, additional needs and anti-discriminatory practices
- Curriculum for Excellence, including the cross-cutting themes of literacy; numeracy; enterprise; creativity; citizenship; sustainability; ICT (see http://www.ltscotland.org.uk/curriculumforexcellence/index.asp)
- the Assessment is for Learning initiative (see http://www.ltscotland.org.uk/assess/index.asp)
- the HMIE Scoping review of ITE (HMIE, 2002) and Review of Initial Teacher Education Stage 2 (SEED, 2005) and articulation of a model of the teacher for 21st Century
- Student Teacher Placements within Initial Teacher Education (HMIE, 2005); Progress with Student Teacher Placement (HMIE, 2006a)
- How Good is our School ? (HMIE, 2007a, b, 2006b)

- the legacy of 5-14 Curriculum and National Testing
- the Standard for Initial Teacher Education(SITE) (GTCS, 2006) and Standard for Full Registration (SFR) (GTCS, 2007)
- developments in induction, continuing professional development, life long learning, Chartered Teacher, Standard for Headship
- the collaborative review process and the GTCS framework for accreditation and review.

These topics and initiatives informed discussion of the processes, content and design of the programme. Some led to structural changes, some to conceptual change and some to perceptual change. These changes were important in terms of the culture, emphases and orientation of teacher education, and the need to modify content and operational strategy in response to further influences in the years ahead. They informed the revision of the content and process of assessment, placement, and the nature of university teaching. A number of themes were identified as emerging from this macro-context and were taken up in discussions with the intention of refining and establishing their contribution to the programme. These themes included: health and well-being; creativity; global citizenship; education for sustainability; enterprising teaching and learning; learning beyond the classroom.

The predominant aim of the review had been to consider how the B.Ed. (Hons.) Primary could raise further the achievement of students, while retaining its widely acknowledged strengths, and continue to provide the profession with new teachers of the highest quality.

Discussion suggested that the main barriers to raising achievement were:
- insufficient lateral coherence across programme components (education, curriculum and placement)
- lack of interdisciplinary work between curriculum courses
- dissatisfaction with the pattern of school experience
- insufficient preparation across years one to three for students to take up the role of teacher-researcher expected of them in year four
- under-use of emerging technologies and innovative approaches to teaching generally
- lack of support for students to improve and develop their academic writing;
- under-development to date of the potential of school partnership beyond placement matters
- under-development of student self–assessment and formative assessment in promoting student learning
- insufficient ownership by students of their professional learning.

Programme and Course Design

There was a need to reconceptualise how the courses could be configured taking account of the realignment and expansion of traditional subjects, the emergence of new subjects; the priority given to cross-cutting themes; research on the concept of curriculum architecture outlined in policy documents, in particular CfE.

New courses needed to be designed which would allow more flexibility in the way that they are taught. For example, course design could facilitate a range of teaching approaches including both subject teaching and some forms of interdisciplinary teaching. Course design might also be more effective in including Additional Support for Learning and ICT, as well as cross-curricular themes such as global citizenship, sustainability and enterprising teaching and learning.

Partnership

It was believed that strengthened partnerships with schools would optimise student learning on placements and improve the ways in which students connect knowledge from the university to knowledge in schools. Partnership should also be extended to include other organisations working with children in both the statutory and voluntary sectors.

Teaching/Learning Environment

As with any change process it was imperative that those tasked with implementing the change were clear as to its purposes and could see how their expertise could be utilised in bringing about the required change. There was a need to build on tutor expertise. Any radical change requires that careful attention is given to avoid de-skilling those that have to implement the change. Consequently, the subject knowledge of course tutors had to be validated and seen as the foundation on which the new approach was built.

The curriculum component of the B.Ed. (Hons.) Primary programme needed to take account of the emphasis on aspects such as health, enterprise, creativity, sustainability and citizenship, perceived to be important for learners in the 21st Century. Additionally, the new courses needed to reflect curriculum design principles such as deep learning, connectivity, inclusion, choice of learning and quality of teaching/learning approaches identified in CfE guidance. In order to bring this about, representatives from two of the NGOs (SCOTDEC and OXFAM) ran two staff development workshops. The first was with Moray House staff. It involved exploring and clarifying staff views on global citizenship and its associated pedagogies. The second session involved the representatives from the two NGOs team teaching with Moray House Staff in running workshops with third year students on global citizenship. The purposes of these workshops were to raise the student awareness of their own understandings and possible misconceptions in this area, to inform them of available resources and to give them an initial set of useful teaching tools. Additionally, an over-arching purpose was to transfer owned expertise from the NGOs to Moray House Teaching staff, for the benefit of future student cohorts.

Many of these new aspects, like citizenship or sustainability education, seem to have been promoted on the idea that they are essentially founded on values, are permeative in nature, are without subject knowledge and are essentially matters of methodology and context. With this in mind, discussions within the review team explored understandings of 'curriculum' and 'pedagogy' with a view to improving the learning and teaching environment created for students. Acknowledgment was given to the complex nature of both aspects. An audit of current methodologies was carried out and these included:
• Apprenticeship (as experienced by students on placement)
• Demonstration
• Enquiry
• Problem Based Learning
• Discussion
• Reflective practitioner activities
• Micro-teaching
• In-class coaching
• Mentoring
• Subject based teaching.

Teaching teams were established with membership representing a range of 'traditional' curriculum areas. Working with colleagues from different areas of expertise helped develop understandings by recognition of similarities as well as differences. Fostering collaboration, which was necessary for learning for change, required course teams to become learning teams willing to engage in shared reflection, mutual critical and self-evaluation. This was not always straightforward or easy.

The proposals for change that emerged from the planning process were that:
• A suite of courses called 'Curriculum and Pedagogy' courses would be devised which would make use of a range of approaches including subject teaching, interdisciplinary teaching and opportunities for teaching cross-cutting themes of citizenship; education for sustainability; enterprise; creativity; learning beyond the classroom; as well as literacy and numeracy;
• The multidimensional quality of teaching should be examined to ensure that account was taken, not only of the complexity of primary classroom teaching but also of the layers of complexity involved in teaching our students. The need to make these layers explicit, consciously acknowledge them and address them in our own planning was

acknowledged. There was awareness that this examination would require collaboration and therefore it was proposed to make it part of the role of the individual course teams. Guidance from the university's initiative, Scholarship of Teaching and Learning (SoTL) was helpful in this respect.

- The School of Education should engage with the three-year development project 'Taking a Global Approach to ITE'run by the International Development Education Association of Scotland (IDEAS). The project aimed to work with universities in order to support them in delivering Education for Global Citizenship, Sustainability and Learning Outdoors through a variety of methods relating to Curriculum for Excellence. A key aspect of this is highlighting ways in which we can support teachers in delivering on cross-curricular themes.

In order to facilitate planning around these proposals, it was necessary to identify rich, generative learning contexts that tutors would identify with. One such context was the development of understanding of 'Place' as exemplified by Edinburgh's Royal Mile, a rich learning resource on the very doorstep of the School of Education.

This learning context was developed in the course Curriculum & Pedagogy 1b (Social Studies, Expressive Arts, Language) and served to illustrate how students might learn how to help children learn in, through and about their surroundings. A key point in teaching this was to show the students that the approach is transferable to other situations.

A number of approaches are possible, with the following having been considered by the C&P1b team.

The course team could work as three distinct curriculum areas e.g. showing what and how historians, artists and readers/writers might study in the area. It would be possible in this approach for the members of the course team to plan their investigations together and then design activities for the students, ensuring that the work done in each of the distinctive curriculum areas complemented and extended one another. Students might be asked to demonstrate their understandings of how:

- skills and knowledge (e.g. historical enquiry, observation …) can be developed in an interesting context;
- skills and understandings in one subject can support learning in others;
- the teaching approaches/learning activities can be applied to other situations in other places.

Another approach might be to plan the study using a line of enquiry approach based on a set of key questions to encourage observation and challenge thinking:

- Why is there a street here?
- What goes on in the street?
- In what ways has the street changed, and why?
- What does the design of the street convey in terms of values and ideas?
- How do you feel about the street?

In this approach, the study would be based around the key questions with each curriculum area building on work done by the previous one. For example, a visit to the Royal Mile might be made using a social subject perspective to look at architecture and land use, and the evidence gathered (sketches, maps, photographs, film). An artistic perspective could explore how observations might be expressed through different media. Subsequently, the literacy group might use the evidence from both the history and art investigations to stimulate writing or multimedia outcomes.

In any approach consideration would also need to be given to the possibilities of working with:

- informal educators – how and when they could be used across the programme;
- schools – a number of options might be possible, for example students observing tutors teaching children; students working and learning with children.

It was also agreed that all curriculum and pedagogy courses should include subject teaching and also make reference to interdisciplinary teaching, eg by exemplifying possible approaches and contexts. The extent of interdisciplinary teaching would vary among courses but the key themes identified by CfE as the responsibility of all teachers, namely; literacy, numeracy, enterprise, creativity, critical thinking, global citizenship, sustainability, ICT and health, needed to be given careful account across all courses.

Although a course might have a particular focus, all courses would be expected to touch on at least some of the key themes. During the Review Process, the role of informal educators and NGOs was identified as potentially important in supporting the student experience in this respect. The following organisations were invited to participate in discussions about how they might contribute to the courses being developed, in relation to these themes. Those who took part were: Dynamic Earth; Scottish Screen; Royal Botanic Gardens Edinburgh; Scottish Development Education Centre; Museums of Scotland; International Development Education Association of Scotland (IDEAS). Additionally, Learning Teaching Scotland also participated in outlining progress to date in interdisciplinary learning.

Assessing Integrated Courses

Moving from an essentially subject-based approach to a more inter-disciplinary approach generates challenges as well as opportunities in curriculum design, teaching and assessment. The assessment of inter-disciplinary courses presents interesting possibilities in setting authentic tasks. For example:

- devising an upper primary teachers' pack on citizenship, incorporating Social Subjects and RME;
- developing a resource pack to show how both technology and art & design encourage creativity through form and function, and sustainability through the use of materials;
- planning a sequence of lessons to show how expressive arts (e.g drama or art and design) and written language can complement each other in bringing about learning;
- preparing a reflective portfolio (electronic perhaps) containing professional reading, artefacts, models and examples to show how learning in science is supported by understandings in mathematics and how both impact on sustainability;
- designing a teaching pack based on selected locations and aimed at helping children to learn concept(s) such as interdependence, develop skill(s) such as listening and make affective responses;
- designing materials to be used by children and teachers in an out-of-school context such as a museum, gallery or zoo.

Any of the above might also include a theory-based rationale and/or justification.

The use of external experience as a contribution to the course was developed during the review process and a meeting of stakeholders and workshop with NGOs provided a valuable opportunity for tutors to see how to work with informal educators. It also created a chance for educators from the voluntary sector, in this case the Scottish Development Education Centre, to respond to the review proposals and take a view on the adequacy of the global dimension in the new programme.

But what are we teaching – reflections on progress

The rationale for a move from subject-based to more cross-disciplinary courses is easy to understand but is based on little practical experience. There are few education systems across the globe that have successfully moved away from subject courses, even though the need for young people who can move comfortably across subjects and contexts is clear. The aim of the B.Ed Primary undergraduate programme is to build students' professional and personal knowledge in both subject specific disciplines and integrated contexts for learning. The new programme emphasises the importance of; connectedness, generic skills and social values. It also demands students understand the connections between the four capacities of CfE and what they are learning. But this raises issues of how to strike a satisfactory balance between the permeating themes and course content; of where the emphasis should be placed in the tension between 'cross-disciplinarity' and subject rigour; of how tutors can themselves collaborate to ensure no duplication of content; of how coherence can be achieved without losing the distinctive elements of each course component.

These issues were evident in both of the two Curriculum and Pedagogy Courses which were implemented with first year students in the new programme.

Planning in learning teams for both courses took time, and discussions could be slow. However, this was thought necessary to allow genuine sharing of understanding and ownership of change. Disagreement is a natural outcome, with the potential for colleagues to feel that their contributions are not valued. In the process, these situations were evident. Some colleagues were quick to take responsibility to be creative in leadership and to share their ideas. Others found this more difficult to various degrees. The defence of particular subject learning was a particular issue, because of its central importance per se and/ or because of the time/resource and thinking problems associated simply with doing something differently.

The course team for C&P1b embarked on providing the experience ('Place' – The Royal Mile). Whereas this made a very good start based on story dramatisation involving students in interdisciplinary learning using a narrative thread, not enough time was taken to reflect on how this 'worked' and why this was a meaningful experience. Also, there did not seem to be much difficulty in designing meaningful cross-curricular learning activities, which allowed in-depth subject learning, in relation to language, social studies and expressive arts. However, in practice, not enough time was taken to explain or offer a rationale to the students for interdisciplinary teaching. This needs be addressed when the course next runs.

The course team for C&P1c adopted a different strategy, placing emphasis on learning outdoors, with some classes drawing on the expertise of informal educators. A key experience of the course was an inter-disciplinary day either at Holyrood park, the Royal Botanic Gardens or a beach setting in East Lothian. Students were allocated a venue and were challenged to undertake team oral presentations based on their experience there. The presentations were organised to facilitate exchange of learning from each of the three venues. Following that, the written assessment allowed them to analyse selected aspects of their experiences in terms of teaching and learning. Staff were all positive about seeing opportunities for providing worthwhile experiences for the students in outdoor settings. In practice, however, the quality of student activity varied. This was probably due to differing levels of familiarity with outdoor learning amongst staff, along with differing perceptions of the level of management necessary. For example, some staff managed student activity closely and engaged fully with them through preparation, activity and follow-up. Others thought that just providing the task was enough. Again, this needs to be addressed when the course next runs to ensure purposes are clear and consistency of student experience is achieved.

Regarding assessment, there was some concern amongst subject tutors that students were not being assessed in their particular area. This is understandable, despite the list given above on 'assessing integrated courses'. However, there is not enough time available in the programme as a whole to satisfy every interest in this regard. Also, it is not the case that, if there is no assessment (of a particular kind) then nothing has been learned. Assessment approaches will continue to be refined to be fully fit for purpose. One strategy already introduced is that team members have been asked to plot the learning that has taken place in their particular area to show explicitly the progression and continuity in traditional subject areas.

These 'reflections on progress' pertain to two of the year one C&P Courses introduced in 2009/10. What has been been learned from their introduction will be used to help introduce subsequent year two and three C&P courses which will run for the first time in 2010/11.

The strategy employed to enlist the help of NGOs, particularly SCOTDEC and OXFAM, worked very well. In previous years expertise has been brought to the students and they have benefited from that expertise. However, there is an opportunity now for the expertise to be built on amongst Moray House staff. Even simply enhancing familiarity, amongst a range of staff, with a concept like citizenship should result in more effective dissemination across a range of courses.

Experience of staff working in learning teams made up of subject specialists drawn from across subject areas, are at an early stage. Year 2010/11 will see the introduction of a suite of C&P Courses in years one, two and three of the programme. The challenges will be to:
• Plan, monitor and record what is happening across the programme, ensuring some sense of progression in inter-disciplinary teaching towards the key curriculum themes;
• Maintain the momentum of the development at a time of curriculum expansion and probable diminishing resources.

In meeting these challenges, the outlook has to be optimistic since the themes of health and well-being; creativity; global citizenship; education for sustainability; enterprising teaching and learning and learning beyond the classroom are all crucial and are now firmly embedded in the curriculum. Quite rightly, there is consensus that the curriculum is concerned not only with skills and knowledge about the world, but also with the development of healthy, fair minded, considerate and responsible human beings.

References

GTCS (2007) *Framework for Professional Recognition/ Registration, Advice and Guidance for Teachers,* Edinburgh: GTCS.

GTCS (2006) *The Standard for Initial Teacher Education* Edinburgh: GTCS

HMIE (2007a) *How Good is our School?* HGIOS3 Livingston: HMIE.

HMIE (2007b) *How Good is our School? Planning for Excellence,* Livingston: HMIe.

HMIE (2006a) *Progress with Student Teacher Placements* Livingston: HMIE.

HMIE (2006b) *How Good is our School? Part 4 The Journey to Excellence* Livingston: HMIE.

HMIE (2005) *Student Teacher Placements within Initial Teacher Education,* Livingston: HMIE.

SEED (2007a) *Making use of curriculum flexibility in primary schools.* Online at http://www.hmie.gov.uk/ documents/publication/cfps.html (accessed 14/06/10)

SEED (2007b) *Curriculum Architecture- a Literature Review.* Edinburgh: Scottish Government

SEED (2005) *Review of Initial Teacher Education Stage 2,* Edinburgh: Scottish Executive.

SOEID (2000) *Structure and Balance of the Curriculum 5-14 National Guidelines* Edinburgh: HMSO.National Guidelines

Scottish Government (2008) *A unified framework for the children's service workforce – Early Years and Early Intervention Framework* Edinburgh: Scottish Government

Scottish Government (Scottish Centre for Social Research) (2003) *Growing up in Scotland Study* (last updated October 2009). Online at: http://www.crfr. ac.uk/gus (accessed 14/06/10)

Scottish Parliament (2004) *Education (Additional Support for Learning) (Scotland) Act,* Edinburgh: HMSO

2.6 New Twists and Turns: What might the Research Excellence Framework mean for Educational Researchers?

Jane Brown, University of Edinburgh

IN THE PAST 10 YEARS there has been an increasing awareness of the need in education for stronger links between research, practice and policy. Similarly, there is wider recognition of the value of a policy-driven search for answers, and the need for research to contribute more effectively to formulating solutions. Recent developments in the Research Assessment Exercise reflect some of these concerns, and the **impact** of research as well as knowledge exchange is to be assessed in the next exercise. The proposed shifts in weighting raise some timely questions with regard to the nature and purpose of educational research and related criticisms of the applied emphasis in the field. While some disciplines have argued that evaluating impact is inappropriate for their subject areas, it is very much open to debate whether this is the case for education. This chapter addresses the implications of these developments on education, and explores some of the questions it raises for educational researchers.

Introduction

Predicting the impact of the new Research Excellence Framework (REF), on educational research and researchers is a challenging and risky activity. At the time of writing, the REF remains far from finalised, although much has been achieved in setting out its key criteria and components. Some aspects of the new framework involve ongoing consultation, and the piloting of methods of assessment continues. As a result, the original timeline for the implementation of REF, across Higher Education Institutions (HIEs) in the UK was recently delayed until 2014 (Times Educational Supplement 22 April 2010). The fact that the Conservative Party previously indicated that they would re-assess REF, if elected, adds further uncertainty. So what can speculation and reflection hope to achieve at this stage? Inevitably, this contribution will be exploratory in spirit, raising general issues rather than providing definitive answers. It will maintain that the key challenge facing educational researchers remains consistent with the focus of the former RAE which is the quality of research outputs and to a lesser extent the research environment. Critically, however, the new requirement in the emerging REF is the addition of research impact. On this issue researchers will be required: 'to plan to make an impact, to gather data on the impact of their work as it proceeds, and report on its impact '(Delamont 2010:11). Initially, this chapter will provide a brief overview of debates regarding quality of educational research. The new REF framework will then be addressed and its continuing focus on the quality of research outputs will be highlighted. Finally, this chapter will consider the implications of the new category of research impact on educational researchers.

Background: the nature of quality in educational research

The quality of educational research has been the focus of intense political and academic scrutiny, at various periods over the past twenty years (Whitty 2005). This has attracted both justified and unjustified criticism (Rees et al 2007). The critique of educational research was most vocal and reached a peak during the 1990's after the success of the New Labour government and their promotion of the 'what works' agenda. 'Evidence-informed' policy and practice rapidly gained support, influencing research agendas to this day (Furlong & Oneacea 2005). In particular, the usefulness and practical application of educational research for both policy makers and teachers was questioned. Other weaknesses of educational research were identified in the lack of cumulative knowledge, as was a gap in large-scale, quantitative studies (Rees et al 2007). Whitty (2005) lists these criticisms, and adds others:

- lack of rigour
- failure to produce cumulative research findings
- theoretical incoherence
- ideological bias
- irrelevance to schools
- lack of involvement of teachers
- inaccessibility and poor dissemination
- poor cost effectiveness.

(Whitty 2005)

Recent initiatives to promote quality research

In order to address some of these issues a number of research and training programmes have been funded by governments and other bodies (e.g. Higher Education Funding Councils in both Scotland and England). In Scotland the Applied Educational Scheme (AERS 2004-2009) was funded jointly by the Scottish Government and the Scottish Higher Education Funding Council to the tune of two million pounds. The ESRC (Economic and Social Research Council) funded the Teaching Learning Research Programme (TLRP) which continues to undertake research. These initiatives aimed to address research capacity in education with a view to enhancing the quality of research and promoting methodological expertise in the field. Importantly, these schemes and others (e.g. the General Teaching Council Scotland (GTCS) teacher research scheme in Scotland) sought to promote links between research, policy and practice by facilitating the participation of teachers as researchers and forging stronger links with policy makers.

In Scotland, recipients of grants from the government have, in fact, for some considerable time been required to produce, in addition to the traditional end of project report, a short teacher friendly report of approximately 8,000 words. These publications termed 'Insights' highlight the key findings of the research and their implications for practice and were automatically distributed to all schools. Today such outputs are regarded as a 'taken for granted' component of knowledge transfer activities. The extent to which this knowledge has been integrated into teachers' ongoing professional development certainly deserves further investigation. Similarly, the impact of current moves within Initial Teacher Education to ensure that students view their teaching and learning from a research-led perspective remains unclear.

From the RAE to the Research Excellence Framework (REF)

The Research Excellence Framework (REF) builds on its predecessor the RAE which assessed the quality of research outputs primarily through the process of peer review. Criticisms of the 2001 RAE (i.e. see the Roberts Report and the Lambert Report) included the fact that it did not acknowledge the importance of 'knowledge transfer' between universities and industries, neither did it promote 'innovative forms of collaborative university-led research' (Furlong & Oneacea 2005: 5).

A range of stakeholders have been involved in developing REF, including the Scottish Funding Council, the Higher Education Funding Council for Wales, the Department for Employment and Learning (Northern Ireland). REF proposes to focus on three core aspects of assessment, which together are viewed as reflecting the main dimensions of research excellence. These three components include:
• output quality
• impact of research
• quality of research environment.

Assessment and promotion of quality

According to Bridges (2009) the assessment of quality in research is one of the main drivers of the behaviour of staff in higher education institutions across the UK. The quality of research outputs in the new REF will be assessed largely as before on the basis of expert assessment by: 'the expert panels against international standards of excellence'. Some expert panels will continue to make use of metrics and citation information but now this will be supplementary and dependent on decisions made by individual panels. Crucially, quality remains the most important indicator (currently standing at around 60% of REF) in assessing research excellence within the new system. Indications are that quality may now be assessed on 3 outputs rather than the previous 4.

How quality is measured has always been especially problematic for education given that its theoretical basis is eclectic and that there is an applied emphasis in the field (Reiss et al 2010). Today more than ever, education is influenced by a variety of theoretical approaches, as well as methodologies. Inevitably this produces a diverse range of research so that assessing quality poses considerable challenges. There is also potentially an uneasy tension between quality and impact since the more explicitly theoretical considerations are engaged with in research, the less the outcomes are seen as being directly relevant to the work of 'hands-on' practitioners.

Assessment and promotion of impact

The creation of the new category of impact (with a predicted weighting of 25 % by some sources) has been prompted by a number of wider developments. Heightened awareness of the diverse nature of research and the multiple ways it can impact on society, both inside and outside academia (Davies et al, 2005; Bridges, 2009), has been an influential shift in thinking. Debates about the prioritisation of specific research agendas, for example, those around Sustainable Development, are also relevant, contributing to this intensified concern with research impact.

The new framework will give added recognition to circumstances where researchers: 'build on excellent research to deliver demonstrable benefits to the economy, society, public policy, culture and quality of life.' (see http://www.hefce.ac.uk/Research/ref/) While the assessment of impact is now being piloted, how this will be reliably and appropriately measured remains an important question for the humanities, including education.

Debating the meaning of impact for education

Delamont (2010) has recently advocated that there should be open debate in education regarding what impacts are desirable for education. She argues that it is essential for educational researchers to actively engage with, and shape the impact agenda rather than it being imposed on educational researchers. This seems particularly important given that little appears to be documented as to what might be viewed as impact for education (Reiss et al, 2010). REF stresses that impact strategies should be integrated into the early phases of research, including the planning stage, as well as throughout the life of the project. Nevertheless, it can be very difficult to anticipate how research findings may become relevant after the completion a study because impacts can be unforeseen and unexpected.

Discussion and concluding remarks

In recent years there have been a number of concerns about the quality of educational research with a range of strategies to address research expertise, knowledge transfer and user engagement in educational research. Moreover, the model of the autonomous and separate worlds of research, policy and practice is now widely regarded as both outdated and inadequate (Furlong & Oneacea 2005): an idea which is to some extent reflected in the new REF. So what are some of the implications for educational researchers? The continued significance of the quality of outputs underlines the crucial importance of high status outputs (e.g. journal articles, books and chapters). This underlines Martin Hammersleys' (2005) caution that educational research should not be complacent about raising the standard of educational research.

Assessing research impact is contentious but it remains to be seen whether, or in what form, it is included in the new framework. As Delamont (2010) argues, schools of education should be proactive and lead the debate on assessing outputs for their own discipline. This is especially important for educational research where, compared with other disciplines the state of knowledge on effectiveness is at an embryonic stage of development. Appropriate ways of assessing impact need to be in keeping with the concerns of educational research and encompass the diversity of its approaches and outputs. As this publication demonstrates, Initial Teacher Education may be one important avenue where educational researchers can start to identify and explore the impact of their research more fully. The publication also sets out an emergent and promising educational field in terms of integrating research, practice and policy. It remains to be seen, however, exactly how such links may be appropriately and reliably assessed in Higher Education in future.

References

Bridges, D. (2009) 'Research quality assessment in education: impossible science, possible art?', *British Educational Research Journal* 35 (4): 497-516

Davies, H. Nutley, S. Walter, W. (2005) 'Approaches to assessing the non-academic impact of social science research', ESRC symposium on assessing the non-academic impact of research 12th/13th May 2005

Delamont, S. (2010) 'Impact: A Personal View', *Research Intelligence* Spring ISSUE 110: 11

Furlong, J. & Oneacea, A. (2005) *Assessing Quality in Applied and Practice-based Educational Research A Framework for Discussion* see http://www.esrc.ac.uk/ESRCInfoCentre/Images/assessing_quality_shortreport_tcm6-8232.pdf (accessed April 2010)

Hammersley, M. (2005) Countering the 'new orthodoxy' in educational research: a response to Phil Hodkinson, *British Educational Research Journal*, 31(2): 139-156.

Rees, G. Baron, S. Boyask, R. Taylor, C. (2007) 'Research-capacity building, professional learning and the social practices of educational research', *British Educational Research Journal* 33 (5): 761-779

Reiss, M. Tough, S. Whitty, G. 'Measuring Impact in Educational Research', *Research Intelligence* Spring ISSUE 110: 14-19

Whitty, G. (2005) 'Education(al) research and education policy making: is conflict', *Inaugural Presidential Address British Education Research Association* University of Glamorgan, September 2005

SURVEYING ATTITUDES TOWARDS THE GLOBAL

3.1 Introduction

This section comprises chapters that help us to gauge the level of understanding of Education for Global Citizenship and Sustainable Development (EGCSD) within formal education. The investigations reported here examine the perceptions and attitudes of teacher educators, student teachers and practising teachers.

As part of the IDEAS 'Taking a Global Approach to ITE' project, the attitudes of a small sample of ITE tutors in Scotland to the global dimension were surveyed. This indicated significant support for the underlying principles that guide EGCSD, even if these were not always translated into practice. Voting for motherhood and apple pie is, however, not difficult. But, as Souter explains in Chapter 3.5, with regard to science tutors' attitudes, these positive responses are reassuring in terms of tutors' readiness to incorporate these principles into their teaching. The studies with student teachers suggest similar positive attitudes but Britton and Blee's study (Chapter 3.2) reveals the students' difficulties, in a complex policy context, of transferring their ITE experience in relation to the global dimension into their classroom practice. In the next chapter, Fenwick and Munro report on their study of student geography teachers' views. The study highlights the fact that they consider Education for Sustainable Development (ESD) an important issue, but lack confidence in defining and delivering it. The students indicated that more guidance on ESD issues throughout their ITE course would be welcomed. Findings also suggested a very positive attitude to cross-curricular work from these secondary subject specialists. Miller, Wakefield and Dunn (Chapter 3.4) compare the responses to EGCSD of three cohorts of students following different teacher education programmes. Their findings are suggestive of interesting differences in attitude to the global dimension between B.Ed., PGDE and Early Years specialists.

The next three chapters consider specific subject areas, Science, Design and Technology and Geography. As noted above, Souter is concerned with the readiness of science tutors to respond to the changing global context and the correspondingly shifting nature of science and science education. McLaren (Chapter 3.6) considers the potential for radical change within Design and Technology offered by ESD and investigates whether or not practising teachers are engaging with this challenge. Ross focuses on the EGCSD concepts of interdependence and participation and examines ITE practitioners' approaches to embedding these within ITE Geography. He also considers the potential role of ITE as a critical domain between school and university geography, where a foundational geographical imagination can be explored. It is perhaps worth suggesting to the reader that while these chapters are subject specific, the underlying issues and challenges will resonate in other curricular settings. Indeed, McNaughton and King's findings, in chapter 3.8, demonstrate ESD's applicability across the curriculum and all stages of schooling. They consider insights arising from the experience of Chartered Teachers following a specialist interest in ESD. Finally, Miller et al offer the initial findings of a research project aimed at eliciting teachers' views on the benefits of global citizenship in schools. The quote in their title 'They become completely involved' echoes the anecdotal evidence of generations of development and environmental educators.

Pulling studies like these together can allow us to compare findings and identify gaps where further research might be targeted. Large-scale attitudinal surveys around Global Learning have been carried out with teachers and pupils in England (e.g. DEA, 2009, 2008, Ofsted, 2009, WWF, 2009). These offered some startling insights. Encouragingly, 80% of teachers agreed that thinking about how teaching contributes to making the world a better place motivates them to stay in teaching (DEA, 2009) while, more worryingly, only 50% of secondary pupils thought that it was a good idea to have people of different backgrounds living in the same country together (DEA, 2008). The studies outlined in this section could help to guide the development of research of this scale in Scotland. These accounts can also be used to guide the development of EGCSD inputs, in terms of ITE staff development, as well as that of students and teachers. Finally, it is important too that the body of research investigating the impact of EGCSD in schools continues to grow.

References

DEA (2009). *Teachers' attitudes to global learning.* London: DEA

DEA (2008). *Young people's experiences of global learning.* London: DEA

Ofsted (2009). *Education for Sustainable Development: Improving schools, improving lives.*

Online at http://www.ofsted.gov.uk/Ofsted-home/Publications-and-research/Browse-all-by/Documents-by-type/Thematic-reports/Education-for-sustainable-development-improving-schools-improving-lives (accessed on 21/06/10)

WWF (2009). *Learning for Sustainability: from the pupils' perspective.* WWF-UK: Godalming

3.2 Global Citizenship and Course Development: The Experiences of Initial Teacher Education Undergraduate Students

Alan Britton and Harry Blee, University of Glasgow

Introduction

A number of major contextual backdrops informed the development work around global citizenship education at the University of Glasgow described in this chapter. One strong influence (and the origin of the requisite resources) was a new approach to UK development policy; the other was the emergence of a distinctive Scottish approach to Education for Citizenship (LTS, 2000; 2002), and latterly, the publication of *Curriculum for Excellence* (SEED, 2004). Such external policy drivers lent an impetus and rationale for a range of related developments that sought to embed global citizenship within Faculty Initial Teacher Education (ITE) courses.

This chapter provides an overview of this context, together with reference to critiques of such developments; a summary of the strategies employed to achieve the goal of embedding, and the evidence, derived from students' direct experiences and observations, of the extent to which this goal was achieved. The findings are not presented as a case study of flawless practice; rather they are offered with a desire to share experiences of a foray into educational and institutional transformation that enjoyed partial success but was also rendered problematic by a range of factors and circumstances. In this sense it conforms to the wider observation, that,

'Change in education is easy to propose, hard to implement, and extraordinarily difficult to sustain' (Hargreaves & Fink: 2006: p.1).

It is on this basis that it may offer notes of encouragement and caution in equal measure to others wishing to embark on similar journeys.

Context

In 2001, the UK Department for International Development (DFID) embarked on a programme to promote awareness of development issues in the UK. This programme arose from two policy position papers, *Eliminating World Poverty: A Challenge to the 21st Century* (DFID, 1997) and *Eliminating World Poverty: Making Globalisation Work for the World's Poor* (DFID, 2000). The 1999 strategy paper *Building Support for Development* set out DFID's aim of working with the formal education system, the media, businesses, trade unions and faith groups. It is within this context that DFID funded four projects across the UK jurisdictions to look at how changes to the processes of initial teacher education and training might be used to effect longer term changes in the attitudes of teachers towards global development issues. One successful bid was based on a partnership of the University of Glasgow Faculty of Education and the International Development Education Association of Scotland (IDEAS). This *Education for Global Citizenship* Project (hereafter referred to as The Project) ran from 2001-2004, and was followed by a second major development, *Development Awareness and Teacher Professional Development* which was funded for the period 2005-2008.

These developments, driven by a UK Government agenda, took place rather serendipitously at the same time as a new Scottish policy context pertaining to citizenship education and international education was emerging. A range of documents and policies were published from around 2000 that either relates directly or indirectly to the Education for Global Citizenship Project goals [e.g. *The Global Dimension in the Curriculum* (LTS,2007), *An International Outlook* (SEED, 2001), and Education for Citizenship (LTS, 2000 & 2002), amongst others]. Perhaps the single most important document to emerge in education since devolution, *Curriculum for Excellence* (SEED, 2004), places citizenship and global awareness at the heart of the fundamental purposes of education in Scotland, together with four core values that underpin the Curriculum: Wisdom, Justice, Compassion and Integrity. These values help to underpin the importance placed on global citizenship across the various policy frameworks.

The notion that global citizenship and international education ought to be a priority in Scottish education has been reiterated at various stages over the past decade or so, and it is worth noting that the concept has remained robust and has been relatively immune to political and administrative change; note the similarity between the following statements (the first from the then Scottish Labour Minister for Education, the second from his SNP counterpart [as Minister for Schools] seven years later):

'Scottish education must increasingly enable young people to acquire a thorough knowledge and appreciation of international and global issues and the necessary skills to enable them to participate actively and responsibly in the affairs of the 21st Century.' (McConnell,2001).

'Our education system needs to provide [Scotland's young people] with knowledge and understanding of the world and Scotland's place in it... We must ensure that our young people understand, and can respond to, the challenges that are presented by globalisation. If the curriculum is to be excellent, it must incorporate an international perspective; if it does not, our society and economy will be poorer. The Government is, therefore, committed to ensuring that an international education is part of the experience for young people in all our schools.' (Watt, 2008).

Such apparent consensus and shared sense of mission seems to have transcended a notable political divide in Scotland. This would appear to suggest that the notion of global citizenship education could be largely unproblematic. However, this is often far from the case, as will be described below.

Project Aims and Management Strategy

The Project's objectives were as follows:
1. To establish a model for embedding education for global citizenship in ITE
2. To build global citizenship into the philosophy and practice of ITE courses
3. To provide evidence of the effectiveness of this approach in developing global citizens.

'Embedding' was considered to have three levels, each of which could be pursued separately but would be best pursued as part of a unified strategy.
(i) ITE course documentation makes reference to Global Citizenship
(ii) Staff in the ITE institution, through their work, indicate that they interpret documentation in a way more oriented to Global Citizenship
(iii) The general ethos and operation of the ITE institution expresses the principles of Global Citizenship.

These objectives were overseen by a Project Management Team, consisting of representatives from both the Faculty of Education and IDEAS, which led all aspects of the Project over the period 2001-2004.

A number of strategies were developed by the Partnership to achieve the overarching Project aim of embedding Global Citizenship; including an initial audit of existing practice within the Faculty of Education; effecting change to ITE course documentation such that it makes greater reference to Global Citizenship; working with staff in Faculty to support their interpretation of documentation in a way more oriented to Global Citizenship; and seeking to ensure that the general ethos and operation of the ITE institution expressed the principles of Global Citizenship. The extent to which these broader strategies were successful across the Project lifetime is described in detail elsewhere (Blee, Britton et al, 2006) however the desire to monitor any change and progress over a longer timeframe included a longitudinal survey of student perceptions of their global citizenship experiences on the 4 year undergraduate (BEd) course from 2002 to 2008. The most pertinent findings from this study are presented later, however, it may be useful at this point to consider the vexed question of how one goes about pinning down a slippery concept, such as 'global citizenship' in ways that still allow for meaningful educational development.

Defining Global Citizenship

Given the potentially loaded connotations of a concept such as global citizenship, it is inevitable that there are different views on the definition, scope and goals of global citizenship education. The near global turn towards citizenship education over the past ten-fifteen years can be construed either as 'a deep-seated programme that seeks to inculcate critical values, attitudes and dispositions in participating school pupils; or it might be predicated on a shallower approach that provides a knowledge-based grounding in civic structures, perhaps alongside a limited emphasis on skills development for enhanced civic activism' (Britton, 2008). Such alternative views in relation to the praxis of citizenship education reflect a deeper-seated ideological disconnect between conservative and progressive impulses behind such developments (see for example, McCowan, 2009: p.18).

As Tully notes (2008: p.32), 'Global citizenship' has emerged as the locus of struggles on the ground and of reflection and contestation in theory. This is scarcely surprising. Many of the central and most enduring struggles in the history of politics have taken place in and over the language of citizenship and the activities and institutions into which it is woven'.

In the same way as history tends to be defined by the winning side, citizenship or global citizenship tends to be defined by the incumbent political party or the prevailing economic, political and social orthodoxy (see for example Sears and Hughes, 2006, in relation to Canada; Britton, 2006, about *education civique* in France; or Kisby, 2007, for the UK context). As McCowan (2009) suggests, both left and right can find fault with citizenship education. Not surprisingly, there has been something of a backlash against such approaches. In relation to global citizenship in particular there is concern about its apparent intrusion into the integrity of subjects such as Geography:

'…global citizenship education degrades both young people as embryonic political subjects and adults as independent political subjects. It presumes that neither is capable of acting as an independent moral agent by blurring the boundaries between the political world of adults and the world of children' (Standish, 2007: p.49).

Others suggest that it is possible (and indeed essential) for young people to address concepts, values and actions at the same time as imbuing canonical subject content:

'Teachers are probably ill advised to set out to 'change the world' through what they do, but they surely want to change individuals, by challenging them and equipping them to think. Subjects connect us to a range of intellectual traditions, but are also shot through with arguments about how to make sense of the world. Young people need grounding in both' (Lambert & Morgan, 2009).

In the light of such controversies, there was an attempt at the outset of the Global Citizenship Project to arrive at a shared understanding of what we meant by 'global citizenship'. This dialogue exposed potential divergence between perspectives, with the battle lines sometimes (but not always) drawn between the academic and the development practitioner point of view. A pragmatic compromise was reached by drawing upon the *Curriculum for Global Citizenship* framework developed by Oxfam which, while being perhaps philosophically under-stated has the merit of a clear matrix of knowledge, skills, values, teaching methodologies and actions that could be applied to the relevant work in the Faculty's ITE provision. This matrix thus helped to establish some of the core research instruments used in the initial audits as well as the longitudinal surveys. In doing so, the Project team understood that this limited to some extent the different categories and sub-sections of behaviours, knowledge, actions and so on that were considered in the tracking research; this was seen as the price of compromise because otherwise it would have been very difficult to agree on a manageable set of such categories.

The other advantage of Oxfam's definition is that there is scope for some variation on interpretations and the acceptable means of attaining certain goals. The principal difference seems to be one of priority. For educationalists, these goals could be seen as educational goods in their own right; 'experience of political campaigning' might be thought useful as an end in itself. For political campaigning groups the educational goals are only a means to the end of producing active citizens. This difference in perspective reinforces the suppression of what might otherwise have been conflicting or at least variable understanding of the Project's goals and methods.

Methodology

The strategy for data collection consisted of an initial analysis of course documentation (during the period 2001-2002), annual questionnaires to students (from 2002-2007) and semi-structured interviews with course leaders and annual student focus groups. Each year inevitably involved slightly different numbers of finishing students; however, they were consistently targeted during a dedicated session in their final Professional Development Week to ensure a high return rate. The emphasis in this chapter is on the qualitative dimension, namely, course reviews and the views of interviewees and focus group participants during the longitudinal study. This review work has not been undertaken from a specific epistemological standpoint, such as critical discourse analysis; rather it looks at narrative accounts of experiences, as well as some of the face value statements from the documentation.

Detailed analysis of the quantitative component of the research has recently been undertaken and will form the basis of a separate publication[ii]. However, in summary, the findings from the questionnaires seem to show that the development of new course documentation described below had at best a limited *longitudinal* impact on finishing students' exposure to core themes, skills and methodologies relating to global citizenship; in other words, 'improvements' to course documents and parallel developments did not translate into increased awareness/exposure over subsequent years. Notwithstanding, the year on year returns indicated a consistently high level of awareness across the adapted Oxfam matrix, with the exception of 'encouragement to take action' and its associated sub-categories, such as 'volunteering' or 'instigating a campaign'. This trend was consistent over time, suggesting that it is easier to promote change in relation to global citizenship content and dispositions without necessarily impacting upon behaviours.

Auditing Practice and Course Documentation

Change to course documentation was viewed as an important goal of the project, although the Project team were realistic in noting that explicit reference in documentation might not actually impact significantly on practice (as appears to have been vindicated by the evidence summarised above). The key documents were not assessed by looking to see how often global citizenship itself was referred to by name. Rather, the documents were assessed interpretatively, by seeing whether they contained reference to the development of the knowledge, skills, values and attitudes contained within the agreed (Oxfam) definition of global citizenship.

The review of course documentation focused on three of the Faculty's ITE courses: the BEd, the PGCE primary and the PGCE secondary. This analysis established, among other things, that BEd (undergraduate) course documentation at that point focused mainly on rationales, aims and frameworks, not on course content. As a consequence, conclusions about the extent to which courses are meant to contain knowledge, skills, values and attitudes at the basis of global citizenship could not easily be drawn. There also seemed to be obvious areas of omission, where, for example, the course documentation mentioned, 'developing awareness in students of national, regional, and whole school issues', a formulation which excludes the global.

When the BEd course was reviewed in 2001-02, members of the Project Team were involved in the process. The review was explicitly intended to reflect wider patterns of social change, and the new course afforded a central role to education for global citizenship and sustainable development, including strong support for active learning and developing citizenship skills and values through participation in community projects and through fostering student ownership of learning processes. The BEd course seemed to meet the aim of embedding education for global citizenship in Faculty practice. One spin-off from these developments was the creation of an elective specialist study model for third and fourth year BEd students in personal and social development/citizenship, which ran for the first time in 2005. This twin track strategy (general commitment to embedding alongside some specialist inputs and possibly electives) may, in fact, be a preferred model.

After the first year of the Project, the Team settled into a model of collaborative working generally characterised by IDEAS members working with staff rather than directly with students and the object of the collaborations being seen as a mutually beneficial exploration of a variety of methodologies. Work was done with a range of subject areas to enhance the integration of global themes in their courses.

One initial goal that failed to make significant inroads was the aspiration to enrich the culture of decision-making within the Faculty such that student voices would be more readily heard at a strategic level. Very little progress was made here; in part this can be explained by a collective failure (on both sides of the Project Partnership) to fully appreciate the pressures on students taking ITE courses. However, this explanation does not seem wholly satisfactory. More reflection is needed on the nature of decision-making and evaluation in a Faculty of Education, the power relationship between staff, students and senior management, and how it would be possible to make an impact on underlying power structures.

The Views of Students and Tutors

From the outset of the Project, there was some scepticism on the part of Faculty staff with regard to the ability of the students to incorporate global citizenship into their pedagogy or their professional stance. One senior Course Leader (interviewed in 2002) suggested that:

'They [BEd 4 students] are very focused on gaining their degree, and have a very narrow focus in 4th year, whether it's about getting the best degree possible and they are very focused in assignments and stuff like that. It's all very well what's going on in the world, but really it's nothing to do with them at the moment. I think there is maybe a sense, we will worry about this after we are qualified kind of thing.'

This view was subsequently echoed by some of the students, who indicated that the motivation to engage with the agenda might be vulnerable to circumstances such as timing and the intrusion of more pressing priorities:

'I don't know how much was taken on board by the students within the global citizenship component. The events that you had every year, they were always at the end of the year when people aren't around and say 'I'm not going in for that'…So the impact of citizenship within the University requires to be changed, to raise awareness. I think you need to restructure it into the middle of the curriculum because it is coming, they have seen it out in school, I think everybody has now' (BEd 4 student, 2005).

Another student suggested that different priorities might also prevail in the wider teaching profession, indicating that her experience of the level of discourse in school staff rooms concerned:

'whether or not the tea urn has been put on. How little Jack in such and such a primary was behaving today and was he in late today and I don't think ever anything bigger for discussion came up. A Channel 4 programme, Wife Swap, was about the biggest thing that came up for discussion. I think that was about the biggest topic we ever hit upon' (BEd4 student, 2005).

This view might be regarded as overly harsh on hard-pressed teaching colleagues taking a deserved break from the rigours of the classroom. It is also unclear whether schools can create alternative spaces for the kind of critical discussion that this student clearly felt was missing. More generally though there was a view that many practicing teachers lacked global awareness, in comparison to the students who had been exposed to aspects of global citizenship. One indicated that:

'unless they have been on courses for their own professional development and have an interest in it or whatever but I think when you go into most schools I would say our level of awareness is definitely a lot more than what older teachers have' (BEd 4 Student, 2004).

Another suggested that: 'For most of my placements I have been in a class with an older more experienced teacher and I definitely found that when I have come to do anything about globalisation or citizenship in the class it has been, 'oh yes, you do that kind of thing because I am not as comfortable about doing that" (BEd 4 Student, 2004).

And: 'I was in a school where there was said to be ten different languages spoken at any one time and this was new to most of these teachers, but I don't think they learned off the children, they were forced into a situation where they had to find out where the children had come from and I don't think they would have done it otherwise, I think they were forced into it. Some were more reluctant than others' (BEd 4 Student, 2004).

However a number of examples that the authors viewed as promising practice emerged: 'In my BEd3 placement one of the teachers was an enthusiastic music teacher and rather than just do a normal school play whatever she made it round the world with the music and she learned songs and music from around the world but every week she would do a lesson and then put on the culture for that country and then teach music from it, so the school play was music around the world and that was fantastic' (BEd 4 Student, 2007).

With regard to the impact of the course there were a number of positive comments. This observation suggests that a disposition towards global awareness was emerging as a result of the focus on global citizenship:

'There are things I have learned here that I thought to myself why did I not know that... but there are still so many things that I still have to learn about the world and what is going on... sometimes it takes me all my time just to watch the news and things like that... because I feel now I have a duty to know about these things... it should be part of our life now I would say' (BEd 4 Student, 2004).

Another student stated that: 'The course has made me more globally aware. Before I came onto the course I wouldn't say that I really, I knew about more than I was aware, but I was busy getting on with my life, working bringing in a living, ending a day, starting another day and so that any real concern or look at it was never taken on board' (BEd 4 Student, 2005).

In overall terms, there was a certain consistency in the annual accounts of finishing (year 4) students on the undergraduate course as expressed through the focus groups. There was a great deal of enthusiasm for global learning and a sense that it ought to be a significant aspect of their ongoing professional lives and values. However there were frustrations about the time available to learn about these themes in a crowded ITE curriculum as well as in a schools context where other apparently competing priorities (such as literacy and numeracy) held sway.

Conclusions: Learning Lessons for Future Work

The combination of course documentation reviews, interviews and focus groups, as well as the longitudinal quantitative research has created a relatively complex picture both of the original goals and strategies of the Project and the extent to which these aspirations were achieved. A number of tentative suggestions are offered here, based on the experience within

Glasgow's Faculty of Education, for those who wish to develop similar approaches elsewhere: A disconnect was consistently identified between the democratising impulses of the citizenship agenda, and the lack of authentic consultation and engagement with the student voice during the course (although many students suggested their peers were as much at fault for this as any other inhibiting factors). This is an area that requires further thought, and a genuine commitment on both sides to foster a culture of dialogue and genuine engagement.

The issue of whether to focus global citizenship work directly with students on specialist inputs is perhaps dependent upon the core goals of global citizenship developments within ITE. This should generally be avoided in a project aimed at embedding, since students ought to carry the fruits of the work away with them when they leave. However, carefully arranged work with students can be an essential part of effective delivery of these goals, and clear opportunities have emerged in this regard with the strongly asserted place of citizenship and global awareness within CfE. They can be justified, and located within the ITE curriculum on the basis of CfE values, capacities, curriculum design principles, cross-cutting themes and interdisciplinary strategies. As with any educational development it is a question of motivation and creativity on the part of ITE institutions; to work shrewdly within the limited flexibility of the system and to identify those aspects that might be truly transformative in ITE and beyond into the teaching profession.

As noted earlier, political support for education for global citizenship and international education has remained robust, has been relatively immune to political and administrative change and remains a priority in Scottish education. However, the necessary levels of political and economic awareness do not appear to prevail either in faculty or in schools. Nor do curriculum frameworks alone, however well devised or justified, capture the full richness, value and complexity of effective global citizenship education.

Consequently, our main recommendation is that it should be the aim of ITE to actively develop a higher quality, better educated and more critically adept teacher than in the past, i.e., one who is fully aware of citizenship education and international education. In order to achieve this, there is a need to provide for all new student recruits learning opportunities in global citizenship and international education (it may also have implications at the earlier stage of student recruitment). This should be complemented, at postgraduate Masters level, by a range of accredited (and non-accredited) courses in the areas mentioned. It is by experiencing excellence in teaching within a challenging student-centred learning environment, supported by engagement with leading-edge research that will in turn ensure pupils of the future are equipped with the knowledge, skills, values, and actions necessary for critical participation in a globalised society.

References

Blee, H., Britton, A., Davis, B. and Young, B. (2006). 'Never the twain shall meet'? Breaking barriers through a global citizenship partnership between NGOs and a higher education institution. Policy and Practice: *A Development Education Review*, Issue 2 Spring 2006.

Britton, A. (2006) 'The Auld Alliance is just a shot away.' *Times Educational Supplement* (Scotland), 20.1.06

Britton, A. (2008). Book Review: Roth, K. & Burbules, N.C. 'Changing Notions of Citizenship Education in Contemporary Nation-states', in the *Journal of Moral Education*, Volume 37, Issue 2, 2008.

Department for International Development (DFID): *Eliminating World Poverty: A Challenge to the 21st Century* (1997)
Building Support for Development (1999)
Eliminating World Poverty: Making Globalisation Work for the World's Poor (2000).

Hargreaves, A. & Fink, D. (2006). Sustainable Leadership. San Francisco;Jossey Bass.

Kisby, B. (2007). 'New Labour and Citizenship Education' in *Parliamentary Affairs* Vol. 60 No. 1, 2007, 84-101.

Lambert, D. & Morgan, J.(2009). 'Corrupting the curriculum? The case of geography', *London Review of Education*, 7: 2, 147-157

LTS (2000). *Education for Citizenship – A Paper for Discussion and Consultation*, Dundee: Learning and Teaching Scotland

LTS (2002). *Education for Citizenship – A Paper for Discussion and Development*, Dundee: Learning and Teaching Scotland

LTS (2007). *The Global Dimension in the Curriculum*. LTS, Glasgow and Dundee.

McConnell, J. (2001). Foreword to *An International Outlook: Educating Young Scots about the World*. Edinburgh, HMSO/The Scottish Executive.

McCowan, T. (2009). *Rethinking Citizenship Education: A Curriculum for Participatory Democracy*. London and New York, Continuum.

Sears, A. & Hughes, A. (2006). 'Citizenship: Education or Indoctrination?' *In Citizenship and Teacher Education*, Vol 2, No. 1, July 2006, 3-17

SEED (2004). *A Curriculum for Excellence*. The Curriculum Review Group. Scottish Executive.

SEED (2001) *An International Outlook: Educating young Scots about the world* Edinburgh: Scottish Executive

Scottish Executive (2004). A Curriculum for Excellence; *A Curriculum for Excellence – ministerial response*. Scottish Executive.

Standish, A. (2007). 'Geography Used To Be About Maps' in Whelan (ed.) *The Corruption of the Curriculum*. Civitas, London

Tully, J. (2008). 'Two meanings of global citizenship: modern and diverse', in Peters, Britton and Blee (eds), *Global Citizenship Education: Philosophy, Theory and Pedagogy*. Rotterdam, Sense Publishers.

Watt, M. (2008). Extract from Debate on International Education to Scottish Parliament, 24th April 2008. Official Report, Col. 7881. Online at: http://www.scottish.parliament.uk/business/officialReports/meetingsparliament/or-08/sor0424-02.htm#Col7881 (accessed 14/06/10)

Acknowledgements

This chapter draws in part on previous work by the authors, as well as their Faculty colleague Bob Davis, and IDEAS representatives Ben Young and Claire Duncanson. Some of the work relating to evaluation of the original 2001-2004 Project appeared in the Spring 2006 edition of Policy and Practice Journal. Data analysis from the longitudinal study was supported by Jon Hall, the SCRE Centre, University of Glasgow.

Footnotes

[i] Available at: http://www.oxfam.org.uk/education/gc/curriculum/

[ii] For further information, contact the authors at the University of Glasgow: a.britton@educ.gla.ac.uk

3.3 Early Career Scottish Geography Teachers' Perceptions of Education for Sustainable Development

Ashley Fenwick, University of Stirling and Bob Munro, University of Strathclyde.

International context

At the start of the 21st century the global pace of change and challenge continues unabated (Cullingford and Gunn, 2005). Headlines relating to climate change, resource depletion and the consequences of disproportional wealth distribution reflect the rising global and political prominence of issues relating to sustainable development (SD). The importance of Education for Sustainable Development (ESD) in helping individuals navigate increasingly uncertain futures is progressively part of the political agenda (Bourn and Wade, 2008). However, translating political rhetoric into meaningful policy and policy into practice remains challenging. An international study (Learning and Teaching Scotland (LTS, 2005) examining sustainable development education (SDE)in 10 countries reported:
'a great deal of good practice... but... also a need to appreciate and signpost the embryonic and fragile nature of the position of SDE (pp. 49).'

The launch of the UNDESD in 2005 has instigated several key policy documents linked to SD and ESD within the UK (Department for Environment, Food and Rural Affairs DEFRA, 2005a; DEFRA 2005b) and Scotland (SE, 2005a; SE, 2006). The strategic role of education as a vehicle for change and the pivotal role of Initial Teacher Education (ITE) has been emphasised (UNESCO, 2005). This chapter will provide a current Scottish case study exploring early career Geography teachers' views, attitudes and experiences of ESD.

Scottish education context

McNaughton (2007) provides a recent summary of the Scottish policy context linked to ESD in the formal education sector - identifying three phases – emergence, stagnation and re-emergence. Learning for Life (Scottish Office Environment Department, 1993) was a comprehensive and timely response to the United Nations Conference on Environment and Development (UNCED) Earth Summit in Rio which signalled the emergence of a structured and phased approach to ESD in Scotland. However, translating policy to practice proved problematic resulting in a piecemeal approach to ESD in schools. A stagnant period followed which saw the dissolution of the Scottish Environment Education Council in 1999. ESD seemed low on the new Scottish Parliament's agenda and was mainly subsumed under citizenship with Eco-schools largely fulfilling the ESD requirement in schools. Scotland's newest curriculum initiative, *Curriculum for Excellence* (CfE) (SE, 2004) signalled a policy change away from a traditional, knowledge-driven curriculum towards a more skill-based, flexible and creative system. The Scottish Government also indicated their commitment to ensuring: 'that the new *Curriculum for Excellence* integrates education for sustainable development across subject areas' (SE, 2005a, pp. 68).

ESD is specifically mentioned in four of the eight curricular areas - Social Studies, Science, Health and Well Being and Technologies covering topics such as climate change, food production, transport development, recycling, resource selection and renewable energy. Could CfE herald the re-emergence of ESD? Lavery (SDELG, 2006) states that policy and practice have lacked coherence and direction to date, but suggests that CfE knits well with ESD. A recent publication by HMIe (2009) noted that:
'most schools have been increasing their emphasis on sustainable development education, through eco-activities and recycling. Only half have reviewed the extent to which the curriculum promotes sustainable development education on a coherent and sustained basis' (pp. 7).

While ambitions are high at governmental level, concerns have been raised around the lack of consultation and clear rationale linked to the values which underpin CfE (Gillies, 2006). Curriculum architecture, too subject focused approaches and an assessment centred curriculum have been identified as challenges (McCracken, The Sunday Herald, 2008; MacIver, Teaching Scotland, 2007; Priestley, 2005). Changing departmental structures in some Local Education Authorities (LEA) leading to a lack of subject specialist guidance and management of curricular change have also been identified as practitioner concerns (Cairns, TESS, 2004; Henderson, TESS, 2006; Buie, TESS, 2007; SSTA, 2008). The Teachers' Agreement Communications Team (SE and Convention of Scottish Local Authorities, 2006) provided a more optimistic view of the restructuring process, concluding that communications within schools with faculty structures had generally improved and collegiality was promoting sharing of knowledge and practice. As a result of considerable lobbying relating to the above concerns, the Cabinet Secretary delayed implementation of CfE until 2010 (SG, 2008). This move has been welcomed by the majority of stakeholders as creating time for unresolved issues relating to content, assessment and staff development. (McCracken, The Sunday Herald, 2008) However, the OECD Report (2007) warns that Scotland's six-year lead up to curricular change, compared to countries like Finland that have undergone three reforms in 19 years, could lead to a loss of momentum, enthusiasm and commitment amongst practitioners (pp. 121).

Several of the changes and challenges shaping Scottish Education have been outlined. Priestley (2005) highlights the power that schools and practitioners have to mediate change. New teachers have been singled out as 'catalysts' of curriculum change linked to the implementation and delivery of CfE (Hulme et al., 2008). It is, therefore, an apposite time to consider new teachers' opinions linked to ESD.

Qualitative and quantitative questionnaire data was gathered from a group of 42 secondary Geography students from four of Scotland's seven ITE establishments. They represent 60% of new Scottish Geography teachers entering their induction year in August 2009. Their views will be explored in relation to three areas: defining ESD, ESD and ITE, and ESD and CfE. Each of these headings will be considered briefly.

Defining SD and ESD

SD is a difficult term to define, open to multiple interpretations (Scott and Gough, 2003) and continually evolving. One of the most frequently used definitions is proposed by the World Commission on Environment and Development (WCED, 1987):
'Sustainable development is development that meets the needs of the present without compromising the ability of future generations to meet their own needs' (pp. 43).

While a host of meanings abound, and are largely encouraged (Scott and Oulton, 1999), there is a growing consensus that SD must be conceptualised at least in terms of three overlapping dimensions: environment, society, and economy. (Summers et al.,2004).

Students were asked to identify key words they associated with the term SD. As Geography teachers – the majority of words reflected this background. Five terms dominated and accounted for almost 50% of responses. 'Environment' and 'Green' appeared most frequently followed by 'Renewable', 'Eco' and 'Future'. The economic dimension of SD was also evident in some student responses, for example, 'economy' and 'industrialisation'. 'Future generations' and 'responsibility' reflected the social aspect. The varied list highlights the breadth and multi-faceted nature of SD and the challenges associated with agreeing upon a clear definition. 19 out of 42 students stated that they found SD difficult to define.

In 2005 the UK produced a shared framework entitled One future – different paths (DEFRA, 2005a) to be used as the basis for each country to develop their own SD strategies. Their definition of SD reflects the three overlapping dimensions: 'Living within environmental limits and ensuring a strong, healthy and just society by achieving a sustainable economy, promoting good governance and using sound science responsibly' (pp. 8).

85% of students felt that this definition of SD was acceptable. A minority were suspicious of the political agenda and choice of wording. Questions such as who sets the limit were posed. Others felt that the tone lacked urgency and suggested a continuation of the status quo.

'It doesn't recognise the present predicament and the need for radical changes required. It represents a position of no real change'. (Student 7)

Speaking at the UNESCO World Conference on Education for Sustainable Development (2009) Graça Machel summarised the importance of ESD:
'In tackling the current global economic crisis, we have an opportunity to build a new world order, not simply tinker at the edges of a failed system or recreate the corrupt systems that have imploded on us. And education has a crucial role to play in restructuring. We know that education is key to individual growth as well as social, economic and political development'.

A range of views and perspectives exist relating to ESD (Sterling, 2001; Scott and Gough, 2003; Hicks, 2001; Morgan, 2000). However, the SE defines SDE as developing knowledge, skills and attitudes based on six principles of SD:
'Interdependence, Diversity, Carrying capacity, Rights and Responsibilities Equity and Justice, Uncertainty and Precaution' (SE, 2006, pp. 2-3).

80% of students found this definition useful. The six headings were viewed as wide ranging and helpful when planning programmes and selecting topics, whilst still allowing autonomy linked to delivery. The headings were thought to promote inter-disciplinary working. A minority of students commented on the difficult vocabulary and felt that the headings needed clarification and were inaccessible to pupils.

'Not very detailed, just fancy words, needs explained and elaborated upon in order to be able to develop a planned programme of ESD' (Student 4).

Students were able to provide a range of topics that might be covered as part of an ESD programme. 'Climate change' (17) and 'renewable energy' (11) were the most frequently identified issues associated with ESD. Other significant groupings were observed for 'Environment', 'Environmental impact', 'Environmental consequences '(9) and 'Farming/ Farming Practice' (6). Students viewed Geography as playing a central role within ESD programmes and most were clear about the benefits of inter-disciplinary working and delivery.

Education for sustainable development and initial teacher education in Scotland

The structure of Scottish ITE will now be outlined and the place of ESD in relation to this framework. Scottish secondary ITE has been dominated by the one-year model to a greater extent than most other European countries (Eurydice, 2002). Only one of the seven ITE providers in Scotland, the University of Stirling, offers a combined degree in Education and Geography. Despite, numerous discussions and alterations, the fundamental shape and purpose of secondary ITE programmes in Scotland have undergone little major change. For example, progressively from the early 1990s all teacher training establishments became affiliated with universities. Rather than re-energising programmes, the main results have been tensions in relation to teaching hours and school visits versus research demands (Nixon et al.,2000). Similarly, changes in the outcomes of ITE, towards competences and then standards, which occurred in the late 1980s and early 1990s, left Scottish ITE establishments with considerable freedom over the design, delivery and assessment of the training programme (Christie, 2008). Whilst the structure of teacher training programmes is determined by the General Teaching Council of Scotland (GTCS), teacher education institutions can be as innovative and flexible as they wish, so long as their programmes comply with the national guidelines issued from time to time by the First Minister, who is accountable to Scotland's Parliament for the quality of education in Scotland. Guidelines for teachers published by the Scottish Office Education and Industry Department (Scottish Office Education and Industry Department, 1998) state that teachers should be knowledgeable, competent and able to contribute to ESD, however, the extent and mode of coverage is left to individual teacher education institutions to determine. The SE and GTCS believe that it is through the acquisition of The Standard for Initial Teacher Education (SITE) (GTCS, 2006b) and the Standard for Full Registration (SFR) benchmarks (GTCS, 2006a) that students will develop the necessary skills and abilities to provide a high quality of teaching for all pupils. ESD is not a key benchmark heading but is referred to twice in the SITE under the expected features for benchmark 1.1.2 and 3.3:

'1.1.2 Have knowledge and understanding of, for example, sustainable development, equal opportunities, additional support needs, citizenship, international education, education for work, enterprise'(pp. 17).

'3.3 Know about environmental issues and be able to contribute to education for sustainable development' (pp. 25).

As with any public sector activity, government and its agencies have scrutinised teacher preparation. ESD was briefly mentioned in the two most recent reports:

A Scoping Review of ITE (HMIE, 2003) indicated that early career teachers' views on education for sustainable development were relatively polarised, with 44% of probationers suggesting that ITE had provided some understanding and a similar proportion (45%) claiming that ITE had not provided any understanding at all' (pp. 20).

The follow up review stated that whilst ITE establishments were largely equipping students successfully to meet the needs of 21st Century pupils, they did not feel well prepared in relation to ESD (SE, 2005b, pp.4). The report concluded that too many expectations were being placed on ITE and that courses did not have the capacity to respond positively to all the demands for greater emphasis on topics such as ESD, concluding that ITE was 'only the initial phase in a continuum of teacher education' (SE, 2005b, pp. 7). An international report indicated that Scottish ITE (OECD, 2007)' training remained too subject-centred and too little focussed on the challenges of diversity and inclusiveness' (pp. 40) and lacked 'cross-professional training'(pp. 89).

If we are to ensure that ITE supports learning that incorporates a global dimension and prepares young people to contribute to the sustainable development of society, the way teachers are trained and the extent to which they feel prepared to meet this challenge must be examined. The IDEAS network launched a 3 year project in 2007 entitled 'Taking a Global Approach to ITE' which seeks to foster an active and growing network of teacher educators, engaged with global issues, who are developing and promoting quality teaching and learning approaches for Global Citizenship/Sustainable Development throughout all ITE courses. This small scale piece of research will contribute to this larger body of knowledge. The initial findings from this study suggest that this sample of new Geography teachers do not feel well equipped to deliver ESD. 40% of students felt that ITE had not prepared them for teaching ESD and 60% requested more ESD in ITE preparation. There were a significant number of neutral responses - 38% and 36% respectively. 52% lacked awareness of resources available to support teaching ESD.

30 students indicated that they had not observed/taught any aspects of ESD during ITE school placements. Given the relevance and wide range of topics encompassed within ESD and commonly taught in Geography classrooms in Scottish secondary schools, this result seems questionable. This may be because the term ESD was not specifically linked to the topic; and students had earlier identified a long list of ESD issues such as climate change, land use conflict and development issues associated with this area. A minority of students provided some examples of good practice they had observed linked to ESD. For example, a climate change week within a school, an environmental based first year unit and successful inter-disciplinary project involving Geography and Art.

Almost half of the early career Geography teachers indicated a lack of confidence if asked to teach ESD and seven of these considered it a difficult topic to teach. They requested greater guidance in relation to exploring key topics, suitable teaching and learning strategies and ideas for delivering ESD lessons. They considered that ESD should be accorded a higher priority in the ITE course; more opportunities for inter-disciplinary working would be welcomed as well as time to share placement experiences. Resources such as websites which provided up to date information on initiatives and included examples of good practice relating to discrete and inter-disciplinary ESD strategies were requested. Conferences and continuous professional development opportunities were also seen as beneficial.

Education for Sustainable Development and *Curriculum for Excellence*

There was overwhelming support for the Government's intention to promote a planned programme of ESD in Scottish schools. 76% of students agreed that CfE was a good vehicle for delivering ESD. They indicated that the inter-disciplinary nature of ESD and contemporary content was in line with CfE and the four capacities linked with many aspects of ESD such as responsible citizens and respect for others. However, some concerns were noted in relation to the vague nature of the outcomes which could result in multiple interpretations.

All students indicated that more than one subject area should deliver ESD, 6 students felt that all departments within a secondary school had a valuable contribution to make. Subjects that were viewed as best equipped to deliver ESD were: Geography, Biology, Modern Studies, Personal and Social Education, Home Economics and Business Studies. Collectively, these subject areas reflect the three key areas associated with ESD – economy, environment and society. It was surprising given the strong focus on literacy and numeracy within ITE and schools that these areas were largely overlooked by students.

All students stated that ESD should be embedded in the secondary curriculum. They view ESD as an inter-disciplinary topic and 36 students felt that ESD was well suited to inter-disciplinary working. Most believe that primary and secondary schools can play a valuable part in the delivery of ESD - 83% indicated that it was suited to primary and secondary stages. However, only 45% felt it should be delivered from nursery, this runs counter to agreed policy on ESD and the 3-18 philosophy advanced by CfE.

Conclusion

Our data indicates that early career Geography teachers view ESD as an important issue which should be embedded within the new Scottish curriculum and experienced by all pupils. CfE is viewed optimistically and presents a valuable opportunity for enhanced inter-disciplinary working designed to promote ESD. However, there was little evidence these new teachers would act as 'catalysts of change' (Hulme et al., 2008). Instead greater direction from ITE and schools was requested, linked to learning and teaching strategies, clearly identified resources and CPD support. The new teachers are demonstrably receptive to ESD related issues and ideas. A lack of confidence has been highlighted in relation to defining and delivering SD/ESD. This lack of confidence may be eased if greater collective responsibility and commitment to ESD were displayed by key stakeholders – policy makers, HMIE, ITE and LEAs. ITE has a responsibility to model good practice and create more opportunities for inter-disciplinary working.

'Sustainable development education is not about transmitting a set of answers to pupils, but about engaging them in learning and in activities that will allow them to develop the skills and explore the issues in ways that will enable them to make up their own minds on some of the issues which will shape the world' (Sustainable Development Education Liaison Group, 22-23rd August 2006, pp. 3).

The same is true for ITE – it is not only about meeting the SITE but engaging students in challenging, meaningful debate and discussion. It should provide opportunities for students to:
• 'investigate and interrogate the discourse of ESD
• develop a critical and holistic understanding of ESD
• reflect on and analyse their own views of ESD
• apply this understanding to planning, using and evaluating classroom materials (which meet curriculum requirements) in ESD
• rethink ways of teaching geography that take account of complex social and political issues
• move from promoting transmissive learning to promoting critical and creative transformative learning '(Smith, 2007).

A more joined up approach is required if ESD is to become embedded within the Scottish curriculum. ITE is only the first phase in teacher development (HMIE, 2003) and there is clearly potential for CPD linking CfE and ESD. This could provide a valuable opportunity for schools and ITE to work together to create partnerships which would support and sustain teachers.

Acknowledgment
Please note that this chapter was based on a presentation given at the 2009 conference of the 'UK Teacher Education Network for Education for Sustainable Development/Global Citizenship'. It was published previously in Inman, S. & Rogers, M. (Eds.) (2009) Developing Critical Perspectives on Education for Sustainable Development / Global citizenship in Initial Teacher Education. UK Conference July 2009. Conference Proceedings. London: CCCI, Southbank University.

References

Bourn, D. & Wade, R. (2008) Teacher Education: Education for Sustainable Development and Global Citizenship: The Challenges of the UN Decade. In: *Proceedings of the UK ITE Network for Education Sustainable Development/ Global Citizenship. London, 10th July*, UK ITE ESD/GC Network, pp. 4-24.

Buie E. (2007) Faculties a backward step. *Times Educational Supplement Scotland.* 1st June. Online at http://www.lexisnexis.com/uk/nexis/results/docview/docview.do?docLinkInd=true&risb=21_T5482775718&format=GNBFI&sort=BOOLEAN&startDocNo=1&resultsUrlKey=29_T5482737845&cisb=22_T5482775720&treeMax=true&treeWidth=0&csi=235865&docNo=11 (accessed 10/2/ 2009).

Cairns, G. (2004) Faculties Won't Work. *Times Educational Supplement Scotland* 7th May. Online at http://www.lexisnexis.com/uk/nexis/results/docview/docview.do?docLinkInd=true&risb=21_T5482853863&format=GNBFI&sort=BOOLEAN&startDocNo=1&resultsUrlKey=29_T5482853866&cisb=22_T5482853865&treeMax=true&treeWidth=0&csi=235865&docNo=3 (accessed 10/2/ 2009).

Christie, D. (2008) Professional Studies in Initial Teacher Education. In: Bryce

T. G. K. & Humes, W. M. (Eds.) *Scottish Education: Beyond Devolution.* Edinburgh, Edinburgh University Press, pp. 830.

Cullingford, C. & Gunn, S. (eds.) (2005) *Globalisation, Education and Culture shock.* University of Huddersfield, Athenaeum Press.

Department for Environment, Food and Rural Affairs (2005a) *One future – different paths. The UK's shared framework for sustainable development.* London, DEFRA Publications.

Department for Environment, Food and Rural Affairs (2005b) *Securing the future: delivering UK sustainable development strategy.* The Stationary Office.

Eurydice (2002) *Key topics in education in Europe. The teaching profession in Europe, Report 1: Initial training and transition to working life.* Brussels, European Commission.

Gillies D. (2006) A Curriculum for Excellence a Question of Values. *Scottish Educational Review*, 38, pp. 25-36.

GTCS (2006a) *The Standard for Full Registration.* Edinburgh, General Teaching Council Publishing.

GTCS (2006b) *The Standard for Initial Teacher Education.* Edinburgh, General Teaching Council Publishing.

Henderson, D. (2006)). Faculties meet resistance. *Times Educational Supplement Scotland* 26th May. Online at http://www.lexisnexis.com/uk/nexis/results/docview/docview.do?docLinkInd=true&risb=21_T5483178125&format=GNBFI&sort=BOOLEAN&startDocNo=1&resultsUrlKey=29_T5483178128&cisb=22_T5483178127&treeMax=true&treeWidth=0&csi=235865&docNo=1 (accessed 5/3/2009)

Hicks, D. (2001) Envisioning a better world. *Teaching Geography*, 26, pp. 57-60.

HMIE (2003) *Evolution or Revolution? HMIE Scoping Review of Initial Teacher Education.* Livingston, HMIE.

HMIE (2009) *Improving Scottish Education - A report by HMIE on inspection and review 2005-2008.* Livingston, HMIE.

Hulme, M., Elliot, D., McPhee, A. & Patrick, F. (2008) *Professional culture among new entrants to the teaching profession Report to the General Teaching Council for Scotland and the Scottish Government.* University of Glasgow.

Learning and Teaching Scotland (2005) *Sustainable Development Education Liaison Group - an international study.* Learning and Teaching Scotland.

McCracken E. (2008) Delay on cards for flagship schools policy. *The Sunday Herald*, 26th October. Online at http://www.lexisnexis.com/uk/nexis/results/docview/docview.do?docLinkInd=true&risb=21_T5556765709&format=GNBFI&sort=BOOLEAN&startDocNo=1&resultsUrlKey=29_T5556765712&cisb=22_T5556765711&treeMax=true&treeWidth=0&csi=172807&docNo=3 (accessed 23/01/09).

MacIver, M. (2007) *Teaching Scotland.* Edinburgh, General Teaching Council Publishing.

McNaughton, M. J. (2007) Sustainable development education in Scottish schools: the Sleeping Beauty syndrome. *Environmental Education Research*, 13, pp. 621-638.

Machel, G. (2009) *UNESCO World conference on Education for Sustainable Development.* Online at: http://www.esd-world-conference-2009.org/en/whats-new/news-detail/item/graca-machel-addressed-world-conference-participants-in-keynote-speech.html (accessed 20/05/09).

Morgan, J. (2000) Geography teaching for a sustainable society. In Kent, A. (Ed.) Reflective Practice in Geography Teaching. London, Paul Chapman Publishing.

Nixon, J., Cope, P., McNally, J., Rodriques, S. & Stephen, C. (2000) University-based initial teacher education: institutional re-positioning and professional renewal. *International Studies in Sociology of Education*, 10, pp. 243-261.

OECD (2007) *Reviews of National Policies for Education: Quality and Equity of Schooling in Scotland.* Paris: OECD.

Priestley, M. (2005) Making the most of the Curriculum Review: Some Reflections on Supporting and Sustaining Change in Schools. *Scottish Educational Review*, 37, pp. 29-38.

Scott, W. A. H. & Gough, S. R. (2003) *Sustainable development and learning: framing the issues*, London, Routledge Falmer.

Scott, W.A.H. & Oulton, C. (1999) Environmental Education: arguing the case for multiple approaches. *Educational Studies*, 25, pp. 119-125.

Scottish Executive (2004) *A Curriculum for Excellence – The Curriculum Review Group*. Edinburgh, Scottish Executive.

Scottish Executive (2005a) *Choosing our future: Scotland's sustainable development strategy*. Edinburgh, Scottish Executive.

Scottish Executive (2005b) *Ministerial Response to the Review of Initial Teacher Education Stage 2*. Edinburgh, Scottish Executive.

Scottish Executive (2006) *Learning for Our Future: Scotland's first Action Plan for the UN Decade of Education for Sustainable Development*. Edinburgh, Scottish Executive.

Scottish Executive & Convention of Scottish Local Authorities (2006) *Teachers' Agreement Communications Team: Evolving Career Structure in the Secondary Sector*. Edinburgh.

Scottish Government (2008) *Report of the Teacher Employment Working Group*. [WWW] Available from:http://www.scotland.gov.uk/Resource/Doc/242958/0067605.pdf [Accessed 20/01/09].

Scottish Office Education and Industry Department (1998) *Guidelines for initial teacher education courses in Scotland*. Edinburgh, SOEID.

Scottish Office Environment Department (1993) *Learning for life: a national strategy for environmental education in Scotland*. Edinburgh, HMSO.

Scottish Secondary Teachers Association. (2008). SSTA *Calls for a Delay in Curriculum for Excellence*. Online at http://www.ssta.org.uk/PressReleases/pressrelease_CfEdelay.htm (accessed 23/01/09).

Smith, M. (2007) GTIP Think Piece – Education for Sustainable Development. Online at http://www.geography.org.uk/projects/gtip/thinkpieces/esd/ (accessed 30/03/09).

Sterling S. (2001) *Sustainable Education: Revisioning learning and change*, Totnes, Green Books.

Summers, M., Corney, G. & Childs, A. (2004) Student teachers' conceptions of sustainable development: the starting point of geographers and scientists. *Educational Research*, 46, pp. 163-182.

Sustainable Development Education Liaison Group (22-23rd August 2006) *Discussion Paper Sustainable Development Education in A Curriculum for Excellence Network Event*. Stirling Management Centre.

UNESCO (2005) *Guidelines and recommendations for reorienting teacher education to address sustainability*. Paris, UNESCO.

World Commission on Employment and Development (1987) *Our common future*, Oxford, OUP.

3.4 Where Are They Coming From? Education Students' Knowledge and Attitudes towards Global Issues

David Miller, Peter Wakefield and Brenda Dunn, University of Dundee

Introduction

The current emphasis on global education (see, for example, LTScotland, 2010; Scottish Government, 2009) has many implications for universities, in terms of initial teacher education (ITE) and continuing professional development (CPD) programmes. This chapter looks at one aspect of ITE provision, although as will become clear, it also draws upon data from a smaller group of students following a post-qualifying course. Essentially, it focuses on the knowledge that beginning teachers bring with them as they start their primary teaching courses.

In common with many other countries, pre-service teacher education in Scotland has two main routes: the four-year undergraduate Bachelor of Education programme (B.Ed.) and the one-year post-graduate diploma in education (PGDE), which requires the student to hold a first degree. There is some commonality of approach across Scotland in terms of course structure and experiences, and this is currently being encouraged via partnership agreements.

Within individual institutions also, there exist natural pressures towards congruence between the aims and structures of their B.Ed. and PGDE programmes. Drivers here include the overall framework provided by the Standard for Initial Teacher (SITE) benchmarks (GTCS, 2006) and concerns about efficiency of programme delivery. There is also likely to be similarity in terms of underlying ethos, reflecting institutional hegemony and shared beliefs of the teaching staff. These factors often lead to a broadly similar focus being adopted in terms of content knowledge, placement experiences and teaching and learning style on pre-service courses.

This is clearly only a partial picture, since the temporal dimension alone means that the lived reality of the two student bodies is very different, with students on the one-year course having to assimilate information and develop skills in a significantly shorter period of time. Additionally, those individuals who undertake the four-year course (often, but not exclusively, direct from school) may have had very different life experiences from those who take the one-year course – all of whom have already obtained at least one degree, and some of whom have given up other careers to enter teaching. So, while both groups of students are working towards the same goals, course tutors and programme managers are aware that the student bodies have different pressures. Moreover, they bring different life experiences to the programmes.

Mindful of these and other factors, programme teams are aware of the need to take into account students' starting knowledge. Whether this concern is driven more by beliefs about constructivism and principles of student-centred learning – or by pragmatic factors related to efficiency of teaching and covering an ever-widening curriculum – it is undoubtedly helpful to have a picture of what the students bring with them when they start. In an area where attitudes, as well as factual knowledge, are relevant, this is particularly important. The area of Global Citizenship (GC) is one such area, and this chapter reports some findings from a survey designed to learn more about beliefs and attitudes of student teachers.

What we did

At the start of term, before the pre-service students had attended any classes on global issues, a survey was conducted. This involved students completing a short questionnaire, originally designed to provide teaching staff with some baseline data to inform subsequent teaching and learning on the B.Ed. and PGDE programmes. Shortly afterwards, the opportunity arose to administer the instrument to a group of early years practitioners who were undertaking a post-qualifying course, the B.A. in Early Childhood Studies (BAECS). It was felt that this extra group of students might provide an interesting comparison with the two pre-qualifying groups.

The participants consisted of the entire cohort of B.Ed. and PGDE students (n=94 and 119 respectively), together with 37 students following the BAECS programme. The questionnaire consisted of 12 main items, several of which were sub-divided. Some of these were open-ended questions; examples included: 'What do you understand to be the issues that Global Citizenship covers?' and 'When should the teaching of Global Citizenship start?' Other items involved respondents rating the importance of different global topics on a 5-point scale. Some probed opinions on the language associated with global issues. The range of question types meant that both quantitative and qualitative data were collected. The former were collated as descriptive statistics; the latter were subject to a simple content analysis to identify common themes. The aim was to look for overall trends across all participants, but also for similarities and differences between the student groups. What follows is a summary of some preliminary findings.

What we found
a) Beliefs about the nature and scope of GC

In an open-ended question, students were asked for their understanding of the issues addressed by GC. No limit was set on the number of issues raised, and responses ranged from zero to six. Overall, two main issues were identified: a concern for the global environment, and the need to respect difference and diversity. However, there were interesting differences between the groups. About one third of B.Ed. students and twice that proportion of PGDE students identified a concern for the global environment:

'recycling, learning about global warming and extinction of animals' (B.Ed. f.)
'Understanding global problems such as third-world hunger, ozone layer, ice caps melting, weather, etc' (PGDE, f)
'Sustainable development. Global warming /climate change and individual responsibility.' (PGDE, f)

With the B.Ed. students, although many other issues were also mentioned, none stood out as being chosen frequently. It is perhaps notable that four out of ten B.Ed. students did not respond to this question. However, with the PGDE students, a significant number (40%) identified another priority: respecting difference and diversity:

'the world is very diverse and different ethnicities are increasingly combined. We need to understand inclusion' (PGDE, m)
'(gaining) knowledge of other cultures and diversity' (PGDE, m)
'respecting values and diversity' (PGDE, f)

With the BAECS students, the proportion of respondents identifying respecting difference and diversity was even higher; it was the most frequently mentioned issue, with over two thirds noting this. No other major issue was identified with any regularity by these students:

'to make attempts to understand cultures and customs different to our own' (BAECS, f.)
'It will highlight rights, concerns, human dignity, interests equality, race and religion' (BAECS, f.)
'Valuing what others provide us with and respecting everyone for who they are, not what they possess' (BAECS, f.)

In a related question which asked which of the topics were 'most important', the patterns were very similar, with the same issues being highlighted. In terms of the number of suggestions, it would appear that the PGDE students had most to say on this topic. Modal figures indicated the typical response for this group consisted of two issues, whereas for the other two groups it was just one. The B.Ed. students seemed less certain in their views here, as reflected in the large proportion that offered no response.

An open-ended question asked which skills one might expect from a global citizen. The most common response related to individuals holding positive attitudes towards people: being caring, understanding, respectful:

'Recognising the rights and beliefs of individuals and nations' (B.Ed. f.)
'Understanding and valuing other opinions, cultures, ways of life and beliefs' (PGDE, f.)

'I think a global citizen should be respectful of others and have a sense of personal responsibility for the world' (BAECS, f.)

Again there were some differences between groups. With the B.Ed. students, almost 4 out of 10 students commented on holding positive attitudes towards people. No other patterns of response stood out, and over 40% made no comment at all. In contrast, with the PGDE students, a similar figure (about 4 in 10) commented on holding positive attitudes towards people, but in addition a further 36% identified other positive personal characteristics. Analysis of these comments showed that they related to other personal characteristics, more general in nature; for example, being open minded, flexible, honest, having integrity:

'showing awareness of issues, communication skills' (PGDE, m.)
'having a drive to make a difference, analytical skills' (PGDE, f.)
'(having) the skill to pass on knowledge/advice to others' (PGDE, f.)

Additionally these students identified a range of other characteristics. Similar patterns were seen with the BAECS students: 70% of respondents identified holding positive attitudes towards others, and 57% mentioned other positive personal characteristics.

The overall picture here seems quite clear. Almost all those who offered a response focused on personal – often inter-personal – characteristics. It seems noteworthy that this emphasis on personal characteristics emerged so strongly, as opposed to a commitment to taking care of the planet, being knowledgeable about environmental concerns, and focusing on sustainability issues.

b) The importance of Global Citizenship in the curriculum
A closed question asked students to rate the importance of Global Citizenship as a curriculum subject in schools today (see Table 1). A five-point scale was used, 1 signifying not important and 5 very important. This was followed by an open-ended question asking for reasons for respondents' decisions. The modal score overall was 4, but once more there was some variation when we looked at mean scores.

Table 1: How important is the teaching of Global Citizenship?

Programme	N	Mean scores
B.Ed.	94	3.29
PGDE	119	4.14
BAECS	37	4.49

Certainly it appears that B.Ed. students see Global Citizenship as being less important than do the other groups. BAECS rated it highest. However, no clear pattern emerged from the reasons offered for the choices, with a wide range of justifications offered. The reasons offered most frequently, with similar patterns in all three groups, were that it is important for the child to become a responsible citizen, and it is important for improved understanding of GC issues generally.

Respondents were given a list, and asked to rate five specific aspects of Global Citizenship in terms of their importance. Scores ranged from 1 (not important) to 5 (very important). Mean scores can be seen in table 2.

Table 2: How important are these aspects of Global Citizenship?

	MEAN SCORES		
	B.Ed.	PGDE	BAECS
Understanding and accepting diverse values	3.5	4.3	4.5
Expanding the scope of knowledge	3.2	4.0	4.4
Raising awareness of global issues	3.7	4.3	4.2
Raising awareness of sustainability issues	3.2	4.2	4.0
Enhancing pupils' future competitiveness	2.5	3.1	3.1

Two trends seem evident. First, the PGDE students tended to rate each item more highly than B.Ed. students. In fact, their views were more aligned with the BAECS students, despite the fact that in terms of professional preparation they had more in common with the B.Ed. students[1]. Second, it can be seen that the lowest means within each group are for the final item here, enhancing pupils' future competitiveness. Clearly this particular aim was not rated highly by these respondents – at least in the context of Global Citizenship.

c) Pedagogy: when and how should Global Citizenship be taught?

An open-ended question asked when teaching in Global Citizenship should start. Overall, there was a clear preference for a very early start, with a high proportion specifically mentioning nursery or 'the earliest years'. Not surprisingly perhaps, the BAECS students spoke with one voice, with almost 90% suggesting starting at the earliest stages. PGDE students followed this trend (60%), but a significant minority (over a quarter) specifically mentioned infants rather than nursery. Once more, there was more variability amongst the B.Ed. students; a wider range of alternative start-times was evident, although the nursery stage was still the most popular suggestion.

[1] A simple one-way ANOVA with post-hoc comparisons indicated that the scores of the B.Ed. students were significantly lower than those of the other two groups ($p < .001$, two-tailed).

One question asked about the basis on which Global Citizenship topics should be chosen. There were some interesting variations here. B.Ed. students offered a range of suggestions, the most popular (about a third of responses) being that work should be based round topical issues. In contrast, PGDE students were roughly split; over 40% thought that projects should be based on topical issues, but a similar proportion favoured basing choices on children's interests and/or their stage of development. With BAECS students, more than half chose the child's interest or level of development, with a further 21% saying it should be based on the curriculum. Given the educational ideology which informs pre-school education, these may well be viewed as similar in emphasis; both relate to a focus on the child's perspective. Taken as a whole, it seems clear that students favoured an early start to teaching Global Citizenship; there was little evidence that the nature of the subject matter called for a later start to this work.

When asked about the challenges which might be associated with the teaching of Global Citizenship, there was again some variation between the groups. With the B.Ed. students, over half made no response at all. Given the fact that they had only just started the course, this high percentage is unsurprising. Of those who did respond, the scope and complexity of the subject matter was identified as the biggest challenge (20% of the group). With the PGDE students, who were at a similar stage of professional preparation, we saw a different pattern; over 90% expressed opinions here. There was spread amongst their responses.

38% referred to the nature of the subject matter:

'difficulties making the issues appropriate to the level' (PGDE, f.)
'younger children may not have a strong enough concept of 'future' to understand sustainability, etc' (PGDE, m.)
'emphasising the fact that individual actions can affect the world – children often think on an individual/family level' (PGDE, f.)

29% identified issues related to child or family values and beliefs:

'Being able to get people to take it seriously' (B.Ed. f.)
'[conflicts with] the values passed down from the community and family' (PGDE, f.)
'Since some of the issues are upsetting, some people may want to keep their children ignorant' (B.Ed. f.)

19% referred to teacher characteristics (her knowledge base, etc.):

' The teacher might not have specialist knowledge' (B.Ed. m.)

' Researching and developing our own knowledge to teach the children' (B.Ed. f.)
' resources, teacher knowledge and understanding' logistics, balancing subjects' (PGDE, f.)

With BAECS students, almost half mentioned child and/or family characteristics, and 27% highlighted teacher characteristics. Some responses from this group are reproduced here because of the reflective nature that is evident:

'Ensuring that practitioners understand the issues themselves and feel confident about how to include global citizenship into their practice.' (BAECS, f.)
'My own opinions and attitudes – as fair minded as one hopes to be we always have some bias' (BAECS, f.)
'One of the biggest challenges is dealing with differing family views and values and this is just one of the reasons that parental participation in the setting is so important. Sensitively dealing with those differences while promoting a positive attitude requires knowledge and understanding of the issues involved' (BAECS, f.)

In many ways the last quote above summarises very effectively some of the important issues.

d) The language of Global Citizenship: what's in a name?
A series of open-ended questions attempted to investigate students' awareness of, and views about, the language often employed when making global comparisons. When asked whether they had any thoughts about the ways in which terms such as 'third world', 'developing countries' and 'the west' were used, between a fifth and a quarter of PGDE and BAECS students commented on the derogatory connotations of the language in this area, and the fact that such statements were simplistic and did not reflect the complexity of the issues:

'It is derogatory language' (PGDE, f)
'It's too simplistic, too generalising, with a focus on GDP/industrial output' (PGDE, f.)
'I think the term 'Third World' is degrading as many assume people who are living in poverty are unintelligent and this I feel is untrue' (BAECS, f.)
' 'The West' gives an indication that we are more civilised but really the west has many problems such as violence, poverty and crime' (PGDE, f.)

Fewer than 10% of B.Ed. students responded to this item.

The next two sets of responses provided perhaps the most striking piece of evidence from the research to date; they certainly help to legitimise the move away from the term 'third world'. First, when specifically asked for their understanding of the 'third world', most respondents tended to focus on issues related to poverty and the consequences of this (lack of basic amenities, poor health/housing, etc). The emphasis was very clearly on deficiency. This was consistent across groups, as reflected in the following definitions:

'Countries which struggle with poverty' (PGDE, f.)
'Poor underdeveloped countries in lots of debt with really poor standard of living' (PGDE, f.)
'poor, exploited people/nations. Generally countries where famine and poverty reign.' (BAECS, f.)

Next though, when asked what they understood by the term 'developing countries',now used in preference to 'third world', the language used was very different. Responses tended to be more positive, with words that reflected progress and improvement:

'countries who are improving economically' (PGDE f.)
' discovering peace and prosperity through more effective governmental measures' (PGDE, m)
'working themselves out of poverty' (B.Ed., f.)
'Technology, communications and economy are changing and improving, newer ideas are being taken on board' (PGDE, gender not given.)
 'countries getting to grips with problems of poverty and famine and, with or without aid, helping themselves to improve generally. (BAECS, f.)

This tendency to emphasise positive features was common across all three student groups. Amongst the B.Ed. students, 65% of comments made reference to countries working to 'improve' quality of life or 'emerging' from poverty. Similar figures were seen with the other groups: 66% of PGDE students and over 80% of BAECS. It was most noteworthy that these positive connotations were very rarely associated with the term 'third world' countries. If anyone needed evidence of the power of a label, these participants would seem to have provided a good example.

Further reflections

The original aim of the survey was to learn more about the knowledge and attitudes of the two groups of pre-service student teachers at the start of their courses: the four-year undergraduates and the one-year PGDE students. Overall, responses were generally positive; very few comments suggested that teaching in this area was unnecessary or in any way undesirable. There were many areas of broad agreement in the patterns of response, notably in terms of pedagogy: a belief that teaching in this area should start very early on in a child's educational career, the relative merit of the different components of Global Citizenship, and the challenges faced when teaching this topic. There were some differences in relation to how topics should be chosen, with B.Ed. students advocating a focus on current issues, whereas the PGDE group seemed to be more aware of the developmental stage and level of interest of children. Interestingly this was the clear message from the BAECS participants, who have the advantage of more experience of working with young children. When considering attitudes towards the language that surrounds global issues, again similar views were expressed by all three groups.

To the extent that there were differences between the groups in the pattern of responses, it was the B.Ed. students who differed from the other two groups. These students rated the importance of teaching Global Citizenship lower than the other groups. They seemed less prepared to offer opinions than the other groups; they were more likely to miss out questions, and when they did respond, they tended to offer fewer suggestions to open-ended questions. In contrast, the PGDE students were more likely to answer all questions, and they offered more ideas and suggestions in response to open-ended questions. In this respect the PGDE students seemed to have more in common with the BAECS students, despite the fact that in terms of their developmental journey as a teacher they had more in common with the B.Ed. students.

The question arises, why might this be? One obvious explanation is that the B.Ed. students, being new to teaching, felt they had insufficient knowledge to share – or were apprehensive of sharing it in this new environment. However, PGDE were at the same stage of their professional journey – but were much more prepared to express their opinions. Of course, this raises a question of whether age may be an important factor here; perhaps these differences simply reflect the relative lack of experience of the undergraduate group. The age profiles were certainly consistent with this view; the modal ages for the three groups were: B.Ed. 18 years, PGDE 23 years, and BAECS 35 years. The question then arises: is age a confounding variable in our investigation?

It will be recalled from discussion above that the B.Ed. students did not rate the teaching of Global Citizenship as highly as the other groups; this applied both to the topic as a whole and to the individual component parts (see Tables 1 and 2). The data in relation to these questions were now revisited to investigate the influence of age on attitudes towards teaching the subject. A simple correlational analysis was conducted. For each individual student, the component scores summarised in Table 2 were totalled to provide an overall score; these scores were then correlated with ages. The results indicated that there was a significant positive relationship between age and attitude towards Global Citizenship ; older respondents tended to be more positive than younger ones. According to this analysis then, the fact that the B.Ed. students as a group were less positive about Global Citizenship simply reflects that fact: they were younger.

Implications and conclusions

What are the messages for professional preparation programmes from what is essentially the first stage of our enquiry into the teaching of Global Citizenship in ITE? Perhaps most importantly, the generally positive nature of the responses is encouraging and suggests that teacher educators have willing students who are already favourably disposed to the teaching of Global Citizenship. We must now capitalise on this fact. However, there is another message in here; it would be unwise to ignore the possibility that the younger undergraduates may be somewhat less positive, less willing to share their views, and possibly less aware of the importance of this aspect of the school curriculum. What are the implications?

Bearing in mind the dangers of over-generalising from such data, it seems that course teams might want to consider some of the findings when planning module experiences for first year undergraduates. One relates to the finding that these students were somewhat less positive about the importance of teaching about Global Citizenship. If this is so, there may be value in a series of awareness-raising activities with this group, trying to highlight the importance of global issues – to society generally, to specific groups and individuals in particular, and to them as teachers and agents of social change. This might involve direct, first-hand messages and eye-witness accounts from individuals: inspirational speakers, those with personal experience in the field, and others who have valuable messages to convey. The aim would be to raise awareness and to begin to win hearts and minds.

But if one of the other findings of the current study is accurate, and the undergraduates as a group do tend to be reluctant to express their own views, the 'nature of the learning experiences' will be important. Three processes may be of interest. First, while there is undoubtedly much to be taught in terms of content knowledge, there may be value in first year in encouraging confidence and autonomy. Being required to undertake independent research on global issues, and then examine and articulate their own personal educational ideologies in the light of this work, should help towards the development of autonomy. Second, following the active-learning theme, if it is the case that older students tend to be more willing to share their views and engage with the issues, there may be value in building in opportunities for peer learning activities. Well-chosen collaborative tasks which involve older students working with younger ones may be of benefit. What we know about peer learning leads us to believe that this will not be a one-way process. Third, there will be value in students learning at an early stage of their programme about the excellent work that is currently going on in this area in some schools. Few things make more of an impression on beginning teachers than seeing authentic learning taking place – particularly when it involves enthusiastic children expressing thoughtful and mature views, motivated to help others.

[2] Using Spearman's rho, there was a medium positive correlation between the two variables, [$r=.33$, $n=250$, $p<.001$, two-tailed]

We have focused on the undergraduate students in this final section, not because the other groups of students are less important, but because it appears that these undergraduates may benefit from extra groundwork on our part. We would not argue that these activities are inappropriate for PGDE students, but given that (in this study at least) those students seem to be a bit more informed – and mindful how time is at a premium on the one-year course – perhaps the focus could safely be on classroom techniques. The good news is that such an approach could be adopted with a degree of confidence, since our findings suggest that overall the PGDE students were not very different in terms of beliefs and attitudes from more experienced practitioners following the BAECS programme.

Finally, it is important to acknowledge that any study of this nature has limitations, as reflected in the fact that investigations are continuing, with different methodology being adopted for future phases. Nevertheless, we believe that the information which we have gained from this initial survey has alerted us to some issues which surround the professional preparation of teachers in this important area. For some of our students, the road to Global Citizenship may be an uncertain one. If we want to lead the way, it helps to know where they are coming from.

References

General Teaching Council for Scotland (GTCS) (2006) *Standard for Initial Teacher Education*. Edinburgh: GTCS

Learning Teaching Scotland (2010) *Global education*. Online at http://www.ltscotland.org.uk/citizenship/creativeteaching/themes/globaleducation.asp (accessed 8/4/2010).

Scottish Government (2009) *Curriculum for Excellence*. Edinburgh: Scottish Government.

3.5 Global Citizenship and the Initial Teacher Education of Science Teachers

Nicky Souter, University of Strathclyde

Introduction and background
Examination of aspects relating to global citizenship in the Initial Teacher Education (ITE) of secondary science teachers took place in the study institution during a time of radical change in Scottish schools when *Curriculum for Excellence* (CfE) was being introduced. The study coincided with the review of the Professional Graduate Diploma of Education (PGDE) programmes for both primary and secondary teachers at the institution concerned.

ITE tutors were invited to consider aspects related to global citizenship as these were to be received in Scottish schools, and also the requirements on new teachers within the reformed curriculum and new teacher education programmes.

Science in Scottish secondary schools
The prevailing tradition in the first two years of Scottish schools was described in 2002 by HM Inspectorate of Education (HMIE):

'In Secondary 1 (S1)/Secondary 2 (S2), most schools taught an integrated science course, although large sections were clearly identifiable as biology, chemistry, and physics. A small, but growing minority of schools taught biology, chemistry, and physics as separate courses, normally in S2.'(HMIE, 2002)

The establishment of this pattern of delivery had been fairly rapid since 1969 and MacLaren (1980) noted that:

'Almost all six year schools in Scotland are now comprehensives and pupils transfer from primary to secondary schools at about the age of 12. For the first two years (S1 and S2) most pupils follow the integrated science course (Curriculum Paper 7 1969), or courses based on it.'

There appears to have been little movement on this during the past decade as evidenced by school inspection reports and other publications. HMIE (2005) raised concerns in relation to challenge and performance in the first two years of secondary. The focus had changed, when HMIE reported that in '... many secondary science departments, teachers were reviewing and developing the S1/S2 science courses.' (HMIE, 2008, p9)

For the remainder of secondary schooling from S3 onwards high numbers of pupils follow courses in biology, chemistry, and physics until at the end of compulsory education at age sixteen and into the upper school. These courses are so popular that the total numbers of presentations each year at 'Higher' grade (pre-university) are only exceeded by those in English and mathematics.

Management structures within school science departments are unusual in that previously heads of department were appointed in each of the three subjects and collaborated on the management of the integrated science course during the first two years and retained autonomy in managing the particular subject. This has changed in many schools. Reforms in management structures followed the implementation of the 2001 McCrone review of teachers' conditions and led to the establishment of 'faculties' in many schools. Policy and practice in science departments had been changing and collaborative practices appear to be continuing with the introduction of the newly reformed curriculum

CfE, Scotland's new curriculum is 'underpinned by the four values – wisdom, justice, compassion, and integrity.' (Learning and Teaching Scotland, 2009a) The curriculum also sets out to broaden 'experience of the world' and promote 'responsible citizenship'. Several science 'experiences and outcomes' resonate these principles and attempt to strengthen those issues associated with globalization. These are compatible with the aims of the IDEAS project and, 'foster knowledge, skills, and attitudes which promote justice and equality in a multicultural society and interdependent world.'

Of the 12 aims which are outlined in the 'Experiences and Outcomes for Science' (Learning and Teaching Scotland, 2009b) for science 4 make specific reference to areas related to the key ideas of the global dimension.

- 'develop curiosity and understanding of the environment and my place in the living, material and physical world
- recognise the impact the sciences make on my life, the lives of others, the environment and on society
- develop an understanding of the Earth's resources and the need for responsible use of them
- express opinions and make decisions on social, moral, ethical, economic and environmental issues based upon sound understanding'.

Global Citizenship and Science Education

A brief literature review related to 'science education', 'global citizenship', and lexical variations of these terms was carried out to provide a context for the study and to corroborate parameters within the selected auditing instrument.

Contemporary curriculum reform across the UK (Learning and Teaching Scotland, 2009a, Qualifications and Curriculum Development Agency, 2010) has raised the profile of developing 'responsible citizens'. It might be that it is inevitable that education in post devolution Scotland should focus on the citizenship issues as well as its place within the world. Banks (2007) points out that:

'The increasing ethnic, racial, cultural, religious, and language diversity in nations throughout the world is forcing educators and policymakers to rethink existing notions of citizenship and nationality. To experience cultural democracy and freedom, a nation must be unified around a set of democratic values such as justice and equality that balance unity and diversity and protect the rights of diverse groups.'

The tradition of integrated science in the first and second year of secondary in Scotland is derived from the visionary publication 'curriculum paper 7' (Scottish Education Department/Consultative Committee on the Curriculum, 1969). In this, Mee acknowledged (p13) the 'explosive rate' of scientific knowledge and that this would alter 'our morals, our ethics, and our whole cultural development.' Attention was also given to 'our desire to expose pupils to this cultural aspect of science'. The attitudinal objectives made reference to the 'awareness of the contribution of science to the economic and social life of the community.' Although these may appear comparatively trivial in comparison to current perspectives, they may be considered as the harbinger of future developments e.g. 5-14, CfE and a progressive broadening of the science curriculum. It is worth noting that the current interest in local citizenship is not particularly new (Harvey, 1977, Jenkins, 2006). Jenkins (ibid.) provided a useful analysis 'on the status, objectives, and needs of global education' clued in to 'perspectives to global citizenship' as well as making suggestions in relation to pedagogical approaches in science learning programmes.

These discussions were not restricted to the United Kingdom. Others e.g. Feinstein (2009) raised the dilemmas that are associated with 'shifting priorities' in science education and asserted that planners required 'to provide a science education that truly prepares students for good citizenship and daily decision making.' Davies (2004) argued the '... potential for collaborative work between science educators and citizenship educators' as well as the associated challenges while Cornwell (2006), reflected on field experiences and explained (p5):

'The good news is that scientific methods of inquiry and analysis foster habits of scalar and systemic thinking. Seeing how very small parts function in larger wholes, and understanding relationships in complex systems, are habits of mind well cultivated in the sciences. The world—its elephants, its flowers, and its people—desperately needs that kind of thinking.' Our task is to produce graduates who are capable of it.

The introduction of CfE has provoked a debate within the community. Jackson (2009) encouraged science teachers to 'seize the day' arguing that *Curriculum for Excellence* should ensure that the outcomes and experiences are updated to better reflect contemporary issues in science, ...' as well as noting that there were particular CPD requirements in the primary sector

Buchanan (2009) raised concerns about the introduction of the CfE and these were related to revised management structures within schools, the support provided by local authorities as well as issues relating to technicians. The CPD required was central; 'Most agree that CfE is about methodology and so continuing professional development, not content change, is key.' Buchanan confirmed that 'Pupils are being encouraged to develop informed views on social, environmental, moral, and ethical issues.'

The Royal Society for Edinburgh (RSE)(2008) was critical of the initial proposals for science and numeracy indicating that the proposals 'to develop and reinforce science knowledge and skills within their teaching activities and work with their colleagues in other subjects to plan inter-disciplinary studies and a coherent approach to the development of literacy and numeracy skills, and to themes such as citizenship or enterprise' is encouraging, but will require an unprecedented cultural change in the teaching profession' and that this would require significant support. RSE was especially critical that structured human knowledge had been poorly defined in the draft guidelines, expressing the view that such knowledge acted as '... powerful drivers of new knowledge'; that 'cross-disciplinary understanding will lack rigour and utility'; as well as highlighting the absence of the 'fundamental concepts, the laws and methods. Their critique led to a revision of the initial proposals for CfE Science.

Schulz (2009), Zeidler et al (2005) and Sadler (2009) echoed the RSE concerns, albeit in alternative contexts, noting the competing approaches that 'continuously [reshape] the identity and values of the discipline' (Shultz, ibid.p225) and proposing that revisiting the philosophy of science education would 'serve to reinforce science education's growing sense of academic autonomy and independence from socio economic demands.' (Shultz, ibid, p. 225)

Opportunities exist to support the global dimension in science teaching e.g. Association for Science Education's 'Science across the world' (2009) established a network of '7,984 teachers in 147 countries where students are collaborating on school science topics.' The aims included 'global perspectives', 'contacts and links', 'develop different pedagogic skills and extend science into cross curricular activities, including citizenship and sustainable development education.' A consortium of British Council, Cambridge Education Foundation, UK One World Linking Association, and VSO (Department for International Development, 2010) supports and provides funding for 'partnerships that promote global education through the curriculum'

The Programme of Study

ITE programmes in Scotland are required (General Teaching Council for Scotland, 2006) to encompass three experiences – those related to subject studies (pedagogy and curriculum), educational studies, and practicum (school experience) during which the clinical practice element of ITE is carried out. Students in the study followed elective study in areas are of professional development and these include ICT, language and literacy, health education, outdoor education, guidance and pastoral care, additional needs etc.

Each pedagogy and curriculum tutor is autonomous in terms of the construction of the pedagogy and curriculum programme for the subject concerned. They recognize that each student teacher's formal, informal, prior learning and life experiences are unique but are comparatively constrained in providing differentiated learning experiences. The experiential nature of Initial Teacher Education (ITE) leads to student teachers discussing, debating, challenging and comparing their previous experiences and increasing insights gained from school experience.

Tutors are constrained in the extent to which they can structure the learning experience in pedagogy and curriculum classes in each teaching subject since these represent a small part of the total PGDE. 18 of the 36 weeks are spent on university based, taught classes. Up to 6 hours a week are spent in multidisciplinary tutorial groups and lectures on aspects related to a core programme of educational studies in the wider context pertaining to initial teacher education in Scotland. 4 hours a week are spent in 'Curriculum and Pedagogy' classes for each subject. A further 24 hours contact is incorporated into a 'General Science' programme, reflecting the practice in secondary schools as required (General Teaching Council for Scotland, 2006).

Methodology

The eight key concepts, (Global citizenship, Interdependence, Conflict resolution, Sustainable development, Diversity, Social justice, Human rights, Values and perceptions), and the sub-concepts describing the global dimension to the curriculum (Department for International Development, 2005) was selected as being appropriate in providing the basis of the auditing instrument. This was considered to have the desirable features of summarizing the area of study, presenting the subjects with a comparatively brief (3 page) response sheet, avoiding researcher bias in question design, and providing data sets from the study group.

The questionnaire responses provided the basis of a subsequent semi structured interview of the respondents. The process raised dilemmas in terms of the vision of the student experience in relation to paradigms associated with the nature of science, its history and philosophy, science technology and society and socio- scientific issues.

The respondents included 4 science tutors. For comparative purposes a social science tutor (geography) and a coordinator of the educational studies programme were invited to complete a questionnaire. Geography was selected since on face value geography and biology are closely related subjects since the content covers aspects of the environment, conservation and so on within the Scottish curriculum. 'Educational studies' was selected since it provided core programme for all student teachers.

Findings

Core Programme Educational Studies

They reported a 'huge degree of overlap and repetition in the concepts and sub-concepts.' They also argued that the context of the Scottish reform '*Curriculum for Excellence*' (CfE) 'covers all or most of these in our consideration of the four Capacities'.

They explained that the core programme included 'three intertwined themes: International and Global Education; Citizenship and Enterprise; and Children's Rights and Child Protection. The audit indicated that these themes appeared in all eight key concepts. They believed that the sub-concepts were almost all the included in the core programme. They did acknowledge the possibility that 'I am claiming too much coverage of International/ Global issues.'

Social studies – Geography

The geography tutor as an undergraduate '... studied anthropology as well so have a slant that really looks at diversity, equality, cultural respect etc as well as the physical geography side of things. Geography is everything. The respect for one another etc is included in the course through the cooperative learning approaches used. The tutor indicated that all areas were covered during the PGDE geography programme – with the exception of 'Human rights'.

Science tutors

The 4 science tutors made 62 entries into the questionnaire. They ranked the key concepts as shown in table 1:

Key Concept Area	N
Sustainable development	16
Global citizenship	14
Values and perceptions	11
Interdependence	9
Diversity	4
Conflict resolution	3
Social justice	3
Human rights	2

All 4 tutors made entries to the 2 most highly ranked areas and 3 tutors contributed to the next two most highly ranked.

Each tutor explained that they anticipated making more use of situational encounters rather than necessarily carefully planning each key concept. They each described a permeation model for the majority of the occurrences. It is worth noting that during each interview it became apparent that all 4 tutors' had been influenced by professional experiences, scholarship, and research.

Chemistry tutor

This tutor made responses in the following three areas; Global citizenship (5), Interdependence (3), and Sustainable development (5).

The tutor explained that some of the input was planned and structured, '... seeking opportunities to include the wider perspective ...' In terms of selecting those opportunities '... it's obvious when you are dealing with issues related to fossil fuels –coal, oil and gas...' The tutor continued, 'Opportunities arise in taught classes, on placement...' as well as those encounters where the students were seeking further guidance on teaching and learning. The tutor perceived part of their professional responsibilities and obligations to the student teachers as one where 'awareness raising' to the wider context of science/chemistry was of great importance.

The tutor also believed that they had developed a broader vision of the subject during the period between completing the questionnaire and taking part in the interview. They reflected that this had been the direct result of their experience during the development of resources for CfE:

'This broader view is frankly missing in current practice. All teachers have a responsibility for delivering those outcomes that are described within the questionnaire. *Curriculum for Excellence* raises this and it makes me think that teachers *should*, not *could* be doing this.'

Physics tutor 1
The tutor made responses in the following three areas Global citizenship (1), Sustainable development (2) and Values and perceptions (3).

The tutor explained that they planned and structured encounters by linking learning to topical sciences presented in the news and media. Opportunities were taken in relation to the exemplifying principles and the impacts of physics on society e.g. wind farms and nuclear fuel. They also addressed students' awareness of the 'nature of science' and the way in which '... they as scientists and as teachers should challenge themselves and encourage their pupils to do the same.':

'They need to unpack, tease out the science and its environmental impact and to challenge the categoric way in which these issues are often seen as being ' good' or ' bad'.'

Physics tutor 2
This tutor made the greatest number (28) of responses of the science tutors and these were in all 8 key concept areas; Global citizenship (5), Interdependence (3), Conflict resolution (3), Sustainable development (6), Diversity (2), Social justice (3), Human rights (2), and Values and perceptions (4)

The tutor believed that they covered content in relation to context of particular topics 'for example teaching energy and energy resources and meeting current industrial needs. The tutor incorporates different perspectives into challenging viewpoints e.g.:

' ...the politics of the Bush administration in the United States or the dilemmas brought about by industrialization and cultural differences –the solutions that I have encountered in Cairo and Malawi are quite different from local responses and actions. In disadvantaged areas of Glasgow the culture of failure, fatalism, life expectancy contrasts markedly with the asylum seeker who achieves 5 A passes at higher; the engagement with education in relation to poverty is quite different – disillusionment on one hand and an escape route on the other.'

Biology tutor

This tutor made responses in 5 of the key concept areas Global citizenship (3), Interdependence (3), Sustainable development (3), Diversity (2), Values and perceptions (4).

Planned interventions in relation to these areas included directly taught classes and tutorials with the inclusion of visiting speakers from schools and elsewhere. An inventory of organizations that contributed to all aspects of biology teaching was distributed through the programme Internet to all students. Key publications e.g. (Baker, 2008) are given to support the student teachers perspectives of the global dimension as well as 'issues related' education. Opportunities arrive specifically in the areas of education for sustainable development, conservation and environmental education to raise the dilemmas associated with the counterpoints of social, economic and environmental stresses. The tutor believes that dealing with dilemmas is part of the nature of science and of biology especially where the empirical investigative approaches of science are challenged by counter scientific debates associated with 'intelligent design' etc.

Discussion
Subject and Interdisciplinary Knowledge

Tensions exist between the advocates of the curriculum integration (e.g. CfE) and the defenders of subject boundaries (e.g. RSE). (Beane ,1995) explained that 'the disciplines of knowledge are not the enemy, but a useful and necessary ally' and goes on to provide a rationale for such approaches as are being included in the CfE drive towards cross-curricular learning, '...the central focus of curriculum integration is the search for self- and social meaning.' Each curriculum reform appears to get caught up in the inadequacy of the subject based curriculum. Competition between subjects in the secondary schools often appears to be no more sophisticated than the territorial scent marking that is used by rutting stags to maintain status and resource.

We recognize the blunt nature of the auditing instrument, the completely open way in which tutors could respond to it, the nature, and location of the study group, and the time lag that existed between completing the audit instrument and the interviews taking place.

Nevertheless we can observe the following:

1. Much is attempted during the PGDES. Whether this is in the core programme for educational studies, during pedagogy and curriculum classes, school experience, or elective study is determined by the individual curriculum.

2. The delivered and received curriculum may be quite different. Learner's receptiveness to teacher's ideas and priorities often appear to be at odds and this is most apparent while completing assessments and marking assignments. 'How could they believe that?' 'Where do they get these ideas from?' and so on. This effect may manifest itself in relation to the claim that educational studies 'covers all or most of these in our consideration of the four Capacities'.

3. The subjects appear to offer different coverage of issues related to the global dimension. Revealing beliefs, values and attitudes is notoriously difficult. The limitations of the auditing instrument and the experiences of the tutors within a subject context suggest that differences do exist between the subjects. Personal and other professional experiences play a significant role in informing the tutor's pedagogy and curriculum module as well as their responses in ad hoc situations.

4. Despite the geography tutor making no entry in the concept area of 'Human rights' this is subject appears to establish different priorities from those that appear in the three sciences.

5. While it might be unsurprising in terms of curricular content to note that 'Sustainable development', 'Global citizenship', 'Values and perceptions', 'Interdependence', were the most highly rated concept areas it is also reassuring in terms of the tutors' readiness to incorporate these into their teaching.

6. It is similarly unsurprising in terms of curricular content to note that 'Diversity', 'Conflict resolution', 'Social justice', 'Human rights'.

7. The personal preferences and priorities were highlighted between the responses provided by the two physics tutors.

8. Tutors understanding of aspects relating to the global dimension changed during the study and this was influenced by three factors

   a. The focus on CfE during the preparation of student teachers.

   b. Their attention to redesigning their pedagogy and curriculum programmes during if the PGDE review.

   c. Through their own scholarship while 'unpacking' the CfE experiences and outcomes.

The Scottish Government (2009) encourages the professional autonomy of teachers: 'Teachers are professionals and have been asking for more freedom to teach. The examples of learning and teaching approaches that the Scottish Government is making available to teachers are designed to provide them with the opportunity to design a deep, active appropriate and enjoyable education experience for each learner. This is not a prescribed, top-down national curriculum.'

Teachers are encouraged to 'unpack the experiences and outcomes' in relation to their own analysis of the content as well as incorporating the pupils' needs and preferences. The outcomes are open to many interpretations in terms of knowledge problem-solving practical abilities and above all attitudes. This is a significant strength of CfE in providing strong elements of choice, freedom, and pupil centeredness. We must note that it is also a potential weakness since this freedom has been substantially removed since the introduction of the 5-14 curriculum and the focus of HMI and local authority inspections, international surveys and the imposition of a fixed and national curriculum. Teachers' confidence in making such decisions requires support, encouragement, and above all investment into their CPD. While it is disappointing to note that that only 4 of the 12 aims which are outlined in the 'Experiences and Outcomes for Science' (Learning and Teaching Scotland, 2009b) make specific reference to areas related to the key ideas of global dimension, we would hope and encourage teachers to take a broader perspective.

Observers require maintaining close scrutiny of developments related to CfE to ensure the achievement of high standards as well as avoiding territorial conflict between the three disciplines. The future and security of integrated science during the early stages of secondary may be challenged during the next few years.

References

Association for Science Education. (2009). *Science across the world*. Online at http://www.scienceacross.org (accessed 03/10/09)

Baker, R. (2008). *Getting started with Global Citizenship: A Guide for New Teachers*. Oxford: OXFAM.

Banks, J. A. (Ed.). (2007). *Diversity and Citizenship Education: Global Perspectives*. Indianapolis: Jossey-Bass.

Beane, J. A. (1995). Curriculum integration and the disciplines of knowledge *Phi Delta Kappan*, 76, 616-622.

Buchanan, D. (2009, February 27, 2009). No signs of warming in science climate. *The Times Educational Supplement Scotland*.

Cornwell, G. H. (2006). Science and Citizenship: Habits of Mind for Global Understanding. *Diversity Digest*. 9(3), 4-5.

Davies, I. (2004). Science and Citizenship Education. *International Journal of Science Education*, 26 (14), 1751-1763.

Department for International Development (2010). *About Global School Partnerships*. Online at http://www.dfid.gov.uk/Getting-Involved/For-schools/global-school-partnerships/about-gsp/(accessed 03/10/09)

Department for International Development. (2005). *Developing the global dimension in the school curriculum*. London: DFID

Feinstein, N. (2009). Prepared for What? Why Teaching 'Everyday Science' Makes Sense. *Phi Delta Kappan*, 90 (10), 762-766.

General Teaching Council for Scotland. (2006). *Guidelines for Initial Teacher Education Courses in Scotland*. Edinburgh:GTCS

Harvey, R. (1977). *Global Perspectives: Some Questions and Answers*. Berkeley, Denver: Center for global perspectives.

HMIE. (2000). *Standards and Quality in Secondary Schools 1995-2000: The Sciences*. Livingston: HMIE

HMIE. (2005). *Improving Achievement in Science in Primary and Secondary Schools*. Livingston: HMIE

HMIE. (2008). Science – *A portrait of current practice in Scottish schools*. Livingston: HMIE

Jackson,J. (2009, January 23, 2009). Seize the day, science teachers. *Times Educational Supplement Scotland*.

Jenkins E. W. (2006). School Science and Citizenship: Whose Science and Whose Citizenship? *Curriculum Journal*, 17(3), 197-211.

Learning and Teaching Scotland. (2009a). *Curriculum for Excellence: Purposes and aims*. Online at http://www.ltscotland.org.uk/curriculumforexcellence/curriculumoverview/aims/index.asp (accessed 03/10/09)

Learning and Teaching Scotland. (2009b). *Curriculum for Excellence: Sciences: Experiences and outcomes*. Online at http://www.ltscotland.org.uk/curriculumforexcellence/sciences//index.asp (accessed on 03/10/09)

MacLaren H. M. (1980). Physics projects in sixth-year studies in scotland. *Physics Education*, 15(1), 44-48.

Qualifications and Curriculum Development Agency. (2010). The National Curriculum. Online at http://curriculum.qcda.gov.uk/index.aspx (accessed 20/02/10)

Royal Society for Edinburgh. (2008). *Curriculum for Excellence – draft experiences and outcomes for numeracy, mathematics and science*. Edinburgh: Royal Society for Edinburgh

Sadler T. D. (2009). Situated learning in science education: socio-scientific issues as contexts for practice. *Studies in Science Education*, 45(1), 1-42.

Schulz R. M. . (2009). Reforming Science Education: Part I. The Search for a Philosophy of Science Education. *Science and Education*, 18, 225-249.

Scottish Education Department/Consultative Committee on the Curriculum. (1969). *Science for General Education : for the first 2 years and the early school leaver: Curriculum Paper 7*.

Scottish Government. (2009). *Curriculum for Excellence*. Online at http://www.scotland.gov.uk/Topics/Education/skills-strategy/making-skills-work/utilisation/CfE (accessed 22/09/09)

Zeidler, D. L.; Sadler, T. D.; Simmons, M. L.; Howes, E. V. (2005). Beyond STS: A Research-Based Framework for Socioscientific Issues Education. *Science Education*, 89(3), 357-377.

3.6 Challenges for Design and Technology Education: A Changing Paradigm

Susan V. McLaren, University of Edinburgh

Introduction: Time for Change

Scottish Education has recently undergone a wide ranging review, based on the recommendations of *'Curriculum for Excellence'* (Scottish Executive, 2004). The very essence of learning has been examined and the contribution of each curriculum subject explored. A rethinking of the curriculum hopes to provide a more coherent, meaningful and progressive experience for students. Aspects to be addressed include transition and coherency between stages and sectors of schooling, progression of and challenge to young people and collaborative teaching approaches, including the use of cross sector teachers. The cross boundary nature of sustainability could make a major contribution to these developments. There are opportunities to influence, support and enhance curriculum developments at a time of change. This requires a sound and informed evidence base to be developed in order that subsequent actions are relevant and appropriate.

At present, there is a growing body of work that explores sustainability in relation to Technology Education from other parts of the world e.g. Canada, Ireland, Australia, Russia, England. (cf. Elshof, 2003, 2005, 2006a&b, 2007; McGarr, 2009; Pavlova &Pitt, 2007; Seemann 2003, Pitt, 2009, Petrina, 2000). There is very little research literature available in Scotland which documents attitudes and world views of practicing teachers and student teachers, particularly in Design and Technology (technical). There is also little evidence of the development from the rhetoric of guidelines, policies and initiatives (Scottish Executive, 2006, 2005,) into reality through effective implementation in classroom practice (McNaughton, 2007). Evidence of design for sustainability and sustainable development, and creative approaches to dealing with controversial issues in current formal Scottish teaching and learning in Design and Technology (technical) is particularly sparse.

Since 1993, there have been various editions of national guidelines for Technology Education in Scotland, namely National Guidelines for 5-14 Environmental Studies (SOEID,1993), Technology Education for Scottish Schools (SCCC,1996), National Guidelines for 5-14 Environmental Studies: Society, Science and Technology Education (LTS, 2000), CfE Technologies (LTS, 2009). In each, it is evident that issues of education for sustainability, design for sustainability and sustainable development have been included.

SCCC (1996) described 'technological sensitivity' as an aspect of technological capability which is about having a habit of mind which asks questions about, and reflects on, social, moral, aesthetic and environmental issues, as well as technical and economic aspects of all technological activity. Teachers were encouraged to help learners to apply considered moral and ethical judgements in evaluating technology and to appreciate that technological developments have consequences for people, society and the environment of the world. The National Guidelines for 5-14 Environmental Studies: Society, Science and Technology Education (LTS, 2000) promoted developing informed attitudes of learners through the consideration of consequences for actions proposed and of those taken. It was concerned with the recognition of the sources of resources and materials and energy transfer used in design and make activities. Generally learners were to be more aware of the full lifecycle of a product from inception through manufacture, transportation, marketing and use to waste disposal. Teachers were to help learners appreciate that although some technological solutions may be acceptable to some they may be unacceptable to others. (LTS,2000, p. 76)

And yet, the 'frame of mind' (Bonnet, 2002) required to embed such concepts into the everyday teaching and learning experiences of the Design and Technology classroom, workshop and studio practice remains elusive. The result is that the current technology curriculum, in secondary school in particular, is not presented as the guidance intends. Implementation tends to focus on traditional workshop-based, practical craft skill development at the expense of issues, knowledge, and authentic and context-based design-centred activities. This perpetuates the 'productivism and product paradigm' (Elshof,2006a) There is little focus on issues of sustainability, values and complexity of compromise (McLaren, 1997).

Supporting Change
Littledyke,Taylor & Eames (2009) attempt to identify the 'issues conspiring against the widespread inclusion' of sustainability in teaching and learning. They suggest that it is a poorly understood concept and often teachers do not recognise the direct relevance to their daily activity. Teachers may lack awareness and understanding of, or interest in, national policies. Alternatively, perhaps awareness has resulted in teachers feeling yet more has to be 'fitted in' to an already overcrowded curriculum.

Van Driel, Beijaard and Vreloop (2001) report research on science teachers' practical knowledge, and conclude that experienced science teachers have developed an integrated set of knowledge and beliefs which manifests itself in how they teach. The content of their practical knowledge is determined by national curriculum, and the school culture. This leads to problems when changes are made to the content of the curriculum, including process, conceptual or philosophical changes. The teachers believe that they do not have the knowledge of the new content nor do they feel they have pedagogy suited to what is expected of them.

Other problems are that teachers' beliefs may not match those that are implicit in the new curriculum. This research also indicates that although continuing professional development workshops (the majority of which are of short duration and outwith the classroom) may support teachers in their content knowledge and understanding, and acceptance of the conceptual ideas behind the new curriculum, problems arise when they are in the classroom situation once again. More is required than simply adding information to personal beliefs and existing knowledge frameworks of a teacher. It is a complex process.

Background to the changing paradigm

Design and Technology Education has long been associated with the manufacture and crafting of products, particularly in secondary schools. The making of stuff has defined Technical Education, more recently known as design and technology, teaching and learning experience, since its introduction to the school curriculum in 1868. Crafted pieces, or product models, are often made in school workshops by learners following an apprenticeship style /lock step approach to develop manual and machine skills.

A seismic shift in thinking came about in 1985, when Technical Education was changed to Technology Education, which was described as being:

'...concerned with the identification of some of the material needs of man (sic) and the endeavour to satisfy those needs of man (sic) and the endeavour to satisfy those needs by the application of science and the use of materials, resources and energy. It is concerned with solving problems where there is no right or wrong answer, only good or bad solutions to a problem. Technological behaviour requires activities that are creative and demanding, where laws and principles of science, the constraints of society and economics are applied to problems to satisfy human needs. Technological behaviour involves approaches and techniques, such as systems analysis, problem identification, decision making, planning, idea communication and solution evaluation, which are more that pure science or craft' (COS, 1985: 3-4).

This resulted in the learner being afforded a degree of choice and personalisation in a 'design and make' project (e.g. SQA Craft and Design, 1989).Technology Education was now to involve thinking about issues (albeit not environmental) and was about taking action to address needs (albeit through material outcomes).

'Technology Education in Scottish Schools' (1996),the revised syllabi for post 16 courses (cf. Higher Still, 1999) and 5-14 Environmental Studies Technology Education national guidance documents (LTS, 2000) did not explicitly perpetuate the necessity for 'design and make'. However, the underlying assumption by those planning the learning experiences was that producing product outcomes remained the most important component of the learning.

More recently, the introduction of new computer technologies to aid the manufacture of products has been welcomed, by some, as an updating of the curriculum as appropriate for the 21st century (ref. CfE, 2009) CAD/CAM, together with the wide range of emerging technologies and smart materials, is promoted as the new media with which to develop relevant and interesting learning for learners.Curriculum guidance encourages learners to engage with contemporary and future processes, materials, innovations, technologies and design ideas (cf SQA 2004, and CfE, 2009). CAD/CAM is now considered the 'must have' facility in a modern Design and Technology department. Such facilities may signal a step change, however they merely support the continuation of the creation of product outcomes in wood, metal and plastics. Anecdotally, we hear, 'They want to take something home... the parents expect to see something being brought home'.

The less talked about

Technological Capability is described succinctly as four mutually supportive and inter-related aspects: Technological Sensitivity, Technological Perspective, Technological Creativity and Technological Confidence (SCCC, 1996). The premise here is that by developing technological capability, greater understanding of the ethical, societal, cultural, environmental, technical and economic values through which critical examination of consequences of actions, past and proposed can be made. This concept of Technological Capability was the key outcome for the Technology curriculum of 5-14 Environmental Studies (LTS, 2000). It aimed to develop technologically capable citizens who were equipped to adopt a holistic, linked up, systems-based approach to thinking, acting and being.

The Sustainable Development Education Liaison Group's advisory paper emphasises the importance of systems thinking. 'The ability to understand the links and relationships between issues is vital for understanding the interdependent nature of our world and for addressing the complex problems that increasingly dominate our lives.' (SDLEG,2006,p.8). They note, however, that although systems thinking has to potential to help teachers and learners to 'address problems in a 'joined-up' way, linking and applying learning to new situations and to make better sense of the world around them' is was not generally taught in schools.

Most designers, technologies, and engineers would consider systems thinking as a core skill for their critical understanding and application of creative and innovative approaches to resolving a design challenge. And yet, is this the case in teaching and learning in Technology Education in school? Is design and technology not about making informed choices and decisions; evaluating environmental, scientific and technological issues and applying critical thinking in new contexts to solve problems and arrive at a proposal through a systems thinking designerly process?

Curriculum for Excellence (CfE) principles and purposes (LTS, 2009) explicitly bring attention to the development of responsible citizens and issues of sustainable development. CfE Technologies (2009) provides a clear 3-15 framework for Technology in Society as a context for developing technological knowledge and understanding. This outlines, once again, significant aspects of the design and technology education experience in direct relationship to sustainability, once again. The purposes of learning in the CfE Technologies, in summary, are to enable learners to:

- develop an understanding of the role and impact of technologies in changing and influencing societies
- contribute to building a better world by taking responsible ethical actions to improve their lives, the lives of others and the environment
- become informed consumers and producers who have an appreciation of the merits and impacts of products and services
- be capable of making reasoned choices relating to the environment, to sustainable development and to ethical, economic and cultural issues.

Working towards these purposes, teachers and learners are supported by a framework of experiences and outcomes which form the focus of learning activities. Below is a sample of experiences and outcomes from CfE Technologies (2009):

- I can investigate the use and development of renewable and sustainable energy to gain an awareness of their growing importance in Scotland or beyond. TCH 2-02b *(approx 7-11year olds)*
- Having analysed how lifestyle can impact on the environment and Earth's resources, I can make suggestions about how to live in a more sustainable way. TCH 2-02a *(approx 7-11year olds)*
- From my studies of sustainable development, I can reflect on the implications and ethical issues arising from technological developments for individuals and societies. TCH 3-02a *(approx 11-14year olds)*
- I can examine a range of materials, processes or designs in my local community to consider and discuss their environmental, social and economic impact, discussing the possible lifetime cost to the environment in Scotland or beyond. TCH 4-02a *(approx 12-15year olds)*
- I can practise and apply a range of preparation techniques and processes to manufacture a variety of items in wood, metal, plastic or other material, showing imagination and creativity, and recognising the need to conserve resources. TCH 3-13b *(approx 11-14year olds)*

The guidelines make direct links with other learning areas of the curriculum to encourage recognition of the mutually supportive and cross platform relationships within the overall framework e.g. from CfE Sciences (2009):

- Through exploring non-renewable energy sources, I can describe how they are used in Scotland today and express an informed view on the implications for their future use. SCN 2-04b (approx 7-11year olds)
- By investigating renewable energy sources and taking part in practical activities to harness them, I can discuss their benefits and potential problems. SCN 3-04b (approx 11-14year olds)

CfE Technologies attempts to broaden the scope and range of contexts for learning and, while championing the experience of creative designing and making, demands that the product outcome is not seen to be the sole purpose of the experience. However, the question that must be asked is, what impact will this new conceptualisation and approach have on classroom practice and learners' experience, specifically pertaining to design and technology education?

It seems there is Potential

Design and Technology offers opportunities to apply systems based, closed loop, designerly thinking, knowledge and understanding and taking action concurrently. The trans-disciplinary nature of Design and Technology promotes learning experiences which draw on all areas of learning. Learning experiences can relate to the design, manufacture, engineering, use and maintenance of everyday products, environments, systems and infrastructures such as power generation, energy transmission, transportation, leisure and entertainment provision, the building and operating of homes, waste disposal; i.e. 'real' world , 21st century issues and concerns. These are often 'back boxes' – unknown entities or services which are taken for granted in the western so called developed world. These things 'just are'. However, these are the very same contexts that incorporate the big issues and big ideas of being human; the issues and ideas that require attention in order to address the depletion of resources, the exploitation of others, the reduction in biodiversity.

Humans enjoy new ideas, challenges and new products. In the rich worlds, humans seem to enjoy 'new' to the extent they discard 'old' for 'new'. Designers and manufacturers coalesce through built-in obsolescence, fashion trends, advertising to encourage consumption and create a culture in the 'developed world' of love it, want it, what is it? Design and Technology Education is also expected to work with thinking related to:

- disruptive technologies – these often create new industries- and eventually change the world e.g. internal combustion engine, transistors, Web browser, pod-casting, open-source software

- emergent technologies e.g. nanotechnology, biotechnologies, cognitive science, robotics, artificial intelligence
- smart materials e.g. chromogenic systems, pH-sensitive polymers, piezoelectric, shape-memory alloys, magnetic shape memory.

Technologies operate in a context that negotiates the co-existence of being human (and all that that entails, such as being consumers, thing users, wanters and coveters, stuff makers, curious creatures) with the drive and need for eco-efficiency, adoption of appropriate technology, global social justice and equity and respect and sustainable strategies.

Critical technological literacy and technological sensitivity are central to developing technological capability. Experiences that involve critique, exploration of values, of products, systems, environments, and ideas resulting from design and technological human actions can help develop this [cf. Elshof, 2003, 2006b; Keirl, 2007; McLaren,1997; Pavlova & Pitt, 2007; Petrina, 2007; Seemann 2006;].

Design and Technology education offers opportunities to explore such issues in context through designerly thinking and activity. It has the potential to explore psychology and sociology through the symbolic and emotional meanings of products, systems and environments. It can examine and debate decisions, impacts and consequences of designing, engineering, manufacturing, and consuming. Design and Technology has the potential to help learners understand how products define identities, create social relationships, signal values, etc. It has the potential to facilitate understanding of interconnectedness and begin to develop learners understanding of responsible actions (LTS Citizenship, 2002)

These are big, and often, controversial, issues for the learners and teachers and yet Design and Technology experiences which ignore such fundamental aspects would be limited. To adopt, plan and present learning that has these embedded within, demands new pedagogical thinking.

This section has outlined, in summary, the changing purposes, expectations of the curriculum, policies and educational initiatives. It has described the aims, the potential and the necessary mindsets for a 21st century design and technology education. Clearly, for a shift in classroom culture and traditional practice to occur, some serious reflection and action is required. In conclusion, there is recognition of the great potential for authentic Design and Technology Education when it embraces the importance of education for, in and about sustainability. What does it take to move from the rhetoric to reality; to move from theory to embedded practice?

Contributions to the Discussion

For transformational change to be possible (Leicester, Bloomer & Stewart, 2009) the worldviews of those involved in creating the reconfigured learning experiences of practice in the Design and Technology education arena are highly influential.

A small pilot, sampling survey set out to seek views of experienced practicing Design and Technology Teachers, beginning teachers and student teachers in Scottish secondary schools, June 2009. This aimed to explore the personal views of Design and Technology (technical) teachers towards education for sustainability. It probed what were thought to be hindrances to teaching sustainability in schools, if any, and who should be responsible for developing learners understanding of the issues. It hoped to identify enablers and positive agents (perceived and / or actual) to embedding sustainability into pedagogy and also what were thought to be the key drivers / influences for inclusion of sustainability in planning and teaching (policy, personal, institutional, learners, disciplinary, sector) with specific focus on Design and Technology Education. The responses from those who participated in this survey are very similar to those from a larger study which involved a broader range of cross sector educators (Grant & Borridale, 2007)

In key findings of the Design and Technology teacher survey, in summary, indicate that:
1) Teachers view sustainability in terms of environmental issues related to manufacture of products, materials, energy, and use of resources generally. There was little evidence of reference to factors beyond the environmental, for example to economic factors or social factors in their responses.
2) Very few *always* plan for and teach Design and Technology with a sustainability focus only about one third *sometimes* include consideration of sustainable education in their planning.
3) Views of potential or current projects that involved sustainability centre on themes of *recycling* or *provenance of materials*.
4) Teachers would like to be more involved in planning and teaching aspects of sustainability but were unsure – *'where it fits in to the courses I teach...'* and *'would like to but SQA are not assessing it'*.
5) Additional resources, more access and availability to professional development, changes to curriculum guidance and SQA assessments were deemed necessary to aid teachers in their teaching and planning for SDE in Design and technology.
6) The majority considered their own enthusiasm towards matter of SDE very much higher than that of their peers, the senior management team of the school, their department as a whole, and the learners.

Elshof (2005) conducted a small scale survey with teachers in Canada to explore Technological Education teachers' interpretation of sustainable development. There are many parallels to the responses given in the Scottish survey. For example, the Canadian teachers also took their focus to be the environment, with less emphasis on social justice & equity, economics. He too reports that the teachers have the perception that learners are less interested in sustainability than teachers. The Canadian teachers conceded that there was very little evidence of critical thinking required in their current approaches and there were no explorations of issues when 'doing' tasks and project work with the learners.

In contrast to the Scottish survey, the results of the Canadian survey indicate that in order to shift thinking and behaviours of society to be come more sustainable the teachers felt there needed to be:

1. A change in political leadership
2. Individual citizen action
3. Citizen awareness through education.

This sample of Scottish Design and Technology teachers felt that the biggest influence was parents and teachers, with only 1in 10 believing that politicians could make the biggest difference. Interestingly, the Canadian teachers noted that the least important in shifting thinking and behaviours was the teachers 'own worldviews'.

As hinted at through the two surveys, teachers may require support to make meaningful links with and develop greater awareness of social and economic aspects of sustainability as related to environmental and ecological sustainability.

Pitt and Lubben, (2009) examined the motives for English and Welsh teachers of A-level Design and Technology to get involved in Practical Action's, Sustainable Design Awards (SDA). They were interested in what ways has the SDA project increased participating teachers' understanding of, confidence in, integrating the social dimension of sustainable development in their Design and Technology teaching. Three groups of teachers emerge from the data:

1. the SD *devotees* – Passionate , committed before involvement - SD provide vehicles for coherency;
2. the SD *seekers* – Looking for something to help join up-thinking in design and technology- new underpinning mindset;
3. the SD *surfers* – Seeking a temporary add on, move on to something else.

Pitt and Lubben, (2009) suggest that some teachers seem to hold the perception of sustainability as a "movement". This reportedly makes teachers hesitant to consider sustainability seriously for inclusion in their teaching, even as a bridge for closing the 'value-action gap' (Bonnet 2002).Bonnet describes 'frame of mind' as being where teachers examine their own and others interpretation, and encourage joint development and interconnections. Common to all methods of research summarised in this section is the interrogation of sustainability development, in terms of understanding of the three dimensions of social, economic, environmental. The studies sought to identify indicators of what it is that can bridge the value -action gap or develop a frame of mind, or a worldview that enables teachers to engage with the holistic nature of the inter-related, systems thinking processes of Design and Technology that are mutually supportive of education for sustainability.

Challenge of Change

Times of transition and change create a sense of discomfort for many. Demands are made on existing knowledge and understanding, values, attitudes and world views. Change in education and curriculum requirements, society and learner expectation often require substantial changes in pedagogy as well as content and learning experiences. Paechter (1995) noted that the very nature of Design and Technology e.g. openness regarding 'content', potential exploitation of change, underpinning philosophy of designerly thinking, dealing with uncertainty and intellectual risk taking,can result in what she called 'sub-cultural retreat.'

Design and Technology teachers are being challenged to incorporate 21st century concepts of design for sustainability, appropriate technologies and democratic design. There are many who write about education for sustainability and Design and Technology, however, the majority focus on the *why* things should change, not necessarily the how to affect change in Design and Technology education. However, as Behrenbruch (2007) cautions, when she cites Dewey,1933, 'Knowledge of methods alone will not suffice: there must be the desire, the will, to employ them. This desire is an affair of personal disposition (p. 30)'. Dispositions form the link between knowledge and action.

This paper has highlighted the need for further support for beginning and practicing teachers in dealing with transformational learning, relational learning, complexity thinking, trans-disciplinary thinking, planning, learning & teaching whilst recognising and valuing the unique disciplinary contribution of Design Technology as a specialist learning area. It is as much about what do teachers need to be as what they need to do.

Recommendations

Initial Teacher Education (ITE) programmes supporting beginning teachers are subject to University re-accreditation and General Teaching Council (Scotland) revalidation every 4 years. A re-envisioning of what it is to be a teacher of Design and Technology is possible.

Greater attention is required to develop deeper understandings of sustainability in respect to the inter-related and mutually dependent aspects of society, economy and environment. With systems-based designerly thinking embedded throughout ITE design and technology programmes, the new entrants will have greater confidence to cast off the traditional design and make conception of the purpose of Design and Technology Education. They will recognise the wider contribution it can make in terms of education for sustainable development and global citizenship.

A rethinking of what may be considered the pedagogical content knowledge related to Design and Technology will be necessary. Encouraging students to examine their own worldviews and explore controversial and topic issues through the lenses of design, technology and engineering serves to develop pedagogical content knowledge more than teaching to existing awarding body syllabus.

ITE can model future thinking, scaffold interdisciplinary groups of students and teachers, and encourage reflection on personal and professional responses to a range of pedagogical approaches. Thus, beginnings of change in practice can be experienced, analysed and examined in a no or low- risk environment, prior to implementation in school. Subsequently, confidence in arguing for alternatives can be underpinned by some evidence rather than perceived as naivety. Thus there is less likelihood of enculturation and subjugation to status quo. ITE programmes, including school and work based placements, combine to develop capable education professionals with critical understandings of the holistic nature of learning through the experiences offered by Design and Technology, in collaboration with other learning areas.

References

Bonnet, M. (2002) Education for sustainability as a frame of mind *Environmental Education Research* 8:1 9-20

COS. (1985). *The Place of Technology in the Secondary Curriculum*. Final report of the SCCs Committee on Technology. Scottish Consultative Committee on the Curriculum. Dundee.

Conference on Technical Education Held at Edinburgh Friday 20th March 1868 Neil and Company, Edinburgh (Publication held in University of Glasgow Special Collection BG57c.17.)

Dewey, J. (1933). *How we think: A restatement of the relation of reflective thinking to the educative* cited in Behrenbruch, M. (2007) Sustainable education through sustainable thinking: No longer an optional extra. Online at http://www.aare.edu.au/08pap/bol08404.pdf (accessed 14/11/ 2009)

Elshof, L. (2003). Technological education, interdisciplinarity, and the journey toward sustainable development: Nurturing new communities of practice. *Canadian Journal of Science, Mathematics and Technology Education*, 3.4, 165–184.

Elshof, L.(2005) Teacher's Interpretation of Sustainable Development *International Journal of Technology and Design* 15:173-186

Elshof, L. (2006a) Productivism and the Product Paradigm in Technological Education *Journal of Technology Education* 17,2. 18-32

Elshof, L. (2006b) From Worldview Reflection to Interdisciplinary, Crucial Paths in Teacher Preparation *Salt of the Earth : Creating a Culture of Environmental Respect an Sustainability* 5-19

Elshof, L. (2007) Moving beyond 'artifactual knowing' : Emergent ideas for a 21st century technology education PATT18 *Teaching and Learning Technological Literacy in the Classroom* Glasgow 176-182. Online at http://www.iteaconnect.org/Conference/PATT/PATT18/fullprog-21a%5B1%5D.pdf

Kierl, S. (2007) The Politics of technology curriculum D.Barlex(ed|) *Design and Technology for the Next Generation* Cliffco pp 60-73

Learning and Teaching Scotland (2000) *National Guidelines for 5-14 Environmental Studies : Society, Science and Technology* HMSO

Learning and Teaching Scotland (2002) *Education for Citizenship*

Learning and Teaching Scotland (2004) *A Curriculum for Excellence* Scottish Executive

Learning and Teaching Scotland (2009) *A Curriculum for Excellence* Technologies Online at http://www.ltscotland.org.uk/curriculumforexcellence/technologies/index.asp

Leicester,G., Bloomer, K., and Stewart , D. (2009) *Transformative Innovation in Education: a playbook for pragmatic visionaries* triarchy press publication

Littledyke, M., Taylor, N. and Eames, C. (2009) *Education for sustainability in the primary curriculum: a guide for teachers* Palgrave Macmillan

McGarr, O. (2009) Education for sustainable development in technology education in Irish schools: a curriculum analysis *International Journal of Technology and Design* Education online first – DOI 10.1007/s10798-009-9087-7

McLaren (1997) Value Judgments: Evaluating Design A Scottish Perspective on A global Issue *International Journal of Technology and Design Education* 7 259-278

McNaughton, M. (2007) Sustainable Development education in Scottish Schools : the sleeping Beauty syndrome *Environmental Education Research* 13.5.621-638

Paechter, C. (1995) Subcultural Retreat: negotiating the design and technology curriculum, *British Educational Research Journal*, 21: 1, 75-87

Pavlova, M. & Pitt, J. (2007) The Place of Sustainability in design and technology education D.Barlex (ed) *Design and Technology for the Next Generation* Cliffco pp 74-89

Petrina, S.(2007) 2020vision; on the politics of technology D.Barlex (ed) *Design and Technology for the Next Generation* Cliffco pp 34-43

Petrina, S. (2000) The political ecology of design and technology education: An enquiry into methods *International Journal of Technology and Design Education* 10, 207-237

Petrina, S. (1998) Multi-disciplinary technology education *International Journal of Technology and Design Education* 8, 103-138

Pitt, J. & Lubben,F. (2009) The social agenda of education for sustainable development within design and technology *International Journal of Technology and Design* 19:2 167-187

Pitt, J. (2009) Blurring the Boundaries – STEM Education and Education for Sustainable Development *Design and Technology Education: an International Journal*, 14:1, 37-48

Scottish Consultative Council on the Curriculum (1996) *Technology Education in Scottish School: A statement of Position* Dundee : SCCC

Scottish Executive (2006) Learning for our Future: *Scotland's first action plan for the UN decade of Education for Sustainable Development*,Scottish Executive.

Scottish Executive (2005) *Choosing our future: Scotland's sustainable development strategy*

Seemann, K.W. (2006) The role values play in forging skill and task performance: case studies in cross-cultural and innovation education *Proceedings of Values in Technology Education: the 4th biennial International Conference on Technology Education*, Centre for Learning Research, Griffith University, Qld., 7-9 December.

Seemann, K.W. (2003) Basic principles in holistic technology education *Journal of Technology Education*, 14, 2, 28-39

Sustainable Education Liaison Group (2006) Sustainable Development Education in *A Curriculum for Excellence: Discussion paper.* Online at http://www.scwg.aaps.ed.ac.uk/docs/open/SDELG.pdf

SOIED (1993) *National Guidelines for 5-14 Environmental Studies* HMSO

Scottish Qualification Authority (1989) *Arrangements for Standard Grade Craft and Design Foundation, General, and Credit levels in and after 1989.* Online at: http://www.sqa.org.uk/files/nq/Craft%20&%20Design.pdf

Scottish Qualification Authority (2004) *Arrangements for Product Design first edition 2004.* Online at http://www.sqa.org.uk/files_ccc/Product_Design_Higher_May04.pdf

Van Driel,J. H., Beijaard, D. and Vreloop, N. (2001) Professional Development and Reform in Science Education: The Role of Teachers' Practical Knowledge *Journal of research in science teaching* 38, 2, 137-158

3.7 Interdependence and Participation/Voice in Secondary Geography: The Centrality of Initial Teacher Education

Hamish Ross, University of Edinburgh

Introduction

This chapter examines a case study of geography Initial Teacher Education (ITE) from the perspective of Education for Sustainable Development/Global Citizenship (ESD/GC). It looks at tutor interviews, the planned ITE curriculum and textbook, and at the official school curriculum. Through these discourses the ideas of interdependence and voice/participation are represented in a range of ways to geography graduates who are studying to become geography schoolteachers. The analysis suggests that, for a variety of reasons, school geography is not the opportunity for ESD/GC that it could be. However it also suggests that ITE geography could make a fundamental contribution to ESD/GC through school geography: not only as a centralized point-of-entry for the ESD/GC agenda; but as a critical domain between school and university geography where a foundational geographical imagination can be explored.

The chapter proceeds from the assumption that the student teacher of geography is involved in a set of curriculum discourses that include: the experience and curriculum of their initial teacher education tutors; the key textbook of their ITE course; and the official school geography curriculum. It draws on analyses of these discourses for a case study of student teachers of geography in a Scottish ITE institution. The analyses focused on some of the key curriculum elements of ESD/GC, by asking in what way 'interdependence' and 'active participation/voice' are represented in the discourses of the case. Common to ESD and GC are the ideas that learners should learn that they live in a world of complex interdependence; and that they can and should engage and act in it through their local circumstances. How these two ideas combine is the subject of other work (Gough, 2002) but their centrality to the agendas behind this book can hardly be contested: Oxfam's (2006) definition of global citizenship is an influential example (Marshall, 2005, Standish, 2009: 70-77).

Case Outline and Methods

Various sources of data were brought together to build this case study. The planned curriculum discussed here was part of a Postgraduate Diploma in General Education (Secondary), which was a one-year (36 weeks) course involving a total of 18 weeks in college and 18 weeks of practice in secondary schools. All the geography ITE students on the programme were geography graduates. In college, they received 4 hours per week of instruction under the geography ITE curriculum, though there were also other aspects of their ITE curriculum.

There have been two consecutive geography ITE tutors managing this curriculum: Alex and Phoebe (pseudonyms). They each have about 30 years teaching experience in a wide range of schools and roles. Phoebe ran the course from 2007 to 2010 after Alex moved to related duties in the institution. A coherent time boundary for the case therefore covers the period 2005-2010, allowing both tutor perspectives to be brought together. Each was interviewed separately and the interviews were recorded and analysed.

The official school curriculum referred to as part of this case was the Scottish 5-14 Environmental Studies Guidelines (Learning and Teaching Scotland, 2000), and Scottish examination syllabuses for older pupils of geography. This curriculum was relevant to the ITE students' school practice experience for much of the case period. The analyses of these curricular documents were undertaken for related purposes by the present author (Ross, 2007, Ross and Munn, 2008). Although this school curriculum is now being succeeded, for various reasons the analysis is likely to remain pertinent until at least 2014/15.

As part of their course, the geography ITE students were each loaned a copy of The Secondary Geography Handbook (Balderstone, 2006) – hereafter SGH - an edited collection that is used as a key text for the geography ITE part of their course. This book was a regular (though not exclusive) reference source for the students in both tutors' work with them. The book was analysed thematically for this chapter, using the 'start codes' (Miles and Huberman, 1994: 58) of 'interdependence' and 'participation/voice' as sensitising concepts.

The kinds of claims that can be made from analyses of this limited set of discourses are discussed later. The findings of the analyses are given next.

Interdependence in the Geography ITE curriculum
From the perspective of interdependence, the concepts of society and environment should perhaps be understood as meshes of causal connectivity. However the analysis of the official school curriculum showed that these concepts were fragmented and that there were limited expectations of pupils' ability to articulate a mesh- or web-like concept of interdependence. These claims are expanded upon here.

First, 'geography' is a product of curricular division. In the school where he worked in the late 1980s, Alex was involved in a plan to teach all of S1 and S2 (12-13 year olds) in an integrated away across much of the curriculum, including across geography and science for example. His purposes included the repair of curriculum fragmentation. However, the idea ultimately fell in the face of specialist professional constituencies who maintain curriculum divisions of this kind (Simpson, 2006: 26). The pupil who is to learn of interdependence across ecology and politics, for example, must do so largely unsupported in the spaces between her school subjects.

Second, long-established divisions in the discipline of geography were identifiable throughout the official curriculum. School geography strands were divided into 'human', 'physical' and 'human-physical interactions' (Learning and Teaching Scotland, 2000: 32). Similar divisions were found in the SGH (Bloomer and Atherton, 2006: 52-53). Phoebe and Alex – as geographers themselves – identified with different sides of these divisions. Phoebe said that the geographers recruited to the ITE programme also often came from either side, and that specialisation in undergraduate geography was more pronounced than in the past, so it was possible that some students on the ITE course had not studied human geography since their own school days. Moreover both Phoebe and Alex said that the planned ITE curriculum did not 'teach geography' and instead used the students' own academic understandings of the subject as context. So at first sight the graduate teacher of geography may be little more ready to articulate interdependence across the divisions of geography than her school pupils are.

Third, in the official curriculum the idea of a holistic or integrated physical environment (which is important in understanding interdependence) was relegated in a range of ways. It tended to appear only contextually in relation to some other pedagogical focus. For example, 'equatorial rainforest' and 'tundra' were background rubrics in an assessment which in fact focused on candidates' climate graph interpretation skills (Scottish Qualifications Authority, 2002b: 10-11). Where 'the environment' was itself the curriculum focus, it tended to be broken into features ('pyramidal peak, hanging valley, arête, corrie' (Scottish Qualifications Authority, 2001a: 3)) rather than being presented as a functionally interdependent assemblage. Where functional interdependence was acknowledged, this was represented by generalised, abstracted and separated models such as 'the hydrological cycle', which are devoid of the contingent detail and inter-model connections of a holistic representation. And where the curriculum had things to say about interdependence explicitly (e.g. Learning and Teaching Scotland, 2000: 62), these were typically in background sections separate from the attainment targets and outcomes that could be thought of as driving and organising teaching activity.

In relation to this last point, however, Alex said that he would object to putting important ideas like interdependence and citizenship into attainment targets and boxes to be ticked-off. He thought they should be woven throughout the curriculum so that they 'grow within children'. This idea of weaving was how both Phoebe and Alex sought to incorporate ideas such as globalisation or environmentalism into their work with ITE students. They were not headline goals of the planned ITE curriculum, but they were planned nonetheless.

A final relevant feature of the official school curriculum analysis concerned the complexity of causal connections that pupils were expected to articulate, even while dealing with interdependence. For example, pupils might be asked in an exam: 'What are the main causes of desertification?' (Scottish Qualifications Authority, 2002b: 12). Exam marker instructions revealed much about what was expected of the candidates:

'One mark for each valid point. Two where developed. Maximum 1 mark for list. E.g. failure of rainfall (1 [mark]) and high evaporation rate (1). Overgrazing by cattle/goats/sheep (1). Cultivation where rainfall low (1). Clearing of woodland areas (1) for firewood (1). Or any other valid point. (Scottish Qualifications Authority, 2002a: 5)'

Although the desire for 'development' rather than a list is clear, the expectation appeared to be a set of proximal causes rather than the kind of reasoning that might articulate international interdependence with, for example, UK supermarkets or climate change. This observation was repeated elsewhere in the curriculum (Ross and Munn, 2008) and the analyses used the code 'shallow causality' to describe the phenomenon.

The next section considers findings related to pupil participation/voice. For reasons that will emerge, there are overlaps with the findings above but also a shift in emphasis from the official school curriculum and into the other discourses that make up this study.

Participation and voice in the Geography ITE curriculum
From the perspective of pupil participation/voice, the concepts of society and environment should perhaps be presented as being personally and contextually knowable, so that it is meaningful to act, or express one's view, as an intervention in the world. The absence of contingent detail in official curriculum models of the world would present a challenge to the possibility of personally knowing it, as in the case of knowing the world through 'the hydrological cycle' in the example given previously. Moreover, a key finding of the official curriculum analysis was that learners were progressively expected to see themselves as abstract models, and people in general as instances of categories, and the world as a big place. Various authors have observed the latter 'expanding horizon' curriculum model (Davies, 2006: 12, Marshall, 2005: 82, Richardson, 2008: 115-116), but a key element is the progression, with increasing age, towards the scientific gaze – the so-called 'view from nowhere'.

For example, the Scottish 5-14 Environmental Studies Guidelines (Learning and Teaching Scotland, 2000) showed at least two age-related progressions in the language of the outcomes. Table 1 (Ross, 2009) can be read to suggest that younger learners will understand a worldview in which they are potential local actors (they learn of their local area while understanding it from their own perspective), whereas older learners are expected to understand a worldview from an abstract perspective of the kind that allows system-analysis of global interdependence (they learn to see themselves as instances of categories of people on a large planet – perhaps as 'global citizens').

Strand:	*People and needs in society*	*The physical environment*
Younger (5 yrs) ↓ Older (14 yrs)	...own needs ...family ...friends ...the elderly...community ...individuals ...extended family ...health care providers ...different groups ...young people ...citizens	...nearby physical features ...local physical features ...features of the Scottish landscape ...features outside Scotland ...global tectonics

Table 1: changes in the language of attainment targets in two strands of the Scottish official curriculum (abstracted from Learning and Teaching Scotland, 2000: 32 & 37).

This progression continued beyond the age of 14. Although geography Standard Grade candidates were expected to develop 'awareness of problems facing the environment at all scales from local to global' (Scottish Qualifications Authority, 2001b: 40), 'Scotland' was the smallest area within which the key ideas were to be studied, and even then only one of 17 key ideas was assessed at this scale. Project work was a potential way to bring the local back into the school curriculum. Phoebe recommended to her Advanced Higher pupils that they focused their 'issue' study (see below) on something local or regional, such as a new Edinburgh Airport runway or primary healthcare and malaria in Kenya. But she also said that such independent project work, involving the study of local places like rivers and shopping centres, had been removed from the lower levels of the examination system.

It could be argued that this increasingly global gaze, with age, suggests an increasing opportunity for pupils to understand interdependence (although 'shallow causality', above, mitigates this claim). However Table 1 also suggests a decreasing opportunity to envisage participating (if this is understood to be local and personal) because in the global gaze the learner looks down upon herself as an insignificant speck in global systems that appear indifferent to her presence. This representation of the 'global citizen' is not, surely, what is intended by the concept. One interpretation of this problem is that environment and society in this representation do not surround the learner, who is instead a detached observer. This problem was recognised by several contributions to the SGH that were concerned with developing an emotional or affective connection with places (Caton, 2006: 61). Fieldwork, for example, could achieve this by dispensing with the generalising, quantitative, data collection approaches of 1970s geography that tended to de-generalise places and people into abstract models (Holmes and Walker, 2006: 218). According to Alex, fieldwork was unusually significant in the case institution's geography ITE course, but its purpose and methods were not discussed in the interview.

There was also a set of discourses that contested pupil participation/voice per se. With few exceptions (e.g. Massey, 2006, in the SGH), most accounts separated political content from pupil voice/participation as pedagogical process. For example, in the SGH there was a sense of pupil participation/voice as a progressive pedagogical strategy involving pupils in their own learning in various ways (Marvell et al., 2006: 240, Freeman and Miller, 2006: 249, Freeman and Hare, 2006: 308). Phoebe had seen such shifts in classroom pedagogy over her career and said they were driven by the need to make schooling more inclusive and school subjects more relevant and interesting. In neither case was pupil voice/participation seen as a matter of involving pupils politically in the world about which they were learning.

There were alternative assertions in the SGH that students should aim to participate in the world itself, having come to their inevitably value-laden views of it (McPartland, 2006: 174). Most often, though, this outcome was planned so that geography pupils would learn the 'tools' of action and participation in the world but in the context of 'balanced' content about the world (Wellstead, 2006: 161, Morgan, 2006a: 285-286). This was also the sense articulated by Alex and Phoebe. Phoebe said that at Advanced Higher level pupils were required to investigate some form of controversial issue. She explained that the syllabus said that the pupils were 'to get three robust viewpoints from at least three different sources' which they then:

'summarise, analyse and then they have a conclusion about – not necessarily saying 'I agree most with this' – but they have to have a critical analysis within the body of the thing, so that they are saying that 'this one's a bit more robust because it seems to have real statistical data that's been properly collected and it's free from exaggeration and it's free from bias' (which very few are), and the kids should be able to identify that'.

She also used role-play with younger pupils, and with ITE students, to focus on issues of seeing things from another person's point of view. In her view the geography curriculum involved a lot of areas where conflict could be explored. She thought that teachers had a responsibility to tolerate pupil views that they personally found difficult, so that pupils were allowed to think for themselves. Alex said that a classroom teacher should not be planning to indoctrinate a cohort of eco-activists but should allow for the possibility that such activism might emerge. In part both tutors were concerned with inclusion. Alex used an example of classroom discussions of the nuclear industry in schools where the local economy and families might be reliant on that industry:

'in terms of boundaries I think it is quite important that we alert [the ITE] students to the kind of controversial issues that some of these topics evoke and the kind of feelings that can be raised and the kind of – it's not dangerous ground – but to make them aware of the pitfalls in teaching some of the controversies that surround citizenship and globalisation.'

And yet, neither Alex nor Phoebe saw schooling as apolitical. In his first teaching post Alex spent 3½ years under a Head Teacher who lead the school on a social justice agenda in the face of the local effects of inequality. The geography syllabus at the time was heavily dominated by 'regional' or 'capes and bays' geography (unaffected by global, environmental or citizenship agendas). But Alex was encouraged to undertake fieldwork and he talked of the obviousness of inequalities between the places they visited and his pupils' communities. And both Phoebe and Alex have worked with the Scottish Development Education Centre and Eco-Schools in their geography ITE courses. Perhaps there was a sense here that radical variants of pupil voice/participation were an out-of-classroom matter, or maybe an out-of-geography one.

Conclusions

All of the above discourses are part (and only part) of the discursive material with which ITE students will fashion their teaching activity. The above analysis has suggested various ways in which the important ESD/GC ideas of interdependence and pupil voice/participation are represented, and perhaps muted, therein. What role such discourses play in any given teacher's teaching would be a matter of speculation for this study (though see for example, Summers et al., 2005).

For the purposes of this chapter, some thoughts on the mediating role of ITE can be presented by way of conclusion. The ESD/GC agenda, to some extent, sees the significance of Scottish ITE as a centralised 'point of entry' into schooling. Even if this were ITE's only significance for ESD/GC, the possible diversification of routes into the teaching profession should therefore be a matter of major interest because it would entail a diversification of the discourses in which ITE students were involved. This would matter especially if there were reasons for thinking that geography ITE had an unexpectedly critical role to play in the ESD/GC agenda. If at present school geography is not all that it might be in respect of ESD/GC, as perhaps suggested in the analysis above, ITE is at least one place where this can be addressed. Moreover, it may be the only place. It is to this important possibility that the remaining paragraphs turn.

Alex noted that some students over the case period could not reconcile the emphases of their recent geography degrees with a school geography curriculum that appeared largely unchanged since the 1970s. The SGH contains similar observations (Caton, 2006, Morgan, 2006b) and it is a well established issue (for a recent summary see Hill and Jones, 2010). There is also evidence that ITE students reconcile these differences in favour of the official school curriculum (Firth and Winter, 2007: 612) . However, even if the reconciliation were in favour of the university curriculum it is not clear that ESD/GC would benefit. While the human/physical divide in school geography makes interdependence more difficult to illustrate (and expectations of pupils' ability to articulate it are low), this divide may also be growing in university geography through academic specialisation. The analysis hinted that it was growing between geography ITE students at any rate, whose own ability to articulate interdependence may therefore be in doubt. Yet school geography remains a single subject and is the material across which ESD/GC expects those same geography ITE students to help pupils to understand interdependence. In a similar experience of discordance, undergraduate human geographers can tend to see a 'balanced content' as only one of multiple views of the world, and geographical enquiry and content themselves as a 'tools' of political participation and voice. The discourses described in this chapter, in contrast, tended to separate content and pedagogy, world and learner, in both school and ITE. Just as with interdependence, then, the human geographer might therefore wonder how she is to help her pupils develop their participation and voice, as ESD/GC also demands.

Initial Teacher Education geography lies between school and university geography. There may be nothing more to this fact than the confusing liminality just described, a transitional state of ambiguity and indeterminancy. But that liminality in ITE may in fact be critical, offering a space in which student teachers can consider their own geography educations and those of their pupils, including in the context of ESD/GC.

An even more intriguing conclusion would be that ITE geography amounts to something vital for geography as a whole, and moreover that what it amounts to is unexpectedly critical for ESD/GC. According to this conclusion, ITE is not only liminal between school and university geography, but a space in which students can pause and consider a particular sense of geography (perhaps even the sense in which the word is somehow used both by university and school despite their differences). What they might have the opportunity to pause upon is the development of a 'geographical imagination' and the possibility that this should be a goal of school geography. This in fact made a brief appearance in the SGH (Massey, 2006). It draws on a re-imagining of space that cannot be developed in the present chapter (though see Massey, 2005). But crucially it is a re-imagining of space through which geography could handle and combine interdependence and participation/ voice. The development of such a geographical imagination in ITE would be a very positive intervention in schooling for ESD/GC. Indeed, from this perspective school geography, as a single subject, may even be a better point of intervention for ESD/GC than a highly differentiated undergraduate geography: this idea of the 'geographical imagination' is not a perspective that is central to every, or even most, geography graduate(s) recruited into ITE.

It might be a perspective with which they could leave ITE, however. Initial Teacher Education may be the site where this critical geography can be encountered, precisely because ITE students are tackling the problems of moving from a specialist to a general subject, considering its educational purposes and identity, and their own identification with it. In discussing these problems, Alex expressed satisfaction that ultimately the ITE geography students were 'all geographers at heart'. It would be worth investigating whether they are particularly liable to discover that heart in ITE and in their decisions to become teachers, which echo with the refrain: 'because I love my subject'. If such a geography – ITE geography – could thus be defined by the development of a geographical imagination that captures interdependence and voice/participation, then advocates of ESD/GC would have an interest in seeing ITE less as a central point of influence and more as a critical developmental moment.

References

Balderstone, D. (2006) *Secondary Geography Handbook*, Sheffield, Geographical Association.

Bloomer, D. & Atherton, R. (2006) Understanding landscape. In Balderstone D. (Ed.) *Secondary Geography Handbook*. Sheffield, Geographical Association.

Caton, D. (2006) Real world learning through geographical fieldwork. In Balderstone, D. (Ed.) *Secondary Geography Handbook*. Sheffield, Geographical Association.

Davies, L. (2006) Global citizenship: abstraction or framework for action? *Educational Review*, 58, 5-25.

Firth, R. & Winter, C. (2007) Constructing education for sustainable development: the secondary school geography curriculum and initial teacher training. *Environmental Education Research*, 13, 599-619.

Freeman, D. & Hare, C. (2006) Collaboration, collaboration, collaboration. In Balderstone, D. (Ed.) *Secondary Geography Handbook*. Sheffield, Geographical Association.

Freeman, D. & Miller, S. (2006) Homework and independent study. In Balderstone, D. (Ed.) *Secondary Geography Handbook*. Sheffield, Geographical Association.

Gough, N. (2002) Thinking/acting locally/globally: western science and environmental knowledge in a global knowledge economy. *International Journal of Science Education*, 24, 1217-1237.

Hill, J. & Jones, M. (2010) 'Joined-up geography': connecting school-level and university-level geographies. *Geography*, 95, 22-32.

Holmes, D. & Walker, M. (2006) Planning geographical fieldwork. In Balderstone, D. (Ed.) *Secondary Geography Handbook*. Sheffield, Geographical Association.

Learning and Teaching Scotland (2000) *Environmental Studies. Society, Science and Technology*. 5-14 National Guidelines, Dundee, Learning and Teaching Scotland.

Marshall, H. (2005) Developing the global gaze in citizenship education: exploring the perspectives of global education NGO workers in England. *International Journal of Citizenship in Teacher Education*, 1, 76-92.

Marvell, A., Holland, B. & Shuff, K. (2006) Geography's contribution to vocational courses. In Balderstone D. (Ed.) *Secondary Geography Handbook*. Sheffield, Geographical Association.

Massey, D. (2005) *For Space*, London, SAGE.

Massey, D. (2006) The geographical mind. In Balderstone, D. (Ed.) *Secondary Geography Handbook*. Sheffield, Geographical Association.

McPartland, M. (2006) Strategies for approaching values education. In Balderstone, D. (Ed.) *Secondary Geography Handbook*. Sheffield, Geographical Association.

Miles, M. B. & Huberman, A. M. (1994) *Qualitative data analysis. An expanded sourcebook*, London, Sage.

Morgan, A. (2006a) Teaching geography for a sustainable future. In Balderstone D. (Ed.) *Secondary Geography Handbook*. Sheffield, Geographical Association.

Morgan, J. (2006b) Geography - a dynamic subject. In Balderstone, D. (Ed.) *Secondary Geography Handbook*. Sheffield, Geographical Association.

Oxfam (2006) *Education for Global Citizenship – A Guide for Schools*, Oxford, Oxfam.

Richardson G. (2008) Conflicting imaginaries: Global Citizenship Education in Canada as a site of contestation. In Peters, M. A., Britton, A. & Blee, H. (Eds.) *Global Citizenship Education. Philosophy, Theory and Pedagogy*. Rotterdam, Sense Publishers.

Ross, H. (2007) Environment in the curriculum: representation and development in the Scottish physical and social sciences. Journal of Curriculum Studies, 39, 659-677.

Ross, H. (2009) 'Think global, act local' and the need for curriculum critique. In Inman, S. & Rogers, M. (Eds.) *UK Teacher Education Network for Education for Sustainable Development/Global Citizenship Conference*. Southbank University, London, UK TE ESD/GC Network.

Ross, H. & Munn, P. (2008) Representing self-in-society: Education for Citizenship and the social subjects curriculum in Scotland. *Journal of Curriculum Studies*, 40, 251-275.

Scottish Qualifications Authority (2001a) National Qualifications 2001. Geography Standard Grade. Credit Level. [1260/405]. Glasgow, Scottish Qualifications Authority.

Scottish Qualifications Authority (2001b) Scottish Certificate of Education. Standard Grade Revised Arrangements in Geography. Foundation, General and Credit Levels in and after 1999. Glasgow, Scottish Qualifications Authority.

Scottish Qualifications Authority (2002a) 2002 Geography SG General. Finalised Marking Instructions. Glasgow, Scottish Qualifications Authority.

Scottish Qualifications Authority (2002b) National Qualifications 2002. Geography Standard Grade. General Level. [1260/403]. Glasgow, Scottish Qualifications Authority.

Simpson, M. (2006) *Assessment*, Edinburgh, Dunedin Academic Press.

Standish, A. (2009) *Global Perspectives in the Geography Curriculum*, Abingdon, Routledge.

Summers, M., Childs, A. & Corney, G. (2005) Education for sustainable development in initial teacher training: issues for interdisciplinary collaboration. *Environmental Education Research*, 11, 623 - 647.

Wellstead, E. (2006) Understanding 'distant places'. In Balderstone, D. (Ed.) *Secondary Geography Handbook*. Sheffield, Geographical Association.

Footnotes

[i] Standard Grade examinations were Scottish equivalents to English GCSE exams and were typically taken at the end of compulsory schooling, which ran to age 16.

[ii] Advanced Higher examinations were the top level Scottish school qualification, equivalent to English A2 examinations, and were typically taken one or two years after the end of compulsory schooling at ages 17 or 18.

[iii] http://www.scotdec.org.uk/, accessed 12 May 2010

[iv] http://www.ecoschoolsscotland.org/, accessed 12 May 2010

[v] It is worth observing that this work refers to ITE students in England, where such official curriculum frameworks are technically more heavily prescribed.

3.8 Implementing Sustainable Development Education in the School Curriculum: Learning for ITE from Teachers' Experiences

Marie-Jeanne McNaughton, University of Strathclyde and Betsy King, WWF Scotland

Introduction

The purpose of this research was to investigate the impact that planning, implementing and evaluating a classroom-based Sustainable Development/Global Citizenship project had on the participating teachers, particularly in terms of their knowledge and understanding, teaching and learning approaches and strategies, and values and attitudes relating to Sustainable Development and Global Citizenship Education (SDE/GCE). The initial research sample consisted of seventeen teachers who were undertaking a Chartered Teacher module entitled *Education for a Sustainable Environment* at the University of Strathclyde. From the original seventeen teachers, ten provided full sets of data that could be included for analysis.

The implications of this study for ITE

Although the focus of this study is on practising teachers engaged in post-graduate study, rather than teaching students, the data and findings are, we assert, relevant to the ITE sector as they provide ITE staff and management who are planning and teaching ITE courses with up-to-date examples of teachers currently undertaking SDE/GCE in their own classrooms. In addition, the observations and evaluations of teachers who have had recent positive learning experiences can illustrate the importance of continuing professional development. Most importantly, the teachers' detailed reflections allow ITE staff and management, and their students, to engage with authentic practitioner voices, affording them insights into the benefits for both teachers and their pupils of building opportunities for SDE/GCE into their learning programmes. That these teachers were so enthusiastic and positive in their responses to the power of SDE/GCE to transform and revitalise their teaching, and to meet the requirements of Curriculum for Excellence (2004), should also encourage teacher-educators to provide teachers in training with an understanding of the concepts, skills and values that are central to SDE/GCE .

The location of the research

This research is located within two distinct but, often, complementary theoretical constructs: the pedagogy of SDE/GCE and the pedagogy of reflective practice. In an analysis of the literature pertaining to the effective delivery of SDE/GCE in the school curriculum, McNaughton (2007) found that SDE/GCE is underpinned by six pedagogical themes. Effective sustainable development and global citizenship education should be: holistic and integrated; active and participative; based on and in the environment; focused on values;

based on action competence; and systemic. Together, these pedagogical themes might be viewed as describing a model for progressive, transformative education (Sterling, 2001). However, the realisation of this model, Sterling asserts, is not possible without conscious effort by educators to reflect honestly, not only on their teaching, but also on their own learning.

Reflection as learning is not new in teacher education (Dewey, 1910; Whitehead, 1993). It has been viewed as a way of helping teachers to understand and transform their classroom practice. Indeed, reflection is seen as essential in helping teachers to develop new insights and to clarify their ideas. Scott, (2002) stressed that critical reviews of their practice, by environmental and sustainable development educators, can reveal significant and meaningful experiences. The teachers in this study were introduced to the pedagogical principles underpinning the work of environmental educators such as Huckle (2002), Palmer (1998) and Sterling (2001, 2005) and were encouraged to use these principles when reflecting critically on their own work and, importantly, learning. Specifically, the teachers were asked to keep on-going reflective learning logs to record their critical thinking in relation to their classroom practice over the course of their planned topic. A final summative evaluation was to include an overview of what they had learned: about themselves as teachers; about the pupils as learners; and about the teaching and learning in SDE/GCE. The analysis of this reflective writing would, it was hoped, offer insights into aspects of SDE/GCE from the perspective of the non-specialist teacher.

Research method

This research was predicated on the view that it is important to illustrate, for ITE staff and management, criteria for what might be considered to constitute successful teaching and learning in SDE/GCE. In this small-scale qualitative study, the main research strategy involved the close and systematic analysis and interpretation of the teachers' on-going research logs and summary project evaluations. At the end of the project, the accumulated data was sorted and decisions were made about analysis strategies. In order to view the data as completely as possible, two distinct but complementary strategies were employed. Firstly, a closed, top-down analysis was conducted of the teachers' responses in terms of the eight module Learning Outcomes. Secondly, there was an analysis, using open coding (Flick, 1998), that allowed ideas, themes and categories to emerge from the teachers' reflective summative evaluations (see Table 2). Some additional triangulation was provided through data from semi-structured, informal interviews with a small sample of three of the teachers when the textual analysis was completed.

Sample and module task

The teachers in the study, all of whom had at least five years teaching experience, and some considerably more, were part of a Chartered Teacher (CT) cohort undertaking a module entitled *Education for a Sustainable Environment*. They taught in a range of school contexts: primary, secondary and additional support needs. The assessment for the module required them to plan, implement and evaluate a series of SDE/GCE-based lessons within their own educational context. They were particularly encouraged to create and to take advantage of cross-curricular opportunities and open-ended, learner-centred activities. At the end of the topic, they were asked to submit a portfolio of evidence containing a record of their classroom planning and implementation, examples of the pupils' responses and their own reflective commentaries. They were also required to write an academic essay on the place of SDE in the Scottish curriculum, but this aspect of the assessment is outside the scope of this study.

Ten assessment portfolios were selected for analysis on the basis that these provided the most complete sets of data identified for close analysis: rationales for their topic selection, on-going reflective commentaries in the form of learning logs and a final evaluation of the topic in terms of both their own and the pupils' learning. Ethical approval procedures were completed and all teachers gave permission for their work to be analysed and findings published and disseminated. Table 1 provides a summary of the topics and pupils sectors/stages of the ten portfolios selected for analysis.

Chartered Teacher Assessment Portfolios included in this Study	
Sector/Stage	Project Title
Primary – P2	The School Grounds: Willow Tree Garden
Primary – P2	Taking Action to Make a Difference to Living Things
Primary – P3	Waste
Primary – P7	Global Warming
Primary – P7	Sustainable development in the Context of World War 2: Justice, Equity and Attitudes to Consumption.
Secondary – S2 (English)	Global Citizenship: Malawi
Secondary – S2 (Design and Technology)	The Home and Its Surroundings: Heating and Insulation
Secondary – S1 (Art)	Art Around the World
Secondary –S2 (ASN English)	Re-use and Recycle
Secondary – S2 (ASN Maths)	Travel and Sustainability

Table 1: Scope of the CT Topics

Timescale and scope of the study

The Chartered Teacher module consisted of 25 hours of study over six weeks in the school Autumn Term: two Saturdays on-campus (12 hours) and 13 hours of directed study linked to on-line meetings and tutorials. The module assignment required the teachers to plan, implement and evaluate a topic with a sustainable development/global citizenship theme, lasting between four and six weeks, within their own school context. Assessment for this work was based on a portfolio of evidence: their documentation of the topic and their evaluations of their own and the pupils' learning from its implementation.

The description and analysis of the data

In the following sections, the data and analysis from the project are presented in two complementary ways. Firstly, the teachers' on-going lesson rationales and reflective learning logs are discussed in terms of the module leaders' assessments of the teachers' ability to meet the module learning outcomes. Secondly, the analysis of the summative self-evaluations, completed by the teachers at the end of the project, are discussed in terms of the teachers' perceptions of their pupils' and their own learning. This method of analysis allows the data to be viewed from two perspectives, thus strengthening the validity of any claims for the pedagogical benefits of the inclusion of SDE/GCE in the school curriculum.

The assessors' evaluations of the teachers' cumulative learning in SDE/GCE

University regulations require that all modules provide a list of Learning Outcomes (LOs). These constitute the success criteria for module completion. For this module, eight LOs were designed collectively to allow the participating teachers to demonstrate a broad understanding of SDE/GCE through the planning, implementation and evaluation of their chosen topics. The assessors noted that the teachers' evaluative commentaries on their experiences during the implementation of their topics, particularly in their on-going learning logs, suggested that they were thinking analytically and reflectively at each stage of their work. Individually, the commentaries provided evidence that the teacher had met the assessment criteria set out in the eight module LOs. Cumulatively, these commentaries provided the assessors with a rich source of data on the teachers' learning in SDE/GCE.

Commentary and links with ITE

The assessment of the teachers' work in relation to the eight LOs provided evidence to suggest that, over the course of the implementation of the topics, there was a marked development in their understanding and implementation of the pedagogical approaches to SDE/GCE. Their understanding of the key facts and issues surrounding their selected topics were informed by specific research and reading. However, all of the teachers approached the teaching of their topics not in terms of the presentation of the knowledge, but using issues-based, open-ended approaches. There was clear and specific identification of links between the planning and implementation and the four capacities set out in *Curriculum for Excellence* which aims to ensure that all young people in Scotland become successful learners, effective contributors, confident individuals and responsible citizens. Over the course of the teachers' learning logs, there was evidence of a development in their awareness of the need for planning and teaching to be flexible and responsive to the ideas and interests of the pupils. They reported using a wider range of teaching and learning strategies than they might normally, including discussion, debate, role-play and enquiry based problem solving. However, while they were aware that this might have been because they were being assessed, they all expressed the opinion that the successful outcomes would encourage them to be more flexible in future. One teacher wrote of one lesson:

'It was hard not to just tell them the answer, and I was aware that time was tight, but they seemed to be really involved in finding ways to get it to work so I bit my tongue. I was really glad that I had, as they seemed so pleased with their eventual success.'

The analysis of this data provides ITE staff and management, and their students, with examples of how the criteria for successful teaching and learning in SDE/GCE can be met. It also illustrates for student-teachers, how on-going commentaries, here, in the form of learning logs, are a valuable source of evidence of reflection and learning and, therefore, can contribute to the assessors' knowledge of the progress being made by the writer.

The teachers' summative assessment of and reflection on their own learning
This section focuses on the teachers' summative comments in their final evaluations. The analysis of the teachers' evaluations of their own and the pupils' learning, in their own words, provided insights into the benefits, and problems, of planning and implementation of SDE/GCE topics and lessons in 'real life' contexts. When completing the summative self-evaluation, the teachers were asked to consider the following points:
• Learning about myself as a learner
• Learning about pupils as learners
• Learning about teaching and learning in SDE/GCE
• Any other interesting features.

Although no specific instruction was given about the length of the final evaluation, the number of words was limited by the overall 4000-word requirement of the assignment. The teachers wrote an average of 800 words in this final section. Each text was read, annotated and subjected to open coding (Flick, 1998) from which categories and themes emerged. It was possible to begin to see underlying patterns of understandings and to see how the teachers were able to make connections between what they had been teaching and what they had learned. Column 1 of Table 2 sets out the nine key themes that emerged from this analysis: relevance; thinking skills; active learning; cross-curricular links; empowering learners; collaboration; enthusiasm; values and perspectives; and teacher learning about themselves. In column 2, these are set against examples of the teachers' evaluative statements.

Commentary and links with ITE

The summative self-evaluations provided a rich source of data. They were detailed and each contained thoughtful observations and reflective analysis of the teacher's 'journey of learning' during the implementation of the topic. The general tone of each self-evaluation was very positive. The teachers seemed to be genuine in their enthusiasm for the work they had undertaken with their classes and in many instances they said that the implementation of the topic had re-invigorated their professional commitment. As one teacher put it:

'I had forgotten how much I enjoyed teaching.' (Teacher 2)

It was very evident that the teachers had engaged with the pedagogical principles of SDE/ GCE, and that their own awareness of the benefits of working in a more open, learner-centred way had developed. There was particular consensus on the need to ensure that the topic was presented in ways that were relevant to and meaningful for the pupils. The provision of opportunities for active, participative learning and for the development of thinking skills was also a high priority for every teacher. All of the teachers, both primary and secondary, were aware of the importance of cross-curricular links and connections, and had found that they were able to accommodate these within the topics, to a greater or lesser extent.

Key Themes Emerging from the Teachers' Summative Self-evaluations

Theme	Examples of Statements
Relevance/Meaningful experiences	'The pupils feel that the work they are doing is 'real' and purposeful and this has a positive effect'; 'SDE involves as many people as possible including school staff and the wider community';
Thinking skills	'Teaching and learning are not about telling pupils what to think'; 'Controversial issues often provoked a significant level of debate'; 'I have been heartened by the pupils' ability to acquire new skills';

Active learning	'Direct experience with nature inspired the pupils and linked learning with values'; 'The topic allowed them to participate actively';
Cross-curricular: making connections	'Sustainability helped to make the maths more real for them'; 'I became more aware of the cross-curricular nature of SD issues'; 'They were able to make connections in quite a sophisticated manner'; 'Without realising it they learned the names of various pieces of scientific equipment'; I have been amazed at how easily I could accommodate this topic as a teacher of English;
Empowering learners	'Despite their youth they had the ability to make informed decisions'; 'Through the Learning Wall process the children had a sense of ownership in their learning';
Collaborative/ Participative	'The children collaborated in a way that was respectful and allowed each child to engage'; 'Children like to be pro-active and part of a team';
Enthusiasm	'The work was characterised by enthusiasm and a sense of self direction I have rarely seen'; 'The children were enthusiastic when participating in debates';
Values/perspectives	'I became aware of how caring the children are towards the needs of wildlife'; 'Be careful not to exploit the pupils' sensitivity and natural empathy'; 'It is important to develop an international perspective and to challenge intolerance';
Teacher learning	'I have realised that SDE is a process to be developed not a target to be reached'; 'My own understanding of these issues has developed'; 'I can also learn from the children'; 'Sometimes I spoon feed the children too much';

Table 2: Key themes emerging from summative self-evaluations

A key theme, common to all of the summative evaluations, was the teachers' comments on their learning about, not only teaching and learning in SDE/GCE, but also about themselves as learners. Engaging with the issues involved in the topic had also enabled some of the teachers to think about their own values and behaviours in relation to pedagogy and to the SDE/CGE issues involved in the topic, for example:

'As my aspiration to change the children's thinking and behaviour has developed, so has my desire to change my own behaviour. '(Teacher 3)

'My eyes have been opened to the global perspective.' (Teacher 5)

In terms of ITE, this analysis of the self-evaluations of practising teachers can give ITE staff and programme managers, and their student teachers, an insight into the value that teachers place on the pedagogical approaches and the learning opportunities afforded by SDE/GCE-based topics. The evidence suggests that these also offer excellent potential for schools to engage with the pedagogical imperatives set out in *Curriculum for Excellence*.

Final Comments and Next Steps

The most striking aspect of this research was not the teachers' evaluations of the development of the children's knowledge and skills in relation to SDE/GCE, but their honest reflections on the changes in their own pedagogical attitudes and values. All of the teachers highlighted the tensions between their perceptions of schools' and national assessment priorities, and the adoption of more open-ended approaches to issues-based learning. However, the critical reflection allowed the teachers to articulate and demonstrate the areas of success and seemed to give them confidence in adopting the more learner-centred pedagogy of SDE/GCE. It was evident that the important aspects of the teachers' learning arose not from their planning and implementation but from their critical reflection.

Although this study involved a small sample of teachers, and ones who were already engaged in reflective practice as part of their Chartered Teacher Masters programme, the findings are, nevertheless, encouraging. All of the teachers in the study identified and illustrated how being involved in the SDE/GCE topics helped their pupils to meet the four capacities set out in *Curriculum for Excellence*. More specifically, the evidence from the teachers' assessments and evaluations suggests that many of the aspects of the schematic set out for curriculum planning in *Building the Curriculum* 3 (p.13, 2008), in particular in relation to values for life, integrated approaches to the curriculum, transformative approaches to teaching and learning, and entitlement to a broad general education, were met though their SDE/GCE-based topics. This evidence provides ITE programmes co-ordinators with a justification for offering more SDE/GCE-based, cross-curricular modules that help student teachers to understand and to plan and implement these approaches in their own work. It also provides evidence that teacher educators can integrate SDE/GCE concepts and approaches across a wide range of subject themes.

A next step, here, will be to use these findings to inform two new 20-credit modules for the BEd (Hons.) at the University of Strathclyde, the first of which begins in 2010-2011. These core modules, entitled *Integrated Approaches to the Curriculum*, 1 and 2, will be compulsory for all students and will feature SDE/GCE as a major strand of a multi-disciplinary focus. The ITE students will be engaged in planning and implementing integrated topics and will be supported in undertaking reflection and evaluations of their own learning.

It is also planned that a fuller version of this chapter, with a clear focus on teachers' voices in SDE will be written for submission to the journal, *Environmental Education Research*.

References

Dewey, J. (1910). *How We Think*. Boston: D.C. Health and Company.

Flick, U. (1998). *An introduction to qualitative research*. London: Sage Publications Ltd.

Huckle, J. (2002). *Educating for sustainability: A guide for primary schools*. Birmingham: National Primary Trust.

McNaughton, M.J. (2007). Sustainable development in Scottish schools: The Sleeping Beauty syndrome. *Environmental Education Research*, 13(2), 139-155.

Palmer, J. (1998). *Environmental Education in the 21st Century: Theory, practice, progress and promise*. London: Routledge.

Scott, W. (2002). Minds, gaps, models, and behaviours. *Environmental Education Research*, 8(3), 237-238.

Scottish Executive Curriculum Review Group (SECRG) (2004). *A curriculum for excellence*. Edinburgh: Scottish Executive.

Scottish Government (2008). *Curriculum for Excellence: Building the curriculum: part 3*. Edinburgh: The Scottish Government.

Sterling, S. (2001). *Sustainable education: Revisionary learning and change*. Bristol: Schumacher Briefings.

Sterling, S. et al (2005) *Linkingthinking: New perspectives on thinking and learning for sustainability*. Godalming: WWF Scotland

Whitehead, J. (1993). *The Growth of Educational Knowledge: Creating your own Living Educational Theories*. Bournemouth: Hyde Publishing.

3.9 'They Become Completely Involved.' What Teachers Say about the Benefits of Global Citizenship in Schools.

David Miller, Gwen Boswell, Erika Cunningham, Brenda Dunn, Paola Fallone, Brenda Keatch, Mary Knight, Teresa Moran, Loretta Mulholland and Peter Wakefield, University of Dundee.

Introduction

The concept of global citizenship is one that is gaining in importance within the context of primary education. As we continue to explore its nature and scope, the promotion of global citizenship is likely to figure strongly in the aspirations of curriculum planners in the foreseeable future. 'Global issues are part of children and young people's lives in ways unfamiliar to previous generations.' (DFID et al.,2005). Education for citizenship has been an area of major development in Scottish education in recent years. In many Scottish schools the approach adopted has been one of attempting to embed associated learning and teaching both within the curriculum and across the broader roles of the school, rather than to regard it as a topic to be addressed separately. This has been undertaken in an attempt to better prepare children for their future participation in political, social, economic, cultural and educational decision-making in Scottish society.

The principles underpinning Environmental and Citizenship Education are becoming increasingly embedded within *Curriculum for Excellence*, (Scottish Government, 2009) with its aspiration to enable all children to develop their capabilities as successful learners, confident individuals, responsible citizens and effective contributors to society. Global issues, therefore, have become factors in the lives of young Scottish people quite unlike the issues and concerns of earlier generations. In consequence Scottish primary teachers will be pivotal in preparing and empowering children to assume responsibility for creating and enjoying a sustainable future.

There are obvious implications here for teacher education, and this was the starting point for the work reported in this chapter. The main aim at the outset was to learn more about emerging practice in this area, primarily to inform ITE programmes – but also as an opportunity for further research into classroom practice. Through various contacts we became aware of a number of teachers and schools in the local area where interesting work was going on in the area of global citizenship. We did not have a pre-set agenda or specific research questions. We wanted to see what was 'out there' and to explore the perceptions of the teachers who were leading developments. The expectation was that this initial work would allow us to identify aspects which would then be investigated in more detail.

Methodology

In broad terms, our approach was framed within an interpretivist paradigm. Although we were keen to learn more about what was being done in schools, we were also interested in the perceptions, attitudes and beliefs of the individuals concerned. This approach steered us towards the collection of qualitative data, with an emphasis on open-ended enquiry. Non-probability sampling was adopted; we had learned about schools who were leading the way in developing the curriculum in the area of global citizenship, and these schools and individuals comprised the population from which we drew our sample. Interviews were conducted with teachers in seven schools – six primaries and one secondary school. The sample of primaries included large inner-city schools, a mid-size suburban school and small rural schools. The secondary school was a medium size school in a market town in eastern Scotland. The teachers who took part varied in terms of gender, age, length of time teaching and management experience.

The main data collection instrument was a semi-structured interview which looked at teachers' experiences, beliefs and attitudes towards the teaching of global citizenship. The interview schedule was created in a step-wise manner. After an initial open discussion on a range of issues surrounding global citizenship, the members of the research team drew up a list of issues they wanted to learn more about. Researchers worked as individuals or in pairs, formulating appropriate questions; these were then collated, and the large pool of questions reduced. Firstly duplicate questions were removed. Next, redundant questions were identified and these were also removed. Finally common themes – or underlying factors – were identified. Eight main issues emerged from this process, and these then became the key questions. For each question several probes were identified, based on the initial set of issues raised. The interviews were conducted in the spring term of 2009, and typically lasted for 50-60 minutes.

Findings

Teachers' conceptualisation of the area

It was evident that teachers varied in the way they conceptualised global citizenship. For many the term appeared to be an umbrella concept which encapsulated a range of different initiatives, including eco schools, responsible citizenship and multi-cultural education. When exploring what global citizenship means in practice, many respondents answered by referring to the activities associated with a specific project, usually based on a developing country; examples included Peru and Bangladesh. It was rare for respondents to list a set of underlying principles, although one primary school did this and produced eight key aims, including both cognitive and affective factors. In this case, there were aims related to knowledge acquisition (for example, of specific environmental issues facing the planet, health issues), development of skills (for example, research skills, collaboration skills) and social and personal factors (compassion, responsibility). However, this type of classification was not typical, and most respondents were more general in their description of what global citizenship encompassed. In fact, the discourse seemed to suggest a perspective which was experiential in nature, rather than one based on knowledge or content. Responses were usually framed in terms of activities provided for the children, or the resources used, rather than discussion of principles. Discussion would often focus on a specific resource pack, or an activity the children benefited from, or a product they created, or an inspirational visitor. Generally, affective elements were emphasised by teachers, with descriptions of children's experiences and their consequences.

A theme which recurred was that of helping children to appreciate the reality of the lives of less fortunate children, often focusing on lifestyle and life-chances in other countries. Frequently, the language employed by teachers in this context included terms such as 'comparison', 'recognition' 'appreciating' and 'understanding'. Certainly, a common value which emerged from the teachers' comments was caring for others, and this had both local and global aspects. One teacher stated unequivocally, 'The main benefits are with the children's attitudes'. It was suggested that when children learn more about others, they appreciate the commonality as well as the diversity of experience. The point here was that pupils are learning more about different cultures, but are learning also that (as one teacher put it) 'we share a lot with them; they are real people like us'.

Interestingly the term 'empathy' was not specifically mentioned, but it seems central to much of the discussion here. Another notable finding can be located within child-centred educational ideology. There was clear evidence of a pedagogical perspective which values starting from the child's immediate experiences and knowledge of local community – and then moving outwards towards other cultures and societies. A further theme was the emphasis on the environment at both local and global levels. A message came through in several interviews that concepts of citizenship and personal responsibility are linked. Although it was not specifically stated, the notion of empowerment or agency seemed implicit in much of the discourse.

The motivation for undertaking work in this area
As might be expected, several factors were discussed in relation to the personal motives and/or the professional drivers for undertaking their project work. Most frequently, reference was made to *Curriculum for Excellence* and the emphasis on global citizenship as a focus for development. But additionally, the influence of HMIE was noted; one school had been told that citizenship was an area where development was needed. Various projects (for example, Comenius, KIVA, Connecting Classrooms) were also identified as being significant factors in the decision to develop work in the area. In terms of motivating factors, a message

which came through on several occasions was that visits from individuals with first-hand experience of other cultures were very valuable. In schools in one city, there were frequent mentions of Tom Jolly and the work for Project Colibra. (Tom Jolly is a retired teacher who now lives in Peru and plans to set up a school for street children there.) Other examples were provided, including a local dentist who was able to provide first-hand accounts and share experiences with children. It was also suggested that current news issues often highlight concerns and stimulate new aspects of the work.

The activities related to global citizenship

As suggested above, when discussing the actual work undertaken there appeared to be considerable variation in both content and the activities engaged in. Having said that, a topic based around Peru seemed to crop up frequently, and 'The Peru pack' (a council-wide resource) was mentioned more than once. More recently a project based on jute (the Dakar to Dundee project) has provided curriculum guidance and resources. In terms of learning gains, knowledge, skills and attitudes were all mentioned, including geographical knowledge, (e.g. regions, rain-forests, climate), the wild-life of other countries, health issues for different peoples, and so on. There was an interesting example of children learning Spanish, so they could communicate with children in Peru. As with so many activities reported by the teachers, one cannot fail to make the links here with notions of authentic learning and relevance in the curriculum. But this Spanish example alerts us to another characteristic; the learning exchange is not a one-way process. Certainly, children are learning new things, but they are also communicating with others about their own experiences and their own country. Furthermore, from the perspective of personal and social growth, they are learning about working with, and helping, others. There is evidence that such activities have a positive effect on children's self-perceptions.

Global citizenship work was often incorporated with other cross-cutting themes or initiatives. Many such links were identified, including the Health Promoting School, Fair Trade events, Rights Respecting Schools and Eco-Schools. Links were frequently made with enterprise; indeed the two seem to be very closely related in many schools. The links here are seen in relation to engagement with different local organisations. Several examples were provided of children's efforts through fund-raising events (e.g. salsa evenings, producing a DVD) and also working to secure donations from local organisations to help the community. One school ran a Fair Trade tuck-shop. It is notable that there were several examples of the local dimension of citizenship, for example, supporting a local disability centre and helping local older-age citizens. Another example was one school where the children were collecting rags for recycling – incidentally making links with concepts of sustainability. Apart from the materials specifically produced for schools, several other resources were mentioned by interviewees, including First News (a children's newspaper), the Vine Trust, the Peace Child organisation, and a book *Pachamina – Our Earth Our Future*.

From a pedagogical perspective, a theme that emerged from the discourse was of a process of negotiation between teacher and pupils – and a sense of children having a say in the direction of the work. Quite apart from the resonance with Curriculum for Excellence, there are obvious benefits here in terms of intrinsic motivation and the notion of authentic learning (mentioned earlier). One respondent felt that the success of the work was due to 'real decision-making powers [which] motivate the children''. Of course, from a practical point of view, this degree of collaborative decision making has implications for flexibility in planning. It was also noted that work in the area of global citizenship can raise issues which are challenging and/or contentious. Examples cited included materialism and global health.

In the interview with a secondary school teacher, it became apparent that there was not an official policy on global citizenship in that particular school, although this was under consideration. However, many relevant topics, including those incorporating moral and ethical issues,(e.g. racism, human rights, environmental issues such as global warming and genocide) were part of the formal curriculum. It was explained that such topics were addressed at different times, within a range of different curricular areas and by different teachers. We learned of an interesting example of this work forming a bridging project from primary to secondary school. In this case, an 'Eco Island' activity begins in primary 7 as an induction unit, and is then revisited when the children move up to S1. It was evident also from a long list of fund-raising activities that providing support for those who are less fortunate was very much in the thinking of the school.

Some possible benefits for children
In most schools visited, the discussion of benefits was wide-ranging. It was suggested that increased knowledge about different countries and an understanding of the lives of the children provided meaningful insight into cultural diversity. Stereotypical thinking was often challenged as a result of this. Many other benefits were reported too. Children often showed increased interest in other countries – not just those studied – and more generally in world affairs. It was also pointed out that when children learn about other famous individuals (e.g. Nelson Mandela, Martin Luther King) the links to equality issues become more meaningful. A message that emerged on more than one occasion was that this work made the children reflect on many aspects of their own lives – both at home and in school – focusing on the simple things in life. It was also suggested that the children tend to become more aware of waste. One final point here: after learning about the value placed on education in other countries (often despite many difficulties associated with school attendance) many children seem to be valuing their own education more.

There were reports of benefits in terms of social and interpersonal skills (e.g. co-operation with peers within class, and with children in other classes) and levels of motivation; teachers often commented that the children developed a desire to learn more. Gains in self-esteem were also reported and it was suggested that these are as a result of what children have achieved – not least a sense of pride in helping others. (A range of fund-raising activities was noted across the schools surveyed.) Many other benefits were reported by teachers, including a belief that children seem to become more reflective about what they learn; in some cases this contributes to the development of a sense of responsibility. In another school it was stated that it helps 'promote ethical education for everyone, from nursery to Primary 7'.

Several thoughts are worthy of reflection here. Firstly, reading over the responses, one gains the impression that the value of this work is not limited to new knowledge of other countries and the people who live there – important though such knowledge is. Its value may also be related to a 'springboard effect'; that is, we should consider what this work can encourage children to move towards – further learning experiences and the social and personal development associated with them. Secondly, from the responses of teachers, it seems that attitudinal change is central to this work. Short-term gains have been reported, but on an anecdotal basis. There is a need to measure more systematically attitudes and beliefs so that we may learn more about how these are really affected. Similarly, it will be interesting to learn more about whether any changes in beliefs and attitudes persist over time, given social mores and other influences on children (for example, the media).

Impact on teachers themselves

In one of the interviews, in a small village school in Perthshire, we learned that several teachers had visited Chittagong in Bangladesh, with the Bangladeshi teachers in turn visiting the Scottish village. Further exchange visits are planned, with different staff taking part. This was related to a British Council funded project, Connecting Classrooms. Not surprisingly perhaps, the researcher commented in her notes of a real enthusiasm for the topic work at that school.

Even without such experiences, there were many suggestions that teachers can be influenced at a personal level. In fact, comments suggested a positively reinforcing cycle can be set in motion. The more the teachers learn themselves, and see how the work influences children, the more enthusiastic they become and the more committed to global citizenship; this in turn has an effect on the quality of future teaching and learning. Certainly attitudinal factors can impact on pedagogical beliefs: several teachers indicated a desire to see global citizenship more widely embedded in practice. One teacher explained that she now looks for links even when the topic is not designated as a global citizenship focus. It was suggested that, as with many new or interesting ideas, what one class is doing can have an influence on the other classes. At the very least, there is a greater awareness within the school of what's being done. The process of such organic growth within a school community is one which merits further investigation.

Links with parents and the wider community

Given the underlying community aspect of citizenship, links with those outside the classroom are clearly of interest, and there were many examples of this from the respondents. At the most basic level, parents are informed about the work through their children and through newsletters. In addition, we learned about displays in school for visitors to view; examples included displays showing letters and photographs and pieces of children's work. However, amongst these respondents at least, the impact of the work seems to go beyond this. A notable characteristic was that parents often become actively engaged with the work, for example, by providing support in terms of fund-raising, attending events, buying products, etc. One school in particular reported a range of benefits in terms of parental involvement, with the local community providing materials and resources, helping to develop the school grounds, and being active in other project-related work. Another example was a project with a local repertory theatre, and one school had plans to involve members of ethnic groups in future projects.

Developing a sense of community is exemplified in a comment from one school, where it was reported that planning for global citizenship work is a collaborative venture. It involves work with support staff, parents and pupils: 'Everyone is involved with the process – this is part of the ethos and culture of the school.'

Future directions

A range of goals and plans was evident amongst the respondents; some of these seemed to be very well developed, with others still at an early stage. Some were modest in their aims; others were more ambitious. An example of the former is a group of children in one school who had agreed with the school community to collect change at tuck-shop time and to use this for good causes. A plan which presents greater organisational challenges is to allow children currently learning about Bangladesh in primary 7 to maintain links with their twinned school when they transfer to secondary, with the eventual aim of visiting that school when they are in year 3 in secondary.

In some cases, schools planned to continue with existing projects, but often there was a sense of moving forward to develop work in the area. Examples included plans to establish new links with other countries (Jamaica and Slovenia were specifically mentioned) and steps to integrate an element of global citizenship into a wider range of projects in the school. However, there were differences of opinion in terms of the best way to go about developing this work. One approach favoured organic growth, with the global element infusing different projects as knowledge and interest increased. On the other hand, several teachers clearly favoured a more systematic approach to developing a global citizenship dimension throughout the school. One teacher stated simply, 'There needs to be a set agenda.' An issue raised in this context was the nature of the learning experiences (and the topics explored) at different stages of development, taking into account children's levels of understanding and other issues of appropriateness. Several other points were made as teachers looked to move forward in this area, including sustaining children's interest over time. Some spoke of the links between the local and the global, and helping children to develop their sense of identity and cultural awareness.

Challenges or barriers to global citizenship work

Despite the obvious enthusiasm of the teachers in this investigation, and their success stories, some difficulties or concerns were mentioned. One which recurred is not unique to this area of the curriculum; it was a worry that the learning achieved in primary may not be built upon in secondary school. One teacher who spoke about a group of children learning Spanish as part of their global citizenship work, found out that they were unable to continue with this on transfer to secondary school. There were several complaints about the 'red tape' that sometimes surrounded activities which were planned. One teacher spoke about the difficulties created by health and safety regulations. Another described how, for some reason not fully explained, the children were not allowed to have pen-pals in Peru – an element which would have added an extra dimension to their work. The issue of resources came up on several occasions. Although many good resources could be obtained, there were some problems accessing internet sites (even when previously vetted) because the protective software blocked access in schools.

Having mentioned such difficulties, teachers were often quick to point out that many useful resources are available. In addition to the usual educational sources and many well-known official organisations, local supermarkets were known to be very helpful. It would appear that these committed and resourceful teachers generally overcome the obstacles they encounter, but there will be value in investigating difficulties experienced and solutions found. Certainly, in the interests of encouraging more teachers to become involved in this work, there will be value in collating and disseminating such information.

Some further reflections

Although the information gathered in this study has helped to sketch out some interesting and worthwhile work currently being undertaken, it has also raised a series of issues. A view held by the writers (and evidently shared by most of the teachers) is that attitudinal change is central to the purpose of teaching in the area of global citizenship. While teachers have expressed the belief that children's attitudes can change as a result of this work, these views are impressionistic in nature. This does not make them any less valuable, but it would be helpful to gather more systematically 'hard' evidence to support this belief. Some preliminary work has already been done in this area by the current writers, and it will be important to further explore the issues surrounding the identification and measurement of such attitudes.

Although it was not specifically stated, the notion of empowerment or agency seemed implicit in much of the discourse. One can easily see the links with the purposes of *Curriculum for Excellence*, and a question for further investigation might be the extent to which projects in this area do indeed help to develop a sense of agency (whether conceptualised in terms of efficacy, self-competence or autonomy). Certainly, one of the current challenges for teacher educators is to help student teachers understand the psychological processes involved in the development of such personal qualities.

Issues related to the development of global citizenship arose on many occasions. We heard from schools where global citizenship is being developed systematically from primary one upwards; what are the key factors in terms of a progression here, taking account of developmental issues and how children learn? We became aware of schools whose plan was to 'grow' the global dimension organically within the school community. Certainly it would be interesting to investigate such a change process and to document its development. Given the emphasis in *Curriculum for Excellence*, continuity of experience is an important issue. One question to be asked is how we can best ensure that the work started in primary is developed in secondary, in terms of subject content, associated learning experiences and attitudinal factors. To what extent can – or should – such experiences be mapped out across sectors? How can we ensure we respond to the flexibility that *Curriculum for Excellence* offers, in order to ensure a relevant and meaningful approach to the subject matter?

These questions – and more – emerged from our discussions, both with the teachers and other teacher educators. Some of them are already being investigated; other work is planned. As researchers we are keen to know the answers; but more than this, as teacher educators we are committed to sharing the knowledge gained.

Conclusion

This was very much an exploratory study; it was descriptive in nature and designed to help us understand the perceptions of teachers at the forefront of developments in this area. We should also remember that the scope of the investigation was modest, and no claims are made that these views are representative of Scottish teachers or Scottish schools more widely. On the contrary, it seems more than likely that these findings represent a particular stratum of the teaching force: a group who are actively committed to the principles of global citizenship and who are leading the way in classroom practice in this area. It would be inappropriate to generalise from this group to the teaching force as a whole.

Having acknowledged these limitations, we feel that the data collected create an interesting picture – and a useful starting point for those keen to learn more about the development of work in this area. From the perspective of the authors, the information has helped to inform our teacher education programmes in several ways. It has yielded some important information about what is 'out there', providing insights and promising leads in terms of pedagogy. But this work has another important benefit; it helps to raise the profile of values in education. In the recent *National Framework for Inclusion* document, produced by the Scottish Teacher Education Committee (STEC, 2009), we see an emphasis on social justice, including human rights, the right to education and participation and diversity. Work in the area of global citizenship is clearly congruent with these principles, and it relates to other drivers too. For example, it can be seen that increasing student teachers' knowledge in this area can contribute towards some of the performance criteria for initial teacher education (the SITE benchmarks) (see GTCS, 2006). Benchmark 3.1 for example refers to the need to 'Value and demonstrate a commitment to social justice, inclusion and protecting and caring for children'.

Of course, we are looking at attitudes and beliefs here, and processes of change in this area are not unproblematic. Indeed, one of the challenges facing both teacher educators and student teachers is to develop an understanding of how best to create positive attitudes. One possible approach could be based on Krathwohl's Taxonomy (Krathwohl, Bloom & Masia, 1964). Being aware of a progression – from merely receiving, or being aware of, or tolerating ideas, through stages of responding to and valuing ideas, towards the internalisation of coherent value systems – may provide a framework to understand processes of attitude change. Clearly, while knowledge and understanding are important, if we can't win hearts and minds then our progress may be limited.

Many other questions remain for teacher educators. How can we ensure that issues related to the environment, inequality, poverty, cultural diversity, and participation and access are effectively incorporated into an already packed ITE programme? What are the implications for engaging all tutors in appropriate staff development? These are questions which will have to be addressed, but we close with one final thought. Amongst the many positive messages we received from teachers during the course of the investigation was a belief that the benefits of global citizenship were such that it was worth persevering when difficulties arose: 'It engages the children, they become completely involved and it is worth overcoming any hurdles.' The enthusiasm of these teachers is contagious; teacher educators too must work to overcome any hurdles and take the agenda forward.

References

DFID et al. (2005) *Developing the Global Dimension in the School Curriculum*. UK: DFID.

General Teaching Council for Scotland (GTCS) (2006) *Standard for Initial Teacher Education*. Online at http://www.gtcs.org.uk/Publications/StandardsandRegulations/The_Standard_for_Initial_Teacher_Education_(ITE).aspx (accessed 14.04.10)

Krathwohl, D.R., Bloom, B.S., and Masia, B.B. (1964). *Taxonomy of educational objectives: Handbook II: Affective domain*. New York: David McKay Co.

Scottish Government (2009) *A Curriculum for Excellence*. Edinburgh: Scottish Government.

Scottish Teacher Education Committee (STEC) (2009) Framework for Inclusion. Edinburgh: Scottish Government.

ENACTING THE GLOBAL THROUGH PEDAGOGY

4.1 Section Introduction

The chapters in this section provide a range of perspectives on what might count as effective pedagogy in embedding a global dimension in learning in Initial Teacher Education (ITE). Education for Global Citizenship and Sustainable Development (EGCSD) is built upon active, participatory models of teaching and learning and its engagement with ITE is one way of ensuring as Boyd terms it, 'a confluence of teacher experience and expertise, research evidence and theories of learning'.

In the opening chapter, Boyd argues for a central role for pedagogy in Scottish Education as curricular reform proceeds and for the re-visioning of the classroom as a 'community of enquiry'. Wrigley (Chapter 4.3) provides a wide-ranging account of active approaches to learning from across Europe and specific 'open architectures' for learning that are potentially valuable in securing engaged learning, not least in matters global. Higgins makes a strong case in Chapter 4.4 for the experiential as a necessary component in developing what he describes as 'global intimacy'. Rather than promoting a pre-specified set of values, he argues that students need to be encouraged to develop their own approaches to the ethics of global sustainable development. In Chapter 4.5, Curtis also emphasises the importance of open-ended, democratic learning as a means to understanding how the curriculum can be made real. She argues that such approaches must be internalised if teachers are to feel confident in their use in the classroom.

Issues of democratic process are pointed up in Humes' chapter on the teaching of controversial issues (Chapter 4.6). Recalling the work of Stenhouse and his aim of 'develop[ing] understanding of the nature and structure of certain complex value issues of universal human concern', this chapter argues that student teachers, as well as being well-informed, need to develop certain necessary pedagogic skills. Dunn et al's study of good practice in early years settings (Chapter 4.7) elicits a developing understanding of the potential of the global dimension in pre-school provision among managers. It also demonstrates that, as in other sectors, the impact of EGCSD in terms of encouraging the exploration of values and beliefs, is felt as much by practitioners as by pupils. The study by Collins et al (Chapter 4.8), similarly shows that changing approaches to the use of ICT in the classroom can open up opportunities for methods which allow teachers as well as pupils to explore their own learning processes.

The final two chapters in this section identify an important problem in our concerns with developing a global perspective. The problem concerns the potentially detached, implicitly western perspective of such a 'world view'. Colucci-Gray et al. (Chapter 4.9) make the case for collaborative and interdisciplinary approaches to learning and teaching that encourage multiple perspectives. They argue that, by situating ourselves within natural systems and allowing for the exploration of connectedness, more effective approaches to understanding the challenge of sustainable development may emerge. In a similar vein, I'Anson (Chapter 4.10) suggests that a pedagogical approach based on the philosophical work of Spinoza might offer a means of approaching cultural difference that does not immediately short circuit genuine openness.

4.2 Putting Pedagogy at the Heart of Learning

Brian Boyd, Emeritus Professor, University of Strathclyde

A COMMITMENT TO PUTTING PEDAGOGY at the heart of learning links *Curriculum for Excellence*, the new curricular framework for Scotland, and Education for Global Citizenship and Sustainable Development, the subject of this publication.

Curriculum for Excellence (Scottish Executive Education Department, 2004) was the work of a Ministerial Review Group, set up in response to the findings of a National Debate on school education in Scotland. The Debate, while not taking the nation by storm, drew responses from all of the recognised stakeholders in Scottish education. In essence, it concluded that there was general confidence in the school system, but there were concerns around transitions (pre-school/primary, primary/secondary and secondary/beyond), a lack of real pupil choice and, most importantly perhaps, an overcrowded curriculum.

The Ministerial Review Group was charged with producing a framework for the curriculum for ages 3-18, i.e. the whole of the statutory period of schooling (5-16) and a little bit more. This, in itself was ground-breaking since it was the first time since the Second World War that the whole of the school curriculum was to be reviewed at the same time. On publication, the report inspired some and disappointed others; it was only 8 pages long and did not attempt to look at the detail of the curriculum. Instead it outlined values, aims, principles and purposes and, most importantly of all, put pedagogy at the heart of the curriculum reform. It was not a 'year zero' scenario since the new principles incorporated those of the previous curriculum (the 5-14 Programme); instead, it sought to draw on world-wide research on learning and teaching and stated explicitly that the curriculum was not simply what was taught, but how it was taught.

The word pedagogy has been little used in Scottish educational discourse. Often 'teaching methods' or even 'methodology' seemed to suffice to describe what teachers and others did to help their pupils to become effective learners. But pedagogy is much more than this. It is, above all, the confluence of:

• Teacher experience and expertise
• Research evidence
• Theories of learning

Curriculum for Excellence sought to reinforce the centrality of pedagogy in a number of ways, not least in its new principles: depth, challenge and enjoyment, relevance, personalisation and choice.

Principles

Depth

The 'new' principles introduced by *Curriculum for Excellence* were an attempt to deal with the issue of the overcrowded curriculum. If the curriculum were to be 'de-cluttered' as the then Education Minister suggested on publication of the report, then the rationale must be to enable pupils to move from superficial learning to deep learning. Simply getting through the syllabus, or curriculum coverage as it has been described (Boyd and Simpson, 2000), was no longer enough if learners were to be successful in the 21st century. The work of David Perkins at Harvard (1995), which had grown out of his work on Project Zero with Howard Gardner, had sought to put understanding at the heart of learning. Their research, working with teachers who had been identified as effective, suggested that understanding should be the goal of teaching and that learners should be given opportunities to *perform* their understanding in classrooms.

Shortly before the establishment of the Ministerial Review Group, the publication of 'Inside the Black Box' (Black and Wiliam, 1998) had been the impetus for a UK-wide pedagogical initiative known as Assessment (is) for Learning (AifL). It promoted the use of assessment as a formative process designed to help learners improve and to give them more responsibility for their own learning. Thus while AifL supported Perkins (ibid.) view that goals should be shared between teachers and learners and that learners should actively engage in activities which allowed them to perform their understanding, it also placed an emphasis on peer- and self-assessment, only possible if learners have a deep understanding of the criteria for success.

Challenge and enjoyment

The idea that learning could and should be fun exercised the Ministerial Review Group; some argued that the word fun would send the wrong signals and suggest a 'dumbing down'; others wished to promote the idea, based on decades of research into pupils' views (Rudduck, 1996; MacBeath, Boyd, Rand and Bell, 1996), that pupils enjoyed their learning most when they were appropriately challenged. This was where the broad age-range covered by *Curriculum for Excellence*, i.e. from 3-18, helped. Early years education in Scotland, long the Cinderella of the education system, had, nevertheless often been at the heart of pedagogical progress. 'Active learning' was beginning to emerge as the dominant pedagogy in early years education by the time the report was published and its 'raison d'etre' was to engage all learners.

Relevance

The word 'engagement' is central to a number of the pedagogies which are consistent with *Curriculum for Excellence*. Perkins' (1995) notion of the 'generative topic' is a recognition that not everything teachers wish to teach is inherently interesting to all learners. Our job as teachers to find ways of helping the learners to make connections, between the learning that takes place in the classroom and that which takes place outside; between the issues which affect them locally and what is happening across the world; between their values and those of others; and so on. Thus relevance more than simply introducing learners to experiences with are already familiar to them but to enable them to move from what they already know to new contexts, new cultures, new values and new concepts.

One way of doing this is to look beyond individual subjects as the context for learning and to take an inter-disciplinary approach. Gardner, in 'Five Minds for the Future' (2006), argues that these two approaches are not mutually exclusive; indeed, an interdisciplinary approach must build on knowledge of the individual disciplines and must justify its use by reference to what value is added when disciplines come together. Thus, the 'disciplined mind' and the 'synthesising mind' are both required if young people are to be successful in the 21st century.

Personalisation and choice

For too long, pupils in Scottish schools have had little choice as to what they learned and how they learned it. Now, *Curriculum for Excellence* suggests that learning goals should be negotiated, not imposed and that learners should learn how to learn, have access to a range of strategies on which they can call when 'the going gets tough' and that learning with others, cooperatively, is part of personalisation. Thus, teachers no longer need to be told, from the centre, what to teach, how to teach it, when to teach it, in what order to teach it and for how many minutes a week to teach it. Curriculum for Excellence is about trust in the professional expertise of Scottish teachers, and their ability to work with their pupils flexibly.

Curriculum for Excellence, Pedagogy and the Global Dimension

How then does pedagogy link *Curriculum for Excellence* and the Global Dimension? We know from research (Boyd, 2008, p.162) that global issues concern young people. We also know that many teachers find it difficult to deal with controversial issues in their classrooms. We know that traditional approaches such as didactic teaching, worksheets or rote learning are not sufficient if we wish to promote critical thinking, creativity, problem-solving. Similarly, cooperative learning requires a classroom ethos which promotes dialogue and empathy, where talk is 'collective, reciprocal and supportive' (Alexander, 2006). If we are, as teachers, to gauge whether pupils are reaching an understanding of concepts, then they need, actively, to perform their understanding through, role-play, debates, presentations, mock-trials, exhibitions of research findings, and so on. Active learning is at the heart of both *Curriculum for Excellence* and Education for Global Citizenship and Sustainable Development. The classroom should become a 'community of enquiry' (Lipman, 2003), in which learners of whatever age, can engage in exploring important concepts, as Jerome Bruner (1960) put it, 'given a courteous translation'. Making links across subjects and with the outside world to make learning come alive and a commitment to the exploration of values are a challenge for teachers in schools.

The essential elements of 'The Global Classroom' (Boyd, 2008, pp.173-174) might be said to be:
• Community of enquiry
• Links with the outside world
• Commitment to values.

The pedagogies required to create such a classroom go far beyond traditional didactic teaching or reliance on worksheets and low-level tasks. Rather they promote active engagement, thoughtfulness, judgements based on evidence and empathy. *Curriculum for Excellence* is an opportunity, and a challenge, for teachers to embrace this view of pedagogy and a chance to make learning in Scotland more inclusive, more collaborative and thus more relevant to the underlying principles of global learning.

References

Alexander, R. (2006). *Towards Dialogic Teaching: Rethinking Classroom Talk Dialogos*. Online at www.robinalexander.org.uk

Black, P. and W.D. (1998). *Inside the Black Box*. London: NFER Nelson

Boyd, B. (2008). *The Learning Classroom*. Paisley: Hodder Gibson

Boyd, B. and Simpson, M (2000). *A framework for learning and teaching in the first two years of secondary school in Angus Council*. Angus Council Education Department

Bruner, J. (1960). *The Process of Education*. Cambridge, Massachusetts: Harvard University Press

Gardner, H. (2006). *Five Minds for the Future*. Boston: Harvard Business School Press

Lipman, M. (2003). *Thinking in Education*. Cambridge: Cambridge University Press

MacBeath, J., Boyd, B., Rand, J. and Bell, S. (1996). *Schools Speak for Themselves*. Glasgow Quality In Education Centre, University of Strathclyde

Perkins, D (1995). *Smart Schools: Better Thinking and Learning for Every Child*. New York: Free Press

Rudduck, J., Chaplain, R. and Wallace, G. (Eds) (1996). *School Improvement: What can pupils tell us?* London: David Fulton Publishers

Scottish Executive Education Department (2004). *A Curriculum for Excellence*. Edinburgh: SEED

4.3 New Models and Pedagogy for Education for Citizenship

Terry Wrigley, University of Edinburgh

EDUCATION FOR CITIZENSHIP can be understood both as a specific section of formal curricula and as an overarching effect (or indeed aim) of education. In its former aspect, it takes various names (social education, political education, civics) and is shaped by the educational and political history of specific countries. In the latter form, it is always present, albeit tacitly as 'hidden curriculum', since schooling inevitably shapes future citizens, for good or ill. This chapter seeks to draw upon some experiences of citizenship education, in both senses, in other education systems. The experiences and exemplars are highly relevant to the development of Global Citizenship and Sustainable Development, but are framed in terms of 'education for citizenship' because of the benefits of developing a common pedagogical understanding.

The development of Education for Citizenship as a curriculum subject across the UK is relatively recent. In England and Wales, it was a late addition to a standardised National Curriculum which had largely suppressed the study of contemporary society, and even now it is generally marginalised, including optional accreditation through a half-GCSE. The Scottish decision to emphasise citizenship as cross-curricular provision rather than a discrete subject symbolically rejected this marginalisation, but left practically unresolved the question of where it would actually happen, particularly in secondary schools which are built upon strong subject boundaries. *Curriculum for Excellence* has further raised its standing, as one of the 'four capacities' or key aims of curriculum, though with no greater clarity, as yet, as to where and how it will happen. In this context, we have much to learn from education systems with a longer history of citizenship education or a stronger democratic impetus.

British schools are also working against traditional cultures of schooling which were never designed to promote democratic or critical citizenship. Despite the resistance and innovative practice of many teachers, the dominant traditions of schooling across Britain since the start of compulsory schooling in the 19th Century involved a systematic denial of the voice and agency of the learner, in three fields: disciplinary, curricular and pedagogical. (For a more extended explanation, see Wrigley 2006)

Disciplinary: Though corporal punishment is now outlawed, our schools have strong norms of physical passivity, spatial regulation and containment, with expected self-regulation reinforced by public reprimand and ritualised punishment. There are traditionally strong internal boundaries according to age, subject and academic success, and a rigid demarcation between school and the neighbourhood.

Curricular: Learners have very little say in what they learn. This is largely determined by government agencies, including examination boards, and in recent years through a nationally standardised curriculum.

Pedagogical: Despite decades of academic and professional analysis and concern, the standard pattern of classroom discourse remains much as it was in the 1960s and 70s (Barnes, 1969; Stubbs, 1983). The teacher's voice dominates, pupil utterances are brief, interchanges are rarely initiated by pupils, and most exchanges are restricted by closed and low-level questions from the teacher. Genuine discussion and investigative talk, whether whole class or in smaller groups, remains rare.

We should not underestimate the impact of these three forms of regulation for young people's development as citizens. They establish tacit social norms and promote a habitus of undemocratic and non-participatory citizenship, analogous to the low levels of participation required by parliamentary forms of representation. This restrictive culturing of young people is far more powerful than occasional lessons on global warming or civil liberties, or peremptory consultation through school councils.

Though it would be false to idealise other educational traditions, we can learn from alternative principles and practices elsewhere.

Firstly, the 'custodial' nature of schooling is more marked in Britain than in some other school systems. I say 'marked' because this is partly a symbolic matter (e.g. school uniform, bells, registers) but it stretches into pedagogic and social assumptions which are perhaps best illustrated through examples and anecdotes. When I asked the head of a Norwegian primary school (ages 6-13) about hyperactive children, she said simply 'They go for a walk outside. We do say at the start of the morning when we expect all pupils to be listening to the teacher, for example 10 o'clock for twenty minutes, so that they don't miss anything.' All Norwegian primary schools, urban or rural, have a forest site, where younger children spend a day each week. I visited one secondary school (in Norwegian, 'youth school', for 13-16 year olds) on a maths day, where each activity was organised by a group of pupils, mostly out of doors. 14 year olds in another school were preparing for a two-day Storyline (see below) to improve their understanding of local services and agencies. Each group of pupils was to choose for themselves somewhere to meet up in the two small towns served by the school at the start of the next school day, with the proviso that someone in each group must have their mobile phone switched on to receive phone calls and text messages. It is examples such as this that bring home, by contrast, the structures and norms we take for granted in Scotland, and how they might negatively affect a sense of agency. Beyond this, it is worth noting that division into classes by 'ability' is not permitted in most Scandinavian countries, and exclusion from school is extremely rare. Time divisions are also less rigid in the Norwegian secondary school; because each year group is taught almost exclusively by a team of 5-6 teachers, decisions to suspend the timetable or go on a visit are easily made.

Secondly, Scandinavia also provides various models of greater openness of curriculum. I was startled to find, in Denmark's social studies curriculum (Undervisningsministeriet, 1995), a recommendation to teachers not to overplan the year's activities; the plan should 'consist of broad and open possibilities, which give room for adjustments and changes, and not least to encourage and accommodate pupils' participation and co-responsibility'. The choice of theme 'is made in co-operation between teacher and pupils', based on current events, 'questions or wishes from the pupils' or 'suggestions from the teacher'. More detailed work on each theme also involves considerable autonomy, including choices about specific research and presentations. The frequent use of project method and storyline in various Scandinavian countries creates a pedagogical framework whereby pupils have scope for initiative within an interactive learning community.

A similar tendency towards greater pupil agency was apparent in a Danish curriculum project on differentiation. This was based on pupils co-determining their tasks, rather than the same task being set by the teacher for the whole class, and with the aim of pupils developing an awareness of their own skills and development needs through formative assessment.

'Just as you must formulate a goal for your teaching, so must each pupil formulate a goal which will become a leading thread in the pupil's work.

It will often happen that the learners' goals are inspired by the framework which you planning provides, and often many pupils will formulate similar objectives. However, the essential point is that each pupil or group of pupils will have ownership of the learning process and will know what they want to teach themselves, so that they can find ways of doing it more effectively.' (Krogh-Jespersen et al, 1998:17)

Reflecting on British educational norms, and particularly the (historically recent) standardisation of the English national curriculum, Davies and Edwards (2001) insist on authorship for young people:

'How can we reconceptualise and reconstruct the curriculum in such a way that pupils, at least for part of the time, have an opportunity for fashioning some time for themselves so that they can pursue their own ideas and studies? '(2001:p104)

One pedagogic feature of school learning is that it is seen as discrete and with no real-world consequences. This can be justified philosophically, in terms of the continuity of academic disciplines (Young 2008) or the need for quiet concentration. On the other hand, there are dangers in the universal assumption that academic learning has no real-world outcomes, or that real-world engagement should be limited to extra-curricular or additional activities such as volunteering or charity collections. It is extremely rare in British schools for pupils to engage in any sort of public campaign or to try to influence public opinion as an outcome of their school learning. The German tradition of political education stems in part from a determination to build a strong enough sense of autonomy and political agency in young people to prevent the re-emergence of fascism. Political campaigning therefore, whilst not widespread, is legitimised. German textbooks on methodology (Weissenau and Kuhn, 2000, among others) include activities such as running a memorial ceremony in the city centre to commemorate the imprisonment and death of former Jewish citizens in the early 1940s, or an environmental protest on bikes with appropriate slogans printed on t-shirts. The term 'problem-solving' is explained (ibid) in terms of the town hall or hospital coming to the school with a genuine problem, which the students are invited to help solve. They discuss and research it before presenting their analysis and recommendations to the local policy makers. What is most surprising, on reflection, about such examples is not that they are tremendously revolutionary, but that they can appear so to British teachers.

Dealing with controversial issues

We can learn from other education systems alternative ways of handling controversial issues in schools. In Britain we tend to steer a middle course, avoiding strong opinions and in practice preferring to stage anodyne debates about relatively uncontentious issues such as cruelty to animals or smoking in public places. As Michael Apple has argued:

'There are few serious attempts at dealing with conflict (class conflict, scientific conflict, or other). Instead one 'inquires' into a consensus ideology that bears little resemblance to the complex nexus and contradictions surrounding the control and organisation of social life. Hence the selective tradition dictates that we do not teach, or will selectively reinterpret (and hence will soon forget) serious labor or women's history… It may be rather imperative that urban and working class… students develop positive perspectives towards conflict and change, ones that will enable them to deal with the complex and often repressive political realities and dynamics of power of their society.' (Apple 1979:7)

Alternative practices began to emerge in the curriculum reforms of the 1970s; the Schools Council's Humanities Curriculum Project involved the teacher maintaining a role as neutral chair, whilst pupils developed arguments in response to a pair of opposing newspaper reports.

A good set of principles was developed by a teachers' conference in Germany for dealing with controversial issues. This code of practice, known as the Beutelsbach Consensus, should be read against the norms whereby teachers are seen as the fount of a single 'truth'. Indeed, it is valuable for learners too to be aware of these ground rules.

1. You must not overpower. It is unethical to take pupils unawares, however that is done, in imposing preferred opinions, and thus to prevent learners reaching an independent judgement.
2. Whatever is controversial in social science and in politics, must openly appear controversial in teaching.
3. Pupils must be placed in a position where they can analyse a political situation and their own interests and position, and also look for ways of influencing it.

Few genuine debates result from teachers asking a class a series of closed questions; indeed this is probably the most effective way to reduce pupils to silence. Small group learning can provide greater opportunity than whole-class sessions: an analysis of small group discussions (Phillips 1987) identified that children were more likely to express hypotheses, make tentative statements, build theory and connect with their experience than in whole class teaching. Positioning young people in roles can also provides a kind of protection, for example 'hot-seating' an individual (Barack Obama) or even a concept (the British Empire).

The recent emphasis on pupil voice should also raise wider questions about audience. Whereas writing in British classrooms is generally for the teacher-as-assessor, writing and visual display for a wider audience (peers, parents, politicians etc.) is not only motivating but helps develop the learners' sense of agency and consequence.

If we are serious, therefore, about embedding Education for Citizenship, or Global Citizenship and Sustainable Development across the curriculum, we need to ask basic questions about the normative practices of school learning. There are no easy transfers between education systems and traditions, but we can benefit from a greater openness to alternatives. This applies as much to emergent practices from the years before the national curricula as it does to the experiences of other countries..

Open architectures
The pathway towards a strongly centralised State control of education involved the creation of a moral panic about times past. Amnesia has been officially sponsored; for example, I have heard the head of a leading government agency for the control of teaching in England speak about the days 'before standards and before innovation'. I would not wish to strengthen those voices of derision. Inevitably mistakes are made in a period of

development and experimentation, but this does not provide an excuse for overbearing centralised control.

Some of the problems of that period arose from a tendency towards individualism, including the adoption of Piagetian psychology; subsequently a social constructivism built upon Vygotsky has provided a theoretical foundation and rationale for more collective and situated forms of learning. Terms such as 'discovery learning', 'pupil-centred' and 'open learning' arguably supported a one-sided individualistic form of pedagogical progressivism.

Reflecting on practices such as Project Method, Storyline and Design Challenges, I use the term 'open architectures' to signify ways of structuring the learning of a class as a learning community which include substantial opportunities for individual or small-group decision-making and initiative. They are quite different both from tightly regulated lesson plans and from earlier forms of topic work (alias projects or themes) which were popular around the 1970s and which involved individual pupils collecting and recording data for their own interest. Often this kind of 'project' was low in cognitive challenge – a kind of collection curriculum rather than problem-solving.

The methods which I call 'open architectures' involve individual and small-group research and activity but within a frame of collective activity and discussion. The structure gives teachers and pupils a sense of security and direction and helps build a learning community, but provides substantial flexibility, space for initiative and self-directed learning. When well planned, such learning is cognitively challenging and with strong affective, ethical and aesthetic as well as cognitive dimensions.

Project Method
Project method was developed by John Dewey and W H Kirkpatrick (1918) in the USA in the early 20th century. It takes many forms, but essentially learning is practically oriented and arises from real tasks and situations. A classic structure for project method is described in the guidance for social studies (Undervisningsministeriet 1995) in Denmark. It consists of four stages:

i) The teacher seeks to engage the class's interest in a theme or situation OR a current or local issue is raised by some pupils.
ii) Initial discussion identifies interesting aspects. The teacher draws on disciplinary concepts and skills to illuminate it. This stage ends with small groups (or individuals) identifying questions they wish to investigate.
iii) Small group / individual research.

iv) Groups / individuals present their findings to the class. It is suggested that, whenever possible, this should be more than just sharing information; pupils should design activities which stimulate further discussion.

Many projects involve direct involvement in the world. For example, they can involve a fifth stage, taking pupils' findings and concerns out into the wider community. Alternatively, the project might concern a real problem in the locality.

I have used project method with PGDE students based on the theme of asylum seekers. As stage 1, I used a simulation of a dystopic future Scotland, when tanks roll down the Royal Mile and it isn't the Tattoo. Students differentiate themselves during stages 2 and 3; those with little prior knowledge investigate factual questions such as where asylum seekers come from and why, whereas those with more prior knowledge might choose to explore complex issues such as national identity and xenophobia.

A close cousin of Project Method is Problem Based Learning. It was first developed for medical students, but is increasingly used in various Higher Education degrees. It uses a case study approach to stimulate learning. The problem is contained within a short description or narrative, though photographs or conceptually presented problems can be used.

Storyline

Storyline is a form of thematic work structured by a linear narrative. It was invented in Scotland, at Jordanhill College, particularly for primary children. Ironically, it is now used across Scandinavia for all ages, Primary and Secondary (Falkenberg and Hakonsson 2000) while used much less so in Scotland and almost exclusively in Primary. It can be based on a written narrative such as a novel, with pupil responses at key points, but generally uses only the bare outline or skeleton of a plot.

I. It typically begins with a scene or location, proposed (or better, illustrated) by the teacher.
II. articipants invent roles for themselves – hotel staff, families in a town, for example.
III. The teacher announces events, or organises an intervention (a visitor in role), to move the story on. Each is the stimulus for a type of learner activity such as drama, research, letter writing, art or maths.

Storyline is strongly experiential, using graphic and dramatic representation. Pupils have a part in the narrative, playing characters they have invented. One Storyline invented by Scottish teachers is based on 8th Century Viking invasions. The initial situation is presented as a mural of an empty bay. The pupils, having thought up characters and family relationships for themselves, read about housing in this period, paint houses and stick them on to the mural. One day they arrive at school to find a ship in the bay, which some conclude is a Viking ship. Later in the narrative, they arrive to find the ship missing, and a life-size figure of a Viking warrior on the wall. This triggers an argument: some of the villagers want to kill him, others to make him work for them as a slave; others are more generous. A similar Storyline could, for example, be used to examine the European 'discovery' of America.

Some students designed a Storyline for secondary pupils based on the discovery of oil in the coastal town of Kilgallon. Two teenagers spot some exploratory drilling; a pipeline is laid across the school field; the impact on the town's tourist industry and fishing is examined, etc. Finally, the oil dries up…

Design challenge
There is some overlap with project method, but essentially the learners' activity is determined by an explicit challenge to make or present something to the class after a fixed period of time. Design challenges involve problems that require investigation, and are driven by the need to produce a creative solution.

I witnessed one example in an S1 class, which had two days to present arguments for the continued existence of Planet Earth. This was initiated by showing a video broadcast by the Emperor of the Milky Way, who was dealing with a proposal to drive an interstellar highway from his metropolis to a holiday resort at the other end of the galaxy, and which required the clearance and demolition of the Earth. Pupils would work in groups on sub-themes of their choice, researching and then presenting arguments in terms of animal diversity or architectural achievements, for example. Design Challenges are at the heart of the methodologies promoted in Britain as Critical Skills (www.criticalskills.co.uk, or Weatherley et al., 2003), and which were initially devised at the University of Syracuse (USA) under the title Education by Design.

This approach can be adapted for many different issues and situations. One group of PGDE students modified a BBC News webpage to report that the world's oil had run out early that morning. The challenge was to present policy reports and responses to Parliament.

These various 'open architectures' share a number of important characteristics and advantages, for example:
• engaging learners through a meaningful situation or theme
• integrating skills development with a cross-curricular approach to knowledge

- providing a common framework (a concerned community of learning) whilst giving space for initiative and creativity
- working towards a convincing product or presentation, with the satisfaction that arises from a sense of audience.

Planning is of course crucial for a critical and engaged understanding to emerge. The approaches vary from more conceptual (Project Method) to more experiential (Storyline), though the techniques can also be hybridised (as in the Refugee Project above, which begins with a simulation.

The concept of Open Architectures can be applied to a wider range of existing methodologies, for example, simulations and games, or producing a video or booklet. It provides a conceptual basis for making Design and Technology teaching less individualistic, for example, engaging a class in designing a children's playground, equipment for an old people's centre, or redesigning the school grounds. It can be used to enhance fieldwork, or for a class residential, for example the exploration of resources and technologies needed for human survival or the simulation of a past society.

What I have described here as Open Architectures form strands of a pedagogical development from which schools and learners in Britain have largely been cut off by the era of standardisation and government control, with its overwhelming emphasis on teaching as transmission and learning as replication. There are recent signs of a thaw, including the invitation to experiment with interdisciplinary learning provided by *Curriculum for Excellence*, although it is also possible to use them within the subject timetable supplemented by home study time. Pedagogical development in such a context can also, I believe, be more rapid and more successful if we are able to learn from other education systems. Education for Citizenship or for Global Citizenship and Sustainable Development can be delivered most effectively in the context of this kind of pedagogical shift. (A more extended discussion and examples of project method, storyline and design challenges, especially in the secondary phase, can be found in Wrigley (2007)

References

Apple, M. (1979) *Ideology and curriculum*. London: Routledge and Kegan Paul

Barnes, D. et al. (1969) *Language, the learner and the school*. Harmondsworth: Penguin

Davies M. and Edwards G. (2001) Will the curriculum caterpillar ever learn to fly? In Fielding M (ed) *Taking education really seriously: four years hard Labour*. London: RoutledgeFalmer

Falkenberg C. and Håkonsson E. (2000) *Storylinebogen – en håndbog for undervisere*. Vejle, Denmark: Kroghs Forlag

Kirkpatrick, W.H. (1918) The project method. *Teachers College Record* 19, pp319-335

Krogh-Jespersen, K. et al. (1998) *Inspiration til undervisningsdifferentiering*. Copenhagen: Undervisningsministeriet (Folkeskoleafdelingen)

Phillips, T. (1987) Beyond lip-service: discourse development after the age of nine. In B. Mayor and A. Pugh (eds.) *Language, communication and education*. London: Croom Helm

Stubbs, M. (1983) *Language, schools and classrooms*. London: Methuen.

Undervisnings ministeriet: Folkeskoleafdelingen (1995) *Samfundsfag*. Copenhagen: Undervisningsministeriet

Weatherley et al. (2003) *Transforming teaching and learning: developing 'critical skills' for living and working in the 21st century*. Stafford: Network Educational Press

Weissenau, G. and Kuhn, H-W. (2000) *Lexikon der politischen Bildung*, Band 3. Schwalbach: Wochenschauverlag

Wrigley, T. (2006) Opening the text: voicing a future. In Cooper, K., and White R., *The practical critical educator*. Dordrecht, NE: Springer

Wrigley, T. (2007) Project, stories and challenges: more open architectures for school learning. In S Bell et al. (eds) *Storyline past, present and future*. Glasgow: University of Strathclyde

Young, M.F.D. (2008) *Bringing knowledge back in: from social constructivism to social realism in the sociology of education*. Abingdon: Routledge

4.4 Controversy as a Stimulus to Learning: A Lesson from the Past

Walter Humes, University of the West of Scotland

Introduction

One of the most compelling reasons for including citizenship education in the curriculum is that it introduces young people to issues that will impact directly or indirectly on their current and future lives: issues such as the environment, economic development, energy resources, conflict between nations, rights and justice, poverty and inequality, democracy and freedom. Of course these are complex and difficult topics, which are often contested, and this means that their coverage in schools has to be handled carefully, with due attention to the dangers of bias and indoctrination. It also means that teachers have to be alert to a series of practical pedagogic questions. At what age should pupils encounter different topics, some of which may be potentially upsetting to younger children? What use should be made of material from television and the internet, which may give a dramatic representation of events but which may also be partial or misleading? What are the limits of the teacher's expertise and when might it be appropriate to draw on other people for information and insight? Given the diversity of many classes in terms of ethnicity, religion and cultural background, how can sensitive topics be addressed without causing offence to particular children or their families?

Before offering some thoughts on these challenges, let me say a word about the concept of 'global citizenship' (for a fuller account see Humes, 2008). Traditional conceptions of citizenship, which start from an individual's identification with a nation state, have come under pressure from a number of directions: from the social consequences of population movements which have brought cultural diversity to many countries; from the economic impact of globalisation which has seen the growth of multinational companies, with major consequences for sites of production and patterns of employment; and from political and technological developments which have dramatically changed the landscape within which nation states have to make decisions and plan for the future. The overall result is a world of increasing complexity and uncertainty, reflected in concerns about the threat of terrorism, the future of the planet and the strength of democratic systems of government.

This, then, is the context in which teachers are expected, in the language of *Curriculum for Excellence*, to produce 'responsible citizens'. Good teachers have, of course, always sought to relate their material to topical items in the news, conscious of the fact that there is a world beyond the classroom which youngsters have to understand and learn to negotiate. But if we are to take the citizenship agenda seriously, it must involve a more sustained and systematic attempt to increase awareness of the changing nature of society. In Scotland, unlike in England, citizenship education is not a discrete, compulsory element in the curriculum, though many aspects of it will be referred to in social education programmes. All teachers are expected to embed elements of citizenship education in their work, as opportunities arise. This raises the question of how well-equipped teachers feel they are to undertake this task. Courses of Initial Teacher Education (ITE) are beginning to introduce trainee teachers to some of the resources that are available – including useful material by charities such as Oxfam and Save the Children – but that does not meet the needs of more experienced teachers for continuing professional development (CPD). Here we can perhaps learn from the past.

The Work of Lawrence Stenhouse

In the 1960s an important programme of curriculum development – the Humanities Curriculum Project – was undertaken by a team led by Professor Lawrence Stenhouse of the University of East Anglia (Stenhouse had previously been Head of the Education Department at Jordanhill College in Glasgow). The aim was to look at ways of addressing controversial matters in the classroom and advise teachers about possible approaches. Several key themes were the focus of the project including war, race relations, law and order, and people and work. How could teachers cover these subjects without running the risk of political bias? As authority figures, they might influence pupils unconsciously simply by virtue of their professional role. One option would simply be to avoid any topic that might be seen as contentious: however, this would not only be an abnegation of professional responsibility, it would also be likely to lead to a curriculum that was seen as dull and irrelevant by many pupils. Stenhouse and his team had a number of interesting suggestions that might be adapted to present circumstances. I will first describe the general principles that he recommended and then look at their implications for some current examples of controversial issues that could form part of a programme of global citizenship education.

The overall aim of Stenhouse's project was 'to develop understanding of the nature and structure of certain complex value issues of universal human concern' (Stenhouse, 1969, p. 12). Promoting 'understanding' involved not only access to accurate factual information, but also direct experience (where that was possible), imaginative experience (through drama and literature, for example), serious discussion in which different 'voices' could be heard, critical analysis and independent judgement. The teacher's role was one of 'procedural neutrality', ensuring that different perspectives were represented and heard. There were to be no pre-determined 'outcomes', a feature that might raise difficulties for those inclined to a narrow interpretation of Curriculum for Excellence. A genuinely open approach required that the topic should not be steered in a particular direction: it should develop from the pupil responses to the initial stimulus material, the questions that this raised, the follow-up activities that flowed from it, and the insights arising from group discussion and individual thinking.

Stenhouse was careful not to claim that his method was value-free. Clearly there was a commitment to the principles of free enquiry, fairness and democracy in his whole approach. This meant, for example, that it was not acceptable for pupils to conclude that the views of minorities could simply be disregarded. Equally, values were involved in the choice of curricular resources, though it was thought essential that there should be a large bank of material for each key topic, from which teachers and pupils could choose, and which could be added to as a project developed. Furthermore, classroom procedures required commitment to the educational values of rationality, sensitivity and a readiness to listen to the views of others. But notwithstanding these qualifications, the approach undoubtedly involved a significant shift in the role of the teacher, from an 'expert' who could pronounce authoritatively on matters of fact and on ethical issues, to a facilitator of understanding based on pupil engagement with challenging material and deep thinking about complex issues. That is not to say that the teachers should pretend to have no views of their own, but they should certainly not seek to promote them in ways that might short-circuit the learning processes involved in the project's methods. Building trust, creating a climate in which pupils felt confident enough to contribute to discussions, without fear of a judgemental teacher intervention, was an essential part of the process.

Two Examples

Let me now look at some possible examples of controversial issues and the challenges they might present. Take the financial situation. The economic downturn following the banking crisis of 2009 may have affected some children very directly. Parents may have been made redundant with serious consequences for household bills, mortgage repayments, life styles and family aspirations. Broaching the topic in class would thus call for sensitivity. But it is potentially a very rich topic, one which could stimulate serious thinking about consumerism, about the relationship between 'rich' and 'poor' countries, and about the extent to which established institutions can be trusted to exercise responsible stewardship on behalf of members of the public. Explanations for the crisis are, of course, disputed. One version is that it arose because of a combination of international banking trends which were beyond the control of any one organisation or government. Another is that was the result of greedy, unscrupulous individuals and the failure of regulatory systems. As a basis for encouraging greater 'economic literacy', the subject has much to recommend it.

Again, consider the conflict in the Middle East. A teacher could find that the class contains both Muslim and Jewish pupils. Does this mean that the subject is too controversial to be broached at all? It would certainly require very skilful handling, but if we are concerned to prepare pupils for the world beyond school, including its harsher aspects, we shouldn't shirk from tackling difficult subjects. Such subjects provide a good opportunity to refine the exploratory and questioning approach that Stenhouse recommended (in contrast to teaching which is inclined to move to premature conclusions and judgements). Asking questions is fundamental to the successful teaching of controversial topics. For example, why did the West feel it necessary to intervene in Iraq when it has not been prepared to do so in relation to other oppressive regimes, such as Zimbabwe? Are there situations in which international bodies, such as the United Nations, which seek to encourage conflict resolution, have little hope of succeeding? If so, what are the characteristics of such situations? This might lead to improved understanding of the importance of history, of the strength of religious and ethnic loyalties, of the tortuous nature of many political processes, and of the deep human need for a sense of identity, community and hope.

These examples are clearly more suitable for older than younger children but it would be a mistake to postpone global citizenship education until youngsters reach secondary education. There are already many instances of good work with primary pupils which use as their starting point the principles embodied in the UN Convention on the Rights of the Child. Children are encouraged to help in formulating school rules, to think about the reasons for the difference between children's rights and adult rights, and for the varied customs and practices relating to young people evident in other countries. Again, a subject such as the environment is one that can be introduced to younger pupils, starting with the arguments for re-cycling and alternative energy sources, and the risks associated with global warming. With older pupils, the political dimension of the topic can be given more prominence, perhaps posing the question: 'Why is it so difficult for countries at international summit conferences to reach agreement on environmental issues and policies?'

Conclusion

One of the implications of all this is that future generations of teachers, if they are to be competent to meet the demands of citizenship education, will need to be well informed about a wide range of social, economic, cultural and political matters. They will also need to have the opportunity to acquire the necessary pedagogic skills to handle the delicate nature of many citizenship education topics. That is why it is well worth re-visiting the techniques developed by Lawrence Stenhouse and his team on the Humanities Curriculum Project. A review of teacher education programmes in Scotland is currently taking place and it is to be hoped that, as part of that process, proper consideration will be given to the needs of both novice and experienced teachers in meeting the high expectations involved in equipping youngsters to become 'responsible citizens'. It is unreasonable to expect teachers to achieve that worthwhile aim unless they themselves have been able to develop the knowledge, skills and dispositions that are the mark of an informed, engaged and active citizenry.

References

Humes, W. (2008) The Discourse of Global Citizenship. In Peters, M. A., Britton, A. & Blee, H., eds., *Global Citizenship Education: Philosophy, Theory and Pedagogy*. Rotterdam: Sense Publishers, pp. 41-52.

Stenhouse, L. (1969) Handling Controversial Issues in the Classroom. *Education Canada*, Vol. 9, No. 2, pp. 12-21.

4.5 Pedagogy for Global Intimacy

Peter Higgins, University of Edinburgh

Introduction

Developing an understanding of the global implications of our daily actions is conceptually challenging, and all the more so when extrapolated into a future that can only be predicted by models, which are by their nature imprecise. The lack of any possibility of *direct* evidence that our actions (e.g. energy and resource use) in the here and now of the 'developed world' can have impacts on some distant place (e.g. a 'developing nation' where for example sea levels are rising) or some future where dramatic impacts are felt much closer to home, provides an easy escape for those of us not wishing to make changes to our lifestyle. For educators wishing to address these issues, matters are further complicated by the influence of globalised economies, marketing, media and politics.

These tensions and the educational opportunities as well as the difficulties are explored with students on a range of teacher education and related programmes at Edinburgh University's School of Education[1]. Our approach to this issue is to encourage students to become familiar with, to understand and indeed relish their dependency on the natural systems of the planet. This is in part developed through a place-based approach where students get to know and understand their local environment. They are also provided with academic inputs and practical experiences which make clear the inter-dependence of life on Earth, cycling of nutrients and the flow of energy from the sun. The significance and inescapability of these global phenomena is made plain through a range of intellectual, aesthetic and practical experiences. Rather than a set of values being promoted, the students are expected to develop their own approaches to the ethics of global sustainable development.

The context – globalised disconnection

There seems something of a paradox in the fact that a globalised economy gives rise to many significant anthropogenic 'environmental' impacts (climate change, population growth, loss of biodiversity etc), and that our knowledge of both the science of environmental sustainability issues and the nature of these impacts, now and in the future, is communicated through globalised knowledge exchange. It seems plain that we can 'know' about these issues, and some of us may even believe the science behind the news reports, but this does not necessarily lead to personal actions.

Ben Goldacre, a science correspondent in the Guardian Newspaper (12th December 2009) responded to the outcome of the Copenhagen Summit by asking why 'roughly half of the

---

[1] The approach is also used on teacher in-service programmes in the UK, with groups of European teachers on an EU Comenius programme, and in other international workshops.

people in this country do not believe in man-made climate change, when the overwhelming majority of scientists do?' He suggested the following explanation:

- we are predisposed to undervalue adverse outcomes which are a long way off, especially if we might be old or dead soon;
- we are predisposed to find cracks in evidence that suggests we should do something we don't want to do;
- this is exacerbated because climate science is difficult;
- we don't trust government on science because we know they distort it.

Goldacre doesn't offer a solution, nor should he be expected to as he is neither an 'educator' nor a policy-maker. However, if as 'educators' we are convinced of both the science and impacts of anthropogenic environmental change, we are clearly under a moral imperative to address these issues where possible. In what follows I suggest how an educational approach can address aspects of Goldacre's proposition. However, it is first important to recognise the role an institution (a university) can have in facilitating or presenting barriers to ESD.

An institutional approach to ESD

Both the University of Edinburgh and its School of Education have long and respectable histories in engaging with 'sustainability' and 'sustainable development education'. For several decades now the University has been at the forefront of international research on both the science and social science of a number of 'sustainable development' issues. It has also developed a wide range of taught programmes which are specifically tailored to enable graduates to work within fields that have an impact on sustainable development. But in terms of the day-to-day experience of students and staff it is perhaps the work on issues such as institutional energy efficiency, e.g. through the installation of combined heat and power boilers, a commitment to 'fair-trade' procurement and the establishment of 'Transition Edinburgh University' that are most obvious, and these efforts have led to national recognition and a number of awards.

Through both teacher education and other professional training programmes, staff at Moray House School of Education have made a contribution to Education for Sustainable Development (ESD); in particular through the inclusion of courses in Initial Teacher Education and developments in Masters degree programmes in 'outdoor education' and 'outdoor, environmental and sustainability education'. However, such developments have not permeated throughout all programmes because, as Higgins and Kirk (2006) point out the main drivers for education in Scotland are 'standards' and 'inclusion' and this gives schools little room for manoeuvre in developing ESD.

The School of Education has had a significant role in the national and international 'politics' of ESD through, for example, convening the 'Learning for Life Group[2]' (comprising Scottish Teacher Education Institution (TEI) staff working in ESD), initiating and running the 'SEEPS Project' (Sustainability education in European primary schools) (University of Edinburgh, n.d.), and as initially the only UK TEI in the ongoing UNESCO programme to 'Re-orient teacher education to address sustainability' (UNESCO, n.d.).

Developing a 'pedagogy for global intimacy'

A range of School of Education staff [3] address ESD with students, and in developing our approach to 'pedagogy for global intimacy' we focus on both content and teaching approaches. There is no strict order to the theory or exercises and the overall 'package' is different for each programme. We acknowledge that many students will be well aware of the issues and may have detailed personal knowledge, and our approach is to encourage them to realise they can develop creative approaches to ESD and at the same time deliver important aspects of the curriculum.

Wherever possible our work is mutually reinforced through integrated theory and practice. For example, Robbie Nicol's (n.d.) 'concept-based practice' approach is rooted in the requirement that an educator should first decide on the conceptual issue to be addressed (e.g. anthropogenic climate change) and then decide what activities will help students understand it. Further, he emphasises that there are different ways of knowing and that different learning approaches are necessary for different individuals. These have to be planned for through shared experiences in any learning event, whilst developing theoretical understanding amongst students. However, he emphasises that teachers must be (and be permitted to be) creative in their approach rather than constrained by a set recipe. His approach is modelled through practical (often outdoor) experiences where students take part in integrated exercises such as short walks, short solo observation/reflection exercises etc. Each of these experiences may be described and discussed to consider what conceptual as well as practical and other forms of learning have occurred. In essence the students are being encouraged to integrate theory and practice in ESD through a place-based approach.

In addition to this course students on the two Master's programmes above take several other week-long outdoor academic/practical courses including a 'water-based teaching course' on a canoe descent of the River Spey', an 'interpreting the landscape' course in Edinburgh and

---

[2] This group was one outcome of the Scottish Office 'Learning for Life' project. A document of the same name prepared by a group chaired by Prof John Smyth following the Rio Summit received international praise for its vision though little practical progress was made directly after its publication. See McNaughton (2007) for a commentary.

[3] Primarily Peter Higgins, Robbie Nicol, Simon Beames and Hamish Ross.

the Lothians, 'ecology and field studies' on the Isle of Rum National Nature Reserve, and a 'place-based teaching' course in Argyll. These courses are taught by several staff and built on the common principles outlined here.

The following figure provides a model for a range of further exercises which first acknowledges the complexity of the modern world, then suggests that by establishing a connection with place (the planet) we will become more able to understand the consequences of our actions, and thereby take responsibility for these as active citizens (Higgins, 2009).

Taking Responsibility and the 5 Cs

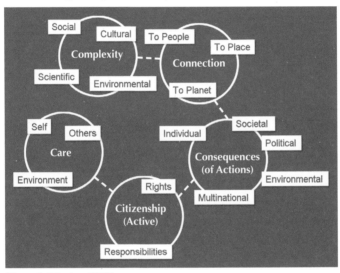

Figure 1 (Higgins, 2009)

A further key theoretical input is an argument that curriculum content should include a focus on 'the elements' upon which life on Earth depends – air, water, earth (and implicitly – biodiversity) and fire (and implicitly – energy flow). The fact that we cannot survive more than 4 minutes without air, 4 days without water and 4 weeks without food is presented as an argument for a focus on these in curriculum design. An image of a leaf is used to discuss the role of plants in cycling nutrients, especially absorbing carbon dioxide and producing the oxygen we depend on (see below). This extends to highlighting the significance of precisely the correct flow of energy from the sun to meet the plant's needs. The fact that these mechanisms are global, as is our dependency on them, is highlighted to emphasise our connection with other parts of the world and other times (past and future).

Students on a range of programmes are presented with these arguments as a means of thinking about issues of sustainability and global and intergenerational social equity, and are provided with challenging examples. The complexity and consequences of everyday decision-making may be exemplified through an image of a cafeteria table with a range of cups, mugs, bottles, cans etc. and the students are asked to discuss what the relative environmental impact is of using one rather than the other. This is developed through consideration of food and drink items, including food production issues (e.g. nitrogen oxides as greenhouse gases), transport, processing, fair-trade etc. In essence, they are encouraged to realise they could even develop a curriculum based on a spoon-full of sugar.

A practical outdoor approach

Theoretical input is underpinned by direct contact with the natural heritage as a means of building a relationship with the environment. Whilst properly understanding it is important, the approach outlined here is intended to encourage a connection to both local and global 'place'. Depending on the programme, students may have practical indoor and outdoor opportunities which build interconnected and interdisciplinary knowledge they can apply in their future teaching roles. The following are examples:

• The significance of solar radiation, including our dependency on this, the causes of seasons and implications for patterns of human settlement are illustrated through a series of indoor and outdoor exercises on sunshine and shadows. See Kibble (2010) for full details.

• Visits to the internationally important 'Hutton's Unconformity' near Dunbar or Arthur's Seat (the extinct volcano in the centre of Edinburgh) are used to illustrate Earth processes, geological time-scales[4] and the rock-cycle. The significance of the growing understanding of 'deep-time' amongst Darwin's geological contemporaries, which allowed him to formulate his ideas on evolution, is highlighted.

• Basic human needs are illustrated through a visit to coastal margin or woodland area where students 'enact' a 19th Century rural subsistence lifestyle. They are set the challenge of finding materials which they could use for food, shelter, warmth, medical purposes etc[5]. The suitability and worth of the materials collected are reviewed in a group discussion. The historical setting is further developed with pieces of plastic sheeting cut to the shapes of the furniture available at the time. The students lay these out on the ground within an area the size of a rural 19th Century home, and their function and significance is discussed. The exercise is drawn together by highlighting our dependency on the fundamental 'Earth processes' that produce materials vital for food and shelter, and that we are as dependant on them today as in the past. Finally, students discuss the proposition that these processes limit population expansion of any species in a geographically discrete area and that without importing goods or ecological services (in stark contrast to contemporary western lifestyles) the same is true of human population growth.

---

[4] A 50m rope is used as a visual scale to illustrate the approximate (4.7 billion year) age of the Earth and various marker cards are used to show the relative timescale of key evolutionary events. Human evolution takes place in the last half centimetre.

[5] This exercise was initially devised by Alastair Lavery and developed by Nev Crowther.

- A basic marine food-web exercise, where the group members are each given a card with a species name and a length of string to connect to prey items, is used to illustrate relationships in the ecosystem. After these principles are established, the significance of over-fishing of e.g. Atlantic cod, is highlighted by removing it from the food-web, and then by subsequent removal of other human food-species such as herring. Further, the controversial proposition that whales and dolphins should be harvested is introduced, student reaction is explored (why do we care more about dolphins than fish?), and the 'relatively modest' impact on the whole ecosystem of over-exploiting them is highlighted. This is contrasted with the potential effect of an environmental change (e.g. change in solar radiation due to atmospheric pollution) which damages photosynthesis and primary productivity of marine algae. The catastrophic effect on the whole ecosystem of such a wide-scale environmental change is immediately evident as there are no food items available for any other species.
- As a practical example of what can be done even in inner-city schools, Simon Beames introduces his 'Outdoor Journeys' programme (Outdoor Journeys, 2009) which explicitly sets out to orchestrate opportunities for young people to take responsibility for themselves, others and the environment through a range of local activities. Through this programme primary and older pupils plan and carry out local journeys which help them to know and understand the place they live, its history and environmental processes.

By leaves we live

A detailed example illustrates the interdisciplinary potential of ESD. The following uses outdoor exercises and prose to illustrate scientific principles and the role of photosynthesis. Throughout the world's terrestrial and aquatic ecosystems, plants absorb carbon dioxide (CO_2) from Earth processes, that we (and other animals) breathe out and we produce through burning fossil fuels etc. In doing so they release oxygen we and other organisms need to breathe [6], whilst plant structure in the form of glucose (as below) and cellulose ($C_6H_{10}O_5$) also of course provides food for ourselves and other animals, and many other materials we depend on.

$$6H_2O + 6CO_2 \rightarrow C_6H_{12}O_6 + 6O_2$$

This equation represents one of the most fundamental processes sustaining life on Earth. The 'carbon cycle' is traditionally represented diagrammatically and illustrated in science classes with experiments. Learning about plants in the outdoors should need no justification, and there are many interdisciplinary opportunities to do so (wood cutting, counting tree rings, fire-making, tree planting etc). Examples of prose and poetry are used alongside these exercises to develop aesthetic appreciation. For example:

[6] Plants also respire at night, though the daily and annual balance is in favour of photosynthesis.

Primo Levi's beautiful essay on 'carbon' is used during both practical identification of rocks and observation of plants as it expresses the immutability of carbon and the cycling of elements within the limitations of planet Earth:

'Every 200 years, every atom of carbon that is not congealed in materials now stable (such as precisely limestone, or coal, or diamond, or certain plastics) enters and renters the cycle of life, through the narrow door of photosynthesis.' (Levi,1984, p. 224-233)

Aldo Leopold's *Sand County Almanac* is used whilst sawing through logs for a fire to encourage students to think of human life-span and history alongside that of a tree. The wood is then burnt in a fire to illustrate how long it takes to grow (even a 20 cm diameter log may be older than the students) and how quickly it is gone, releasing carbon and other elements: 'Fragrant little chips of history spewed from the saw cut, and accumulated on the snow before each kneeling sawyer. We sensed that these two piles of sawdust were something more than wood; that they were the integrated transect of the century; that our saw was biting its way, stroke by stroke, decade by decade into the chronology of a lifetime, written in concentric annual rings of good oak.' (Leopold, 1949, p.9)

A century ago the Scottish polymath Sir Patrick Geddes (1919)[7] elegantly argued that 'by leaves we live'. This epithet is used when observing leaves (living and decaying) to highlight our preoccupation aspects of human existence (e.g. financial markets, fashion, media, marketing, etc.) which are not fundamental to human survival on the planet

'... this is a green world, with animals comparatively few and small, and all dependent on the leaves. By leaves we live. Some people have strange ideas that they live by money. They think energy is generated by the circulation of coins. Whereas the world is mainly a vast leaf colony, growing on and forming a leafy soil, not a mere mineral mass: and we live not by the jingling of our coins, but by the fullness of our harvests. '(Geddes, 1919)

Concluding comments

These exercises and the ones above are summarised through the phrase '*Energy flows, and nutrients cycle*'. Through this process we highlight the fact that as these are global processes our actions here and now may well have consequences elsewhere and in the future.

[7] From 1888 to 1919 Geddes was Professor of Botany at the University of Dundee (Scotland). This passage is from his final lecture in 1919. It was published in a reprint of Cities in Evolution in 1949 (p. 216). He is regarded by many as the originator of the idea of 'think global, act local'. See Stephen (2004) for a recent biography.

However, students are also made aware that the role of the institution and staff (e.g. school and teacher) and their approach to ESD is fundamental to student learning. For example, if a teacher does not take opportunities to place emphasis on ESD in their work, they become as Eisner (1985) suggests, part of a null (i.e. not acknowledged and not valued) curriculum, and are perceived as such by pupils (and incidentally by other staff and the wider public). Similarly, if despite an explicit curriculum with an ESD focus, a teacher behaves in a highly visible contradictory way (e.g. driving a big car a short walking distance to school daily) the implicit curriculum is that the principles of sustainability and social equity are not important. This point is exemplified by the positive efforts the University of Edinburgh has made to address SD in its estates policy and increasingly in its programme provision (as above).

This proposition is used as a both a warning and an encouragement. If teachers acknowledge there is often contrast between policy/curriculum/pedagogy/rhetoric and practice (in schools, education authorities, governments etc) they can encourage their pupils to develop the critical thinking skills that will help them to make personal decisions based on fundamental principles rather than political, media or marketing pressures.

The scientific paradigm has shaped many facets of our civilisation and society, and has also helped us realise many of our impacts on the planet. Hence a clear understanding of 'the scientific method' is essential in making judgements about SD issues. Whilst the fact that scientists generally communicate their findings with caution and explicitly state uncertainties may give their peers confidence in their work and their integrity, this may be seen as weakness or conspiracy by those wishing to present a counter argument, and even poses difficulties for those looking for 'answers' to complex issues. If pupils are to be able to address the complexity of these issues and apply critical thinking skills they will need to understand and respect the scientific approach. Alongside this, 'care' (see Figure 1) must also be fostered because as Wattchow (2010, p. 8) argues 'we damage places not because we fail to understand them, but we are yet to feel for them like kin'.

An integrated approach to learning about SD issues seems essential to help those of us struggling with Goldacre's 'paradox'. If formal education places emphasis not just on the subject matter of SD, but also the ways in which we can link theory with practice, empathy with understanding, and actions with consequences, we may yet help those who make their livings from the 'jingling of coins' and believe in un-tempered growth to think more carefully about their actions; and us as 'consumers' to question this proposition and to resist making decisions that plainly flout ecological principles and ignore intergenerational equity.

References

Goldacre, B. (2009). *Climate change? Well, we'll be dead by then. Guardian Newspaper* (12th December 2009).

Eisner, E. (1985). The three curricula that all schools teach. In E. Eisner, *The educational imagination* (pp. 87-108). New York: Macmillan.

Geddes, P. (1919). Final lecture at the University of Dundee. Published in 1949 reprint of *Cities in Evolution*. London: Knapp Drewett & Sons.

Higgins, P. (1996). Outdoor education for sustainability: Making connections. *Journal of Adventure Education and Outdoor Leadership*, 13(4), 4-11.

Higgins, P. (2002). Outdoor education in Scotland. *Journal of Adventure Education and Outdoor Learning*, 2(2), 149-168.

Higgins, P. (2009). Into the Big Wide World: Sustainable Experiential Education for the 21st Century. *Journal of Experiential Education*. 32(1), 44-60.

Higgins, P., & Kirk, G. (2006). Sustainability Education in Scotland: The impact of national and international initiatives on teacher education and outdoor education. *Journal of Geography in Higher Education*, 30(2), 313-326.

Kibble, B. (2010). *Sunshine, shadows and stone circles*. Sandbach: Millgate.

Goldacre, B. (2009). *Climate change? Well, we'll be dead by then. Guardian Newspaper* (12th December 2009).

Eisner, E. (1985). The three curricula that all schools teach. In E. Eisner, *The educational imagination* (pp. 87-108). New York: Macmillan.

Geddes, P. (1919). Final lecture at the University of Dundee. Published in 1949 reprint of *Cities in Evolution*. London: Knapp Drewett & Sons.

Higgins, P. (1996). Outdoor education for sustainability: Making connections. *Journal of Adventure Education and Outdoor Leadership*, 13(4), 4-11.

Higgins, P. (2002). Outdoor education in Scotland. *Journal of Adventure Education and Outdoor Learning*, 2(2), 149-168.

Higgins, P. (2009). Into the Big Wide World: Sustainable Experiential Education for the 21st Century. *Journal of Experiential Education*. 32(1), 44-60.

Higgins, P., & Kirk, G. (2006). Sustainability Education in Scotland: The impact of national and international initiatives on teacher education and outdoor education. *Journal of Geography in Higher Education*, 30(2), 313-326.

Kibble, B. (2010). *Sunshine, shadows and stone circles*. Sandbach: Millgate.

Leopold, A. (1968). *A Sand County almanac*. Oxford: Oxford University Press.

Levi, P. (1984). *The periodic table*. Chapter on Carbon. London: Abacus.

McNaughton, M. J. (2007). Sustainable development education in Scottish schools: the sleeping beauty syndrome. *Environmental Education Research*, 13(5), 621-638.

Nicol, R. (n.d.). *Outdoor environmental education and concept-based practice: some practical activities designed to consider the relationship between people and place*. Unpublished conference paper.

Outdoor Journeys (2009). Online at http://www.outdoorjourneys.org.uk/Outdoor_Journeys_2/Welcome.html <http://www.outdoorjourneys.org.uk/Outdoor_Journeys_2/Welcome.html> (accessed 20/3/ 2010)

Stephen, W. (editor) (2004). *Think global, act local: The life and legacy of Patrick Geddes*. Edinburgh: Luath Press.

University of Edinburgh (n.d.). Educating for a sustainable future. The SEEPS Project (Sustainability Education in European Primary Schools). Online at http://www.education.ed.ac.uk/esf/project-info/index.html (accessed 20/3/2010)

UNESCO (n.d.). *Reorienting Teacher Education towards Sustainability*. Online at http://www.unesco.org/en/unitwin/access-by-region/europe-and-north-america/canada/unesco-chair-in-reorienting-teacher-education-towards-sustainability-430/ (accessed 20/3/ 2010).

Wattchow, B. (2010). The song of the wounded river. Port Adelaide: *Ginninderra Press*.

4.6 Engaging Student Teachers with the Local Community: A Mapping Approach

Elizabeth Curtis, University of Aberdeen

Introduction

This chapter describes how an Initial Teacher Education(ITE) tutor has approached Global Citizenship Education through the development of fieldwork as a central part of open-ended, democratic learning. This fieldwork was used both in the context of student teachers' preparation for school placements in the first two years of the BEd Primary Programme and in Social Studies teaching across the BEd Primary and PGDE Programmes. The focus of this chapter is on developing students' capacity to become critically aware of ways in which they can explore, 'the values of the global dimension, particularly social justice, compassion and respect for cultural and religious diversity,'(LTS, 2007:7) through fieldwork in the local area.

The introduction of Global Citizenship Education in schools was according to Pykett 'a prime example of a pedagogical form of power that incites citizens to be active and self-governing through instilling participatory democratic forms, involving students in activities of representation, and advocacy and providing opportunities for community involvement,' (Pykett, 2009: 108). A key element of this is the development and nurturing of the democratic classroom in which learners and teachers work together to negotiate paths of learning which allow learners to take responsibility for their own learning in a supported environment. This is reflected in research carried out by Maitles and Deuchar (2006) who identified the role of 'democratic, active forms of learning' in supporting opportunities for promoting pupil voice. It is also reiterated in the opening pages of the Practitioner Resource, the Global Dimension in the Classroom where there is a discussion focusing attention on the importance of the establishment of an 'open participatory ethos...' in schools. (LTS, 2007:7).

Over the past five years there has been a significant change in the way in which the BEd Primary Programme at Aberdeen University is structured and delivered. The introduction of the Scottish Teachers for a New Era (STNE) Programme brought with it an opportunity to critically examine the ways in which both students and tutors experienced the process of learning and teaching, with particular emphasis on student-led participatory learning. In this chapter, I will explore how open ended fieldwork, namely the development of a community walk, has contributed to students' understanding of communities in relation to school placement and to their understanding of the scope of *Curriculum for Excellence* (CfE) Social Studies Outcomes and Experiences in the PGDE Primary Programme.

The Community Walk was developed as part of a series of activities designed to support first and second year Primary Education Students' exploration of the locale of the school in which they were to carry out their placement in order to further their understanding of its broader community context. In addition to the walk, students were also asked to carry out interviews with pupils, staff, parents and members of the wider community who came to the school, for example, the school nurse. The walk was designed as an open–ended piece of fieldwork. Initially students were asked to follow a given trail map around the school in which they were placed, but now the walk is developed by the students themselves.

The methodology for the walk was drawn from Margaret Roberts' work on personal geographies and, in particular, affective mapping (Roberts, 2003), which encourages the learner to map out emotional responses to places. This gave students the opportunity not only to identify key aspects of the school's geographical context for example, people's homes, shops, places to play and places to meet, but it also actively encouraged students to record their emotional responses to the places which they saw. In the first year that the walk was part of preparation for school experience, all of the students were placed in the feeder primary schools for the secondary school local to the university and 4 walking trails were created to take students around the areas close to the schools in which they would be placed. The university campus lies in the heart of the medieval burgh of Old Aberdeen, which is a geographically distinct area of the city and very diverse in nature. The area includes 18th and 19th century housing, 3 large estates of social housing including high rise building and sheltered accommodation. It is bounded by the sea to the east and the main city ring road to the west. For many students it was the first time that they had experienced first hand walking around areas like this.

In preparation for the walk students were given a list of names of places from all over the city and asked to write down the first ideas which came into their heads in relation to the name. Students from outside of Aberdeen had very little idea about any of the places whilst students from the city had opinions and experiences of many places on the list. They were also asked to record how they knew about the places, e.g. from experience, word of mouth, or articles in the local press. This exercise allowed students to reflect on where and how their perceptions of places and the people who lived in them were formed. Students were also encouraged to take photographs which they could then share with the children in school as the basis for a conversation about how children also saw the same places. In a lecture given to the students before going in their walk the following key points were highlighted:

- Personal geography of community and creating an affective map. (Roberts, M. 2003:172)
- Learning from your map: Sharing and discussing your map with children and adults who are part of the community.
- Discussion with members of the community to identify where they place geographic boundaries.

In taking part, the students would be creating an affective personal geography of the area in which they walked i.e they would create a map which linked places to their emotional responses and which would highlight the places which seemed to them to be of importance or places which they would avoid. Once they had completed their map, including photographs of places, they would use this as a basis for learning conversations with both pupils and staff within the school. This would allow students to see these same places from the perspectives of those whose lived experience of the area would provide a deeper, more nuanced understanding.

In addition to Roberts' affective mapping, the Community Walk also drew from the exploration of the idea of 'habitus' and 'being and becoming', (Bourdieu, 1977 and Roth, 2002) and the ways in which student teachers need to learn to 'fit into' the new school community in which they are placed. By thinking about placement in terms of 'habitus', and 'being and becoming', it is possible to help student teachers to actively explore the transitions which they make between being a pupil and a teacher or a parent and becoming a teacher. 'Habitus' is what generates the patterned ways in which we interact with the world. It is what we learn unconsciously from our families, friends and schooling, and it is the shared understanding of these patterns which is one of the factors in shaping vibrant communities. It embodies actions including speech, perceptions and expectations and is formed in time through experience and acquired through co-participation in situations with others who have already acquired 'habitus'. (Roth, 2002). Participation in the walk allows students to reflect on the degree to which they recognise the underlying structures of the community in which they have been placed. It helps to develop students' understanding of self and other through direct experience, in turn helping them to become more aware of their own attitudes towards situations and people whose 'habitus' is unlike their own. It also helps to open discussion with both pupils and teachers in the school, providing a starting point for questions and developing understanding.

The second way in which fieldwork has been developed as a tool for open-ended democratic learning has been in the teaching of Social Studies. This has been used primarily in the PGDE (primary) programme but also in the BEd programme. Here fieldwork is used to support students understanding of both the content and underlying methodologies implicit in the CFE Outcomes and Experience for Social Studies. It is completed by PGDE students in the first 6 weeks of their Programme. Like the Community Walk, the learning takes place on campus and engages students in an active investigation of the local community, but here it is as way of navigating the curriculum. There were several related practical factors leading to the development of the fieldwork task. The first was the need to respond to a significant drop in contact hours with students which led to a review of how face-to-face teaching time was organised. The second related to the author's prior experience as a former development officer with Aberdeen Environmental Education Centre (AEEC). Through this, the author was familiar with the role of fieldwork in supporting children's learning across a wide range of environmental studies relating to investigations of historical, social, environmental and aesthetic features of urban settings. In particular, this meant being aware of the different ways in which pupils engage with different environmental contexts and the range of learning needs which can be met through something as simple as walking down a street (Curtis, 2008). Thirdly, the ways in which local schools had developed fieldwork was also taken into consideration, for example the local secondary school's music department sent pupils out of the classroom to work around the local cathedral to collect ideas for soundscapes, whilst a local primary school contributed to the Imperial War Museum's 'Their Past your Future' initiative through the development of an oral history project through which children came to recognise the contributions of older people to community life (Curtis, 2007). The final factor, as noted earlier, was the geographic location of the University campus which offered a diversity of experiences for students.

In addition to providing a means for students to learn for themselves what constituted Social Studies in *Curriculum for Excellence*, the main aims of the fieldwork task were that students would gain empathy with children as learners, gain direct experience of embodied learning in the environment and make their own links between Social Studies and other areas of the curriculum. The task is designed to be open ended so that each group of students is able to negotiate how they interpret both the places in which they carry out their fieldwork and also how particular features relate to different outcomes presented in the Social Studies Outcomes and Experiences. This is particularly relevant to the PGDE cohort of students as they have studied a particular subject to degree level and some have also come to teaching from other occupations. They are able to learn from each other's wider experiences and build on their own existing knowledge and understanding. In common with the Community Walk, the curriculum fieldwork task is based on a mapping activity in which the students explore the university campus using a historical map from the 1660s as the basis of their exploration. It also emphasises the inclusion of affective and aesthetic responses to places. In order to support this way of working students are provided with a copy of the *Exploring Buildings* pack (Baxter, et al., 2003). This resource encourages participants to incorporate thoughts and feelings in the recording of the built environment through drawings, rubbings and the collection of sounds. Students work in groups of around six and are able to choose for themselves which areas of campus to explore. The main of aims of the task can be summarised as providing students with:

• Situated learning
• Meaningful participation
• Collaborative learning
• Independent learning (Curtis, 2007)

Recent research, which drew on student presentations, a short questionnaire and the on-line discussion of part time students indicated some key areas in which students felt they learned through this task. These included a greater understanding of the experience of working on an open-ended task, with particular reference to the experience as unsettling. One student commented that, 'the criteria need to be clear from the outset for it to work.' Students also commented on learning first hand, through the active participation in a group activity, the complexities of group dynamics. Where their experience of collaboration was positive, students noted that collaborative working, 'helps develop a richer understanding,' that 'communication is important and that 'recognising the ideas of others, helped us to reflect on learning.' (PGDE Questionnaire, 2006). Where students' experiences of collaboration were less successful, they noted 'varying levels of commitment' and 'if some group members do not share, the project loses the enjoyment factor,' (PGDE Questionnaire, 2006). In conclusion, the students discovered that for collaborative investigations to work each group needs clear leadership, each member should be sure of their role within the group and the work should be delegated and prioritised fairly with shared expectations.

In terms of understanding the Social Studies curriculum, the fieldwork task led to a diverse response from students. They felt more able to look at the curriculum in a broad sense identifying some of the overarching themes from *Curriculum for Excellence* (CfE), for example Health and Wellbeing, with particular reference to green spaces and quiet corners around campus. The students clearly identified specific outcomes and experiences from Social Studies that had arisen in the course of their walk and, importantly, could begin to see how working in this way could directly related to the four capacities. For example, one group made links between 'Confident Individuals' and their experience of carrying out the task, noting that this experience would help children to 'share their beliefs and views and 'Listen to opinions and views of others'. Both of these are also very close to the values of the global dimension. (LTS, 2007).

In conclusion, this chapter has shown how fieldwork in the local area can enable student teachers to develop skills that will help them to explore the values and practices of the global dimension for themselves, as well as with children and young people.

References

Baxter, L., Paterson, A., & Pirie, N., (2003) *Exploring Buildings*, Aberdeen Environmental Education Centre, Aberdeen

Bourdieu, P., (1977) *Outline of a Theory of Practice*. (trans Nice, R.) Cambridege University Press, Cambridge.

Curtis, E., (2007) Finding the Curriculum in the Environment: Fieldwork Approaches to Student Learning in Initial Teacher Education. *International Journal of Learning*, 14 (5) (179 – 189)

Curtis, E., (2008) 'Walking out of the classroom: learning on the streets of Aberdeen' in Ingold, T., & Lee Vergunst, J., (eds.) *Ways of Walking: Ethnography and Practice on Foot*, Ashgate, Aldershot.

Learning Teaching Scotland, (2007), *The Global Dimension in the Curriculum*, Learning and Teaching Scotland, Glasgow.

Maitles, H., & Duechar, R., (2006), 'we don't learn democracy, we live it!': Consulting the pupil voice in Scottish schools. *Education, Citizenship and Social Justice*, 1 (3), (249-166)

Pyket, J., (2009) Pedagogical Power: Lessons from school spaces, *Education, Citizenship and Social Justice*, 4 (2) (102-116)

Roberts, M., (2003) *Learning Through Enquiry, Making sense of geography in the key stage 3 classroom*. Geographical Association, Margate.

Roth, W. M., (2002), *Being and Becoming in the Classroom*, Ablex Publishing, Westport, Connecticut, London

4.7 'This Whole Agenda Changes Attitudes and Dispels Myths.' A Study into Global Citizenship and Sustainable Development and its Place in Early Years Education

Brenda Dunn, Jill Shimi, David Miller and Peter Wakefield, University of Dundee

Introduction

Education for Global Citizenship and Sustainable Development has, arguably, two distinct aspects. It deals with specific issues of global interdependence, diversity of identities and cultures, sustainable development, peace & conflict and inequities of power, resources & respect (Oxfam, 2008). But it also requires that these issues are addressed through active and participatory teaching and learning methodologies (ibid.). Such methods are perhaps more strongly embedded in early years education than in any other sector of formal education. There are many ways in which early years settings implicitly consolidate the pedagogical concepts of global citizenship and sustainable development, for example through the promotion and acquisition of such things as 'sharing', working together, taking turns and listening skills. It could be argued that it is the undervaluing of these very fundamental social skills in formal education that has generated the explicit need for Education for Global Citizenship and Sustainable Development to be recognised. Thus, the core work early years practitioners engage in, as a matter of course, can create a profoundly valuable basis for the development of caring, respectful and responsible citizens. The purpose of the current chapter, however, is to examine the explicit place of education for global citizenship and sustainable development in early years education.

Scotland's *Curriculum for Excellence* (2009) stated that 'the curriculum must be inclusive, be a stimulus for personal achievement, and through a broadening of experiences of the world, be an encouragement towards informed and responsible citizenship.' The Sustainable Development Strategy for Scotland, *Choosing Our Future* (2005) sets out a particular requirement for the formal education sector to integrate sustainable development into the school curriculum and across subjects. It is appropriate, therefore, to investigate the pedagogical approaches towards the promotion and understanding of global citizenship and sustainable development in early years education and to consider how work carried out in the early years sector can provide a foundation upon which the primary sector can build.

Curriculum Framework for Children 3-5 (1999) promoted children's development of knowledge and understanding of the world linked closely with other aspects of their learning. It was regarded very much as an 'add-on' to the early years curriculum, acknowledging religious festivals and ensuring that multi cultural resources were provided. *Curriculum for Excellence* (2009) extends this focus and encourages children to view the world with a wider lens. Early years practitioners are currently tailoring their practice to work towards the four capacities identified in *Curriculum for Excellence* – aspiring to develop their capabilities to be successful learners, confident individuals, responsible citizens and effective contributors to society. The study reported here investigated, therefore, how global citizenship and sustainable development are embedded in the early years curriculum and how early years practitioners are engaging with these concepts within *Curriculum for Excellence*.

Through our engagement with our BA in Childhood Practice students, we became aware of some of the interesting work which was going on in the area of global citizenship. We approached the study with general research questions which were open in nature, allowing us to explore current practice and to examine how the concepts of global citizenship and sustainable development were promoted in the learning experiences of young children.

Methodology

The focus of the study was on the beliefs and practices of the early years practitioners. We were keen to find out about practice to promote global citizenship and to explore the values, attitudes and beliefs of the staff involved. In order to do this, we conducted semi-structured interviews and supplemented the information with observations of the settings. Interviews were conducted with experienced managers in three early years settings: one in South Lanarkshire and two in Dundee. The sample of nurseries was chosen based on reports of good practice, and in one instance because of the diversity of the backgrounds of the children and families. Our first community nursery achieved a perfect score from the Care Commission in 2009. Its full capacity is 72, comprising 10 children from birth to three years and 56 children from 3-5 years. The second setting caters for children aged 2-5 years and the total roll is 158 children. It was commended by HMIE in 2006 for its 'Positive and successful approaches to supporting pupils with English as an additional language.' The final setting is a nursery school which has a roll of up to 60 part time children at any one time. The children are aged 3-5 years. This nursery is the holder of the prestigious green flag award under the Eco School scheme and also won a platinum Health Promoting School accolade in 2010.

A semi-structured interview schedule, which was constructed previously by researchers from the University of Dundee in a study relating to global citizenship in schools, was adapted for early years with some questions removed as they related to schools as opposed to nurseries. The questionnaire was also expanded to incorporate questions which related to children from birth to five years. This was designed to identify knowledge, understanding, opinions and values relating to global citizenship and how they were being translated into practice. The visits to the settings were conducted in February/March 2010, ranging from an hour and a half to half a day.

Findings

Practitioners' understanding of global citizenship and key elements

It was evident that practitioners viewed global citizenship as a theme which permeates the curriculum rather than as an appendage to established learning and teaching practice. As one manager reflected, 'We are responding to changes in society and many different cultures.' In the past, the approach appeared to centre on multi-cultural education celebrating religious festivals and ensuring that other cultures were represented in all resources. Generally the discourse suggested that a more integrated approach is now being adopted in early years settings.

One setting described their starting point as 'promoting an understanding of what is going on in the world; children are not citizens in the waiting, but citizens of to-day.' Their initial focus was their *Child at the Centre* audit carried out by staff almost five years ago, which highlighted their tokenism regarding celebrating dates on the calendar rather than having real understanding of culture. There was a desire by the staff team to deepen their own awareness of different cultures and to access information about the many different cultural backgrounds of the children in their setting, to allow them to fully understand and embrace diverse family experiences and traditions. According to one lead practitioner:

'*Curriculum for Excellence* drives us to take a holistic view rather than a subject based approach. This makes it much easier for children to explore similarity and differences and to see the bigger picture'.

Drivers for the promotion of global citizenship

There was general acceptance that *Curriculum for Excellence* was one of the key drivers for the promotion of global citizenship. Interestingly, in one setting political considerations were referred to as possible drivers which, in the long term, would equip children with the necessary skills to prepare them for employability in a global market. Another significant driver was the desire to celebrate the diverse family backgrounds of our global society. Lesson plans centred on events taking place within the families in the setting, the children's interests and upon the promotion of festivals of the relevant different cultures. In the words of one lead practitioner:

'Children drive global citizenship through their own interests and diverse family backgrounds. This leads to a culturally responsive curriculum.'

The activities related to global citizenship and sustainability

There was evidence in every setting that festivals of different cultures were being celebrated as an integral part of the curriculum in the form of posters, food tasting, stories, verse, song and dance. The use of *'All About Me'* booklets completed before the child starts the nursery provided a more holistic approach to understanding the child as part of his/her family. These booklets were used in one setting to identify ways in which parents could be involved and how they could share their skills and talents. Another setting provided questionnaires for the parents at enrolment to capture cultural information to inform practice within the nursery. There was a determination to celebrate the cultures of the children themselves as a key priority. An example which depicted this clearly was the successful Joy to the World Christmas show with its centrepiece banner depicting the phrase 'joy to the world' in the languages of all the children and their families.

In all settings visited, parents were regularly invited to share their own language through story telling. Children from birth to five were being exposed to stories in different languages and the settings encouraged even their youngest children to develop a basic vocabulary. One nursery manager cited the example of a father teaching Spanish greetings to very young children. There was general agreement that it was important to respond to national disasters. All had raised funds for the earthquake victims of Haiti and the Tsunami. This was deemed to have given the children a feeling of 'empowerment' and a sense of their ability to help. Shoe box appeals provided an opportunity to respond to a parent's request to assist with a church appeal. Children filled and wrapped the boxes. This was now an annual Christmas event, which practitioners felt gave the children an appreciation of the life experiences and needs of children in poverty in other parts of the globe. A similar example in another setting was a response to the Belarus appeal, which involved the children donating their books and toys. World news was discussed in all settings and listened to in the playroom. It was acknowledged that media reports, particularly those pertaining to world disasters, can be distressing. The sharing of knowledge was felt to increase understanding and reduce the fear of such events. Links with international schools came about primarily as a result of family connections, which already existed and allowed for the exchange of information through e-mails, letters, web-cam and Skype. There was evidence of relationships developing with settings in Spain, Nigeria and Australia.

Technological tools were being used to access the global world. We evidenced young children exploring the wider world using computers and white boards, giving them the opportunity to take a virtual tour of the world and beyond. GLOW, a Scotland-wide teaching resource, was being used by staff to inform their understanding of global citizenship, to access resources and to open up worldwide education.

Sustainability tended to be addressed in activities centring on healthy eating, planting and growing and recycling. Protecting the world's resources was the particular emphasis of one setting. We discovered grow bags, a mini green house, a nursery garden and a mini-bird sanctuary. Children, families and staff worked in the garden; planting and harvesting fruit, vegetables and herbs, learning about the food cycle and understanding the growing conditions of each plant. This resulted in the creation of a recipe book inspired by the nursery garden. Recycling was evident in the form of bottle banks, rag bags and compost heaps which often generated enterprise activities.

The activities alone do not fully reflect the level to which these early years settings have embraced global citizenship and sustainability. Evidence of the active involvement, the high level participation and genuine partnership working with parents, neighbouring schools and the wider community was seen in the inclusive ethos, which integrated twenty four different languages of the children and their families. There was also evidence of the acquisition of accolades from Local Authorities in the form of awards for Early Years Citizenship, Partnership with Parents and Innovation and Practice. In relation to sustainability one setting had achieved a Platinum Health Promoting School accolade and an eco green flag. Throughout the others there was a determination to work towards Eco School status.

Planning
Planning tended to be carried out on a fortnightly basis building upon evaluations and observations from the previous session. There was general consensus that plans had to be fluid and flexible to allow settings to respond to key world events. Planning in one nursery 'starts with reference to the *All About Me* booklets and develops as the children's interests become clear. This way we make sure that we create a culturally responsive curriculum'. In another setting a Global Citizenship folder was compiled with reference to 'Homecoming Scotland' and joint planning with the local High School.

Future planning included links to Australia as a child had recently relocated to that part of the world. Embedded in planning were opportunities to engage parents to encourage them to bring their skills, experiences and culture into the setting. In the words of their lead practitioner:

'Global citizenship informs our planning, but it must be relevant and pertinent to our children'.

Possible impact on the children and practitioners
The impact of global citizenship and sustainability upon children in their early years was described as cultivating the development of a 'we can do' philosophy and deemed to be responsible for establishing a climate of empowerment. Children were deemed to grow in confidence as they participated in the high quality activities which increased their self esteem and generated a feeling of pride in their achievements. Other possible impacts were

said to include: the opportunity to encourage enterprise skills, language benefits e.g. the learning of basic Spanish phrases, the development of interest in world news, a growing understanding of diverse cultures and empathy for others. Children were said to become motivated, more involved and to feel part of the community as a result of their engagement with global citizenship.

The practitioners themselves were said to have explored their own values and beliefs alongside those of the children and families; this was reported to lead to more effective communication. One lead practitioner referred to global citizenship as a means of expanding the horizons of staff, heightening their own awareness of global issues and the sustainability agenda, which led to an increase in their cultural sensitivity:

'This whole agenda changes attitudes and dispels myths. It promotes children's rights, children's choice, citizenship, enterprise and fund raising. It encourages us to involve parents, ensuring inclusion in policies and that there is nothing offensive to anyone'.

Conclusion

We were keen to discover key messages managers would like to give to others who are at an early stage of work in this area. Advice started with: be open minded about what children can do; begin with their current knowledge and make sure it is interesting and relevant, with links to the experience and understanding of the child.

In the words of the managers:

'Global citizenship is about promoting children's rights and fostering respect for different cultures. It fits in well with the GIRFEC (Getting it right for every child, 2008) agenda, which promotes interagency working and the rights of the child.'

'It is about raising awareness of culture; the 'One Scotland Many Cultures' advert uses many different accents and these voices on radio sum it up for me. It is about not making assumptions about people.'

'Start with your own values and beliefs, self-worth and pride in who you are and then you respect and value others'.

This study was designed to look at the place of global citizenship and sustainable development in three early years settings. The scope of the investigation was limited, but sufficient to provide examples of good practice relating to both global citizenship and sustainable development. Some issues deserve particular attention. Charitable activities such as shoe box appeals and donations of books and toys, if contextualised badly, can reinforce stereotypical views of poverty, promote pity above empathy and cultivate a sense of cultural superiority and pity (Oxfam, 2007). This was certainly not the impression formed from the establishments in this study, however, it is an issue deserving of wider research. A number of references were also made by, practitioners, to work around Scottish Heritage in the context of global citizenship. While teaching and learning about one's own culture and heritage is a profoundly important aspect of learning, it only enhances global learning if framed in terms of how knowing and valuing one's own culture supports one's ability to know and value other cultures. Examination of this would make another interesting question for future study.

Overall, we found that managers had made an active commitment to global citizenship and sustainable development themes and believed that these were now an important part of the ethos of their settings. It is our view that sharing such good practice in the early years could provide a foundation upon which other settings, including the primary sector, can build. By working together, sharing information about previous learning and participating in joint projects there are many exciting opportunities to enrich the curriculum, to ensure continuity and to prepare our children to take their place in global society.

References

Oxfam (2007) *Building Successful School Partnerships*. Online at http://www.oxfam.org.uk/education/teachersupport/cpd/partnerships/files/oxfam_gc_guide_building_successful_school_partnerships.pdf (accessed 05/06/10).

Oxfam (2008) *Getting Started with Global Citizenship: A guide for new teachers*. Online at http://www.oxfam.org.uk/education/teachersupport/cpd/files/GCNewTeacherSCOTLAND.pdf (accessed 05/06/10).

Scottish Executive (2006) *The Child at the Centre: Self-evaluation in the Early Years*. Edinburgh: Scottish Executive.

Scottish Government (2009) *A Curriculum for Excellence*. Edinburgh: Scottish Government.

Scottish Government (2008) *Getting it right for every child*. Edinburgh: Scottish Government.

The Scottish Office (1999) *Curriculum Framework for Children 3 to 5*, Dundee: Scottish Consultative Council on the Curriculum.

Scottish Executive (2005) The Sustainable Development Strategy for Scotland, *Choosing Our Future*. Edinburgh: Scottish Executive

4.8 ICT, Self-Regulated Learning and Web-based Sustainable Development Education / Global Citizenship Resources.

Robert Collins, Marie-Jeanne McNaughton, Moira Paterson & Ethel Anderson, University of Strathclyde

Introduction

The University of Strathclyde has been unusual in having a core integrated Sustainable Development Education (SDE) / Global Citizenship (GC) module as part of its B.Ed (Primary) programme. This article reports on an exploratory study concerning an Information and Communication Technology (ICT) element of this module. It demonstrates a move in ICT provision away from providing a supporting role in knowledge transmission, for example, through offering a research tool to facilitate completion of set tasks, towards supporting a more engaged self-regulatory approach. This is of interest in the context of the current publication because of the concurrent emphasis laid in SDE/GC upon pupil autonomy and active learning. The student task described also demonstrates the effective integration of diverse curricular elements, here SDE/GC and ICT. It is important in initial teacher education (ITE) that additional curricular elements are not dealt with by tacking them onto already crowded programmes but by taking this kind of strategic approach to combining them. Specifically in relation to SDE/GC, the task also offers an approach to dealing with the proliferation of online SDE/GC resources that often leaves student teachers wondering where to begin.

For the past two decades or so, ICT has been consistently envisioned as the ultimate complementary resource, capable of enhancing and transforming learning and teaching across the curriculum in Scottish schools. In the 5-14 National Guidelines (LTS 2000) it figured both as a physically discrete document and as a non-discrete, ubiquitous presence. Within the new *Curriculum for Excellence* (LTS 2009), it is re-imagined and re-positioned within the Technologies component, with the worthy mission of assisting pupils in their acquisition of the qualities of effective contributors, ultimately positioned to communicate equally comfortably on the local and global stage. As Munro (2008) and Condie et al (2005) have stated, however, it is unwise to regard ICT as the magic 'silver bullet' of education, as its much anticipated regenerative qualities on teaching, learning, attainment and even motivation have been far less sustained than anticipated.

Williams et al (1998) reported that most Scottish primary practitioners' typical use of ICT was restricted to the structured use of word processing, followed closely by that of externally produced educational software. Interestingly for ITE, they also suggested that newly qualified teachers were neither more nor less likely to engage in creative and personalised ICT related activity for pupils than established practitioners. Indeed, the ame report explained that studies of final year student teachers suggested that, although entering the profession with good levels of ICT skills, they felt they lacked competence and confidence in utilising it within the classroom in a creative way.

It is important, however, to also acknowledge some important developments in and benefits of ICT within the classroom. Positive effects on the presentation and problem-solving skills of pupils across the curriculum, on their understanding of abstract concepts in areas such as science and in supporting creativity within expressive arts have all been evidenced (as reported in Condie et al, 2005 and Munro, 2008). A strategic and reflective approach, on the part of practitioners, regarding the use of ICT in enhancing learners' understanding and creativity has also been shown to result in higher levels of pupil self-regulation with regard to their own educational development. HMIE (2007) reported that, although provision could still be improved, raised levels of enthusiasm and engagement of pupils had been confirmed in response to the use of innovative approaches to ICT in Scottish classrooms. These pupil-reported innovative approaches included not only a wider use of the internet, but also, significantly, a greater role for pupil autonomy within lessons. It is hoped that, with the onset of *Curriculum for Excellence* (2009), which promotes self-regulation in learning and the contextualisation of learning using current themes in society such as SDE/ GC, there may be a renaissance in ICT's effective use within the primary classroom.

This kind of ICT use resonates more with pedagogies linked to cognitive psychology, to theories such as Piaget's Constructivism or Vygotsky's Social Constructivism, than with more traditional knowledge-transmission approaches in education. The benefit of practitioners considering this prior to planning ICT activity is emphasised by more recent writers on the subject such as Pritchard (2004; pp22-42) who writes that knowledge of the cognitive and social processes involved in learning are, '…essential for those who intend to develop activities which have the potential to lead to effective learning.' (See also Loveless, 1995).

The need for structured ITE inputs to support early career teachers in maintaining progress in ICT use and the benefits of marrying recent cognitive research to ICT classroom practice are recognised and inferred in the numerous policy statements within the new curricular framework in Scotland. The new framework refers to the benefits of wider access to ICT in schools and purposeful curricular subject and interdisciplinary engagement utilising ICT elements (GTCS, 2006 and HMIE, 2007).

The difficulty in achieving all of this, as stated by authors on self-regulated learning theory such as Butler & Winne (1995) is that, for practitioners to teach in such a way, they themselves must experience authenticity of such practice themselves – in other words they must be immersed in an ITE experience which embraces and encompasses such activity.

The task examined in this article was designed to develop student teachers' understanding o how learners learn in a more autonomous, self-regulated manner through the use of specific lesson tools rather than through the transmission of theory (following Brophy, 2002, Butler & Winne, 1995, and Zimmerman,1998). The overall aim was to attend to the student teachers' own mediation and confidence towards learning, to provide aspects that support autonomy and choice and to provide adequate differentiation across the learning situation. This would give the students direct experience of an approach that could subsequently be used with their pupils

To this end, the University of Strathclyde's Faculty of Education established a laboratory based webquest input for third year student teachers aimed at embedding autonomous classroom ICT practice and design. This formed part of the core modular content for the B. Ed. (Hons) Primary within its Integrated Curricular Studies component covering SDE/GC. A webquest is a familiar practitioner-generated tool used in many schools in Scotland. It provides a basic intuitive user-interface contextualised around a common theme, in this case SDE/GC. This helps teachers establish and manage focussed internet access for learners through the use of on-screen text boxes and icons connected to preselected websites relevant to the theme in question. The text boxes offer a variety of planned and prepared on-screen questions, prompts and assistance, giving learners the opportunity to work independently, at their own pace, i.e., to regulate their own learning according to their ability and involvement with the task. The webquest can, therefore, be viewed as a teaching instrument which primarily involves users recognising their own ICT ability level and addressing their development needs in the chosen area through participation in self-regulated web-based activity. Importantly, it can be created on even the most straightforwarc and commonly available software platforms (such as PowerPoint).

Following the self-guided laboratory webquest session, students were required to use a website evaluation tool (adapted from Potter 2002; Pritchard, 2004) to investigate and report upon targeted aspects of one SDE/GC website chosen as a result of the session. The website had to have been designed either for classroom use or to support lesson planning and implementation. The evaluation tool required students to assess the website according to the following criteria:
• purpose and authenticity of task
• creativity
• competence
• issues of accuracy (& security)
• implementation.

n this way the students' evaluative focus was aimed at: aspects of meaningful activity with links to real-world issues, the encouragement of non-passive learner interaction, opportunities for differentiation and engagement, secure and relevant site content and the following of current good practice in terms of lesson implementation, respectively. The provision of the website evaluation tool (Collins & Paterson, 2009) gave students the opportunity to familiarise themselves with a consistent process of assessing the value of specific internet sites for educational purposes. A peer assessment element, an essential aspect of self-regulated learning (Kennedy and Allan, 2008 and Butler & Winne, 1995), was also incorporated, whereby students were required to assess and provide feedback on the evaluations to colleagues through their course intranet. This also served to enhance student discourse within the task. Post-task, cross-cohort sharing of evaluations gave the students a convenient means of tackling the proliferation of potentially relevant sites supporting SDE/GC work as well as modelling the benefits of collegiate working.

The web evaluation tool in question had been used for four years across two separate degree pathways. However, in light of the development of *Curriculum for Excellence* (2009), it was felt that an analysis of its pragmatic benefit in lesson implementation would be prudent and to this end a small scale evaluation study was carried out in October 2008. The main purpose of the study was to gather evidence from students regarding their perception of what key elements of lesson implementation would be addressed through the use of SDE/GC context websites during their school practice. Also of interest was the fact that these students were the first undergraduate year group within the B.Ed. (Hons) degree for whose professional placement experiences were all within primary establishments that were either fully implementing or preparing to fully implement the new curriculum. It was hoped that the ideas of this cohort of students, having been exposed to these environments, would be likely to resonate with current pedagogical change within the field, and that their interpretation of the pragmatic elements of lesson implementation within this area would be particularly useful for the development of the evaluation tool for subsequent year groups.

Method
Design
The study was conducted in Semester 1 of Session 2008-09 with student teachers from the third year cohort of the B.Ed. (Hons) Module PE313 component entitled '*Integrated Studies: Education for Sustainable Development*'. The study was specifically designed to evaluate a section of the established website evaluation tool around 'implementation'. In particular, the tool asked students to openly consider the questions:

- 'How do online tasks tie in with what you want children to learn?'
- 'Will you have to augment these tasks with any external resources?' (and if so how would you achieve this?)

- could your chosen site be used to enhance teaching and learning in the classroom?'
- you recommend any adaptations?'

Students were asked to reflect on the websites they had used in the laboratories according to the evaluative criteria of the tool; to complete the tool in its entirety subsequent to participation in the associated self-regulatory laboratory session; and to submit this to tutors some four weeks later. The students' responses were then collated and examined by the researchers for emergent themes regarding the implementation of SDE/GC focussed ICT lessons. The research team, in their other capacity as the module tutors, also attended focussed discussions regarding the collated material. They were asked to utilise their recollections of observations of and interactions with students during the laboratory sessions in deliberating possible emergent themes. Four follow-up case studies investigating participants' reflections on their use of chosen websites in situ during their third year placement experience (in relation to the emergent themes on implementation) were also planned for the following April-May in 2009.

Instrument

The modular website evaluation tool was initially devised and adapted from advice by Potter (2002) and Pritchard (2004). At the time of the study, it had already been piloted and established as a website evaluation tool for both undergraduate and postgraduate primary Environmental Studies programmes for four years previously. Initially devised for use within any curriculum design, it was felt that various iterations and modifications of the tool over these years may have resulted in a skewed purpose towards its implementation within a 5-14 context. Therefore, any further iteration of the tool in subsequent modules would benefit from in-depth evaluation pertinent to implementation of ICT within the new *Curriculum for Excellence*. With the exception of a final quantifiable scale, from 1-5 (merit) stars used to indicate a personal recommendation level to peers for the chosen site, the tool itself was designed to be open in nature. This allowed for deeper analysis on each section by respondents.

Participants

Although as part of the requirements within established modular content, students were normally asked to conduct a review of the extent and quality of the range of web-based SDE/GC ICT support materials widely available online, participation within the current evaluation study was conducted on a voluntary basis only. Students were also informed that those wishing to withdraw from the study could do so at any time. Ethical consent for the participation in the study was sought and gained from a relevant sample of 113 BEd3 students by the principle investigator in October 2008.

Findings

The initial phases of the research resulted in the collation of the website evaluations submitted by all 113 students. These provided extensive insights into the students' perception across all key themes in the tool regarding website provision. Unfortunately, however, due to limitations imposed on the study involving timescale and participant attrition, the researchers were unable to complete the anticipated follow-up placement-based case studies.

A database was created of the 113 website evaluations submitted by students, and then a subset of data was created consisting of just those student submissions that awarded a highest 'merit' standard (of 5 stars grading) to their chosen website (n = 27). This subset was chosen as, given their highest level of recommendation, these websites were more likely to be revisited and used in the students' class teaching situations. It was this subset that was the focus of the study.

Individual researchers took responsibility for establishing initial themes within the evaluations of the students in this subset who were in their own tutorial groups. The researchers then came together and scrutinised the reasoning behind one another's views of the emergent themes within their sub-group. Justification of individually proposed themes was established via expression of tutor recollection of tutorial observation and discussion with students. The researchers arrived at a total of ten overall emergent themes through this immersion process. Having been discussed, scrutinised and agreed upon, responses held as pertinent to these themes were then collated. Table 1, below, summarises the key themes identified and frequency of statement related to these from within the range of student responses in respect of these sections:

Table 1 Emergent Themes	Frequency of Theme Occurrence within Collated Student Response	Percentage Occurrence within Collated Student Response
Impacting on learning & teaching (e.g used to introduce topic)	24	10.8
Developing research skills/ subject knowledge – teacher	15	6.8
Developing research skills/ subject knowledge – pupil	34	15.3
Supporting collaborative learning – pupil/pupil	22	9.9
Supporting collaborative learning - pupil/teacher	7	3.2
Supporting pupil independent learning	13	5.9
Affording opportunity for personalisation & choice (including ease of navigation)	20	9.0
Engendering pupil motivation/ engagement	44	19.8
Supporting actiave research/ interactive learning	31	13.9
Requiring external self-generated resources / prompts/props by teacher	12	5.4

As stated, ten distinct themes were established. From tutor analysis of the students' responses it became clear very quickly that the themes resonated with intuitively recognisable features of the new *Curriculum for Excellence*, e.g a focus on learner engagement and enjoyment in learning, an assertion of benefits of collaborative group-work, customisation of the curriculum to meet immediate local needs, active and interactive approaches to tasks, and cognisance of pupil personalisation and choice towards task design. This was in some contrast to tutors' subjective recollection of responses from students in the past. That the modal theme related to focus of considerations of motivation/ engagement (19.8 %), is suggestive of this impression.

The data was also viewed in terms of student perception of the application of the desirable implementation behaviours registered, related to the ICT component of lessons in the SDE/ GC context. Through the lens of inferred pedagogical approaches held as stereotypical within knowledge transmission styles or cognitive self-regulation theory, there appears to be a quantitative contrast in student perception of site utilisation within lessons. The shading in Table 1 (above) relates to this question. A notional distinction was made by the researchers between those themes that appear more representative of
– knowledge-transmission styles of teaching and learning
– the prioritisation of knowledge acquisition
 and/or
– ICT's more traditionally reported role (Condie, 2005; Munro, 2008) as solely of use as
   a peripheral pedagogical tool (e.g. as an initial lesson stimulus)
and those that view ICT more as a truly collaborative learning tool within the SDE/GC context. The first three shaded categories of emergent themes in Table 1: impacting on learning & teaching (e.g used to introduce topic); developing research skills/ subject knowledge – teacher; and developing research skills/ subject knowledge – pupil can be seen as resonating with the former approach.

These three categories, when collated, represent 32.9 % of the sample response. Conversely the non-shaded categories can be seen as more representative of the latter approach, those that view ICT more as a truly collaborative learning tool within the SDE/GC context. These categories are more typically associated with self-regulation, and its basis in constructivist or social constructivist approaches (Pritchard 2004). These un-shaded sections: supporting collaborative learning – pupil/pupil; supporting collaborative learning – pupil/teacher; supporting pupil independent learning; affording opportunity for personalisation & choice (including ease of navigation); supporting active research/ interactive learning: engendering pupil motivation/ engagement; and requiring external self-generated resources/ prompts/ props by teacher) constitute some 67.1% of student responses. They also resonate with classroom approaches supported within the new curriculum. This represents a ratio of approximately 2:1 in favour of cognitive considerations over those of traditional knowledge-transmission by students in terms of implementation issues.

As noted earlier, the researchers were unable to complete aspects of in-depth case study around placement learning. This would have offered the opportunity to further establish the relevance of the findings in respect of many of the study's key outcomes, and afforded clearer insight into the students' perception regarding what they identified as key themes prevalent in website provision in situ. It is hoped this will be explored in a future study.

Discussion

The tentative findings discussed above seem to tie in well with messages on the establishment of cognitive approaches and self-regulation in the learning environment espoused by Brophy (2002) and Butler & Winne (1995). This is particularly the case with regard to the stated benefits of self-efficacy and personalisation of choice to the establishment of meaningful learning. It could be argued that the study offers tantalising insight into the impact of student immersion in the self-regulatory learning experience as a means to their own use of it when planning SDE/GC focused ICT inputs, and its eventual realisation within the classroom environment. It seems at least possible that participation within the self-regulated laboratory webquest and subsequent discourse between students therein, may have had some impact upon their view of a similar use of the approach within their own intended classroom practice.

What is evident from the data gathered is at least an initial indication that, when taken as a whole group, cognitive approach aspects surrounding the use of SDE/GC websites in engendering pupil motivation and engagement (the provision of collaboration between pupils, supporting pupil independence and supporting active and interactive learning) would seem to take some precedence at least over more traditional knowledge-transmission approaches such as developing pupil research skills and knowledge. It could then be argued that these aspects are suggestive of key issues of priority, interest or even concern for students in terms of the use of the SDE/GC website provision within the classroom. The findings of the study will impact on the format structure of future iterations of the website evaluation tool. In effect, the section on 'implementation' within the tool will be redesigned to include a greater ratio of consideration advice in terms of cognitive approaches prevalent in *Curriculum for Excellence*, as opposed to that of knowledge transfer integral to its predecessor 5-14.

One other impact of the study has been to further evidence to the module tutors and to a broader range of interested parties the necessity of recognising that the use of ICT in the primary classroom is moving away from its more traditional knowledge-transfer role.

Importantly, this move towards its use in establishing self-regulatory learning by pupils instead seems to be apparent in emerging teachers. The study itself, although limited, should be viewed in the wider context of the task's component position within the core modular programme, with its ongoing focus and commitment to prioritising student awareness of the aspects and principles of the new *Curriculum for Excellence* (CfE) relating to SDE/Global Citizenship.

The main aim of the presentation of this small study is to provide stimulus for future, more stringent research, particularly as the in-situ teaching situation is considered, which may eventually have implications for implementation issues regarding the effective combination of ICT and Education for Global Citizenship and Sustainable Development.

References

Brophy, J. (2002) *Social Constructivist Teaching: Affordances and Constraints*. Oxford, UK: Elsevier Science Ltd

Butler, D. & Winne, P. (1995) *Feedback and Self-Regulated Learning: A Theoretical Synthesis* Review of Educational Research, 65, 245-281

Condie, R., Munro, R., Muir, D & Collins, R. (2005) *Impact of ICT Initiatives in Scottish Schools: Phase 3*. Glasgow: QIE University of Strathclyde

Collins, R. & Paterson, M. (2009) PCs: *A Force for Evaluation?* Primary Science Review ASE Publications: Hartfordshire

General teaching Council for Scotland (2006) *The Standard for Initial Teacher Education* GTCS: Edinburgh

Kennedy, A. & Allan, J. (2009, in press). *The Assessor and the Assessed: Learning from Students' Reflections on Peer Assessment* Journal of Teacher Education and Teachers' Work

LTS (2009) *A Curriculum for Excellence*. LTS: Glasgow

HMIE (2007) *Improving Scottish Education: ICT in Learning & Teaching*. Edinburgh: HMIE

Loveless, A (1995) *The Role of IT*. London: Cassell

LTS (2000) *Information and Communications Technology*: 5-14 National Guidelines. Glasgow: LTS

Munro, R (2008) *Information and Communication Technology* Ch 58 pp509-514 in Bryce, T.G & Hume W.(Eds) Scottish Education (3rd Ed) Edinburgh: Edinburgh University Press

Potter, J. (2002) PGDE *Professional Workbook: Primary ICT*. Exeter: Learning Matters

Pritchard, A. (2004) *Learning on the Net*. London: Fulton

Williams, D., Wilson, K., Richardson, A.& Tuson, J. (1998) Teachers' ICT ICT Skills & Knowledge Needs: Final Report to SOEID available at : www.Scotland.gov.uk/library/ict/append-title.htm

Zimmermann, B. (1998) *Developing Self-Fulfilling Cycles of Academic Regulation*. In D. Schunk & B. Zimmermann (Eds) Self-Regulated Learning London: Guildford Press

4.9 'Science, Citizenship and Sustainability': A Collaborative and Interdisciplinary Approach to Learning and Teaching in Initial Teacher Education to Address Issues of Sustainability.

Laura Colucci-Gray, Elizabeth Curtis, Christine Fraser, Donald Gray, University of Aberdeen

Introduction

Socio-environmental problems are on the increase and becoming more urgent: floods, soil desertification, military conflicts associated with land and water shortages at a global scale are dramatic manifestations of profound changes affecting natural systems. Citizens on the planet feel disempowered because of inadequate ecological competence, power imbalances and lack of democracy (Liberatore & Funtowicz, 2003). In this scenario, a change in the way knowledge is produced with regard to science and technology may be accompanied by changes in social practices. This chapter gives some indications as to how education can provide pointers for deepening perception of multiple inter-connections.

When talking about global citizenship we are effectively handling contrasting visions of the 'global', each one involving different levels of consciousness and responsibility. We may act as 'travellers' on the globe, transporting ourselves from point to point, directing our attention to the world resources like customers in a supermarket. This is the perspective that Ingold (2007) described as the 'straight line': it goes from point to point, in sequence, as quickly as possible, and in principle in no time at all. Another coexisting possibility for us is that of being 'inhabitants' of the world or 'dwellers'. This is the wiggly line of the encounters we make along the way and which leave a sign on our memory and experiences. The wiggly line contains a strong qualitative dimension: the dweller is part of the context which is being experienced and dependent upon it:

'The inhabitant is rather one who participates from within in the very process of the world's continual coming into being and who, in laying a trail of life, contributes to its weave and texture' (Ingold, 2007, p.81).

Human beings as a global species are currently living a paradoxical situation. We have evolved within the web of evolutionary and ecological relationships of the natural world: our anatomical structures and our physiological systems are complex forms which have been shaped by the close contact with and experience of natural contexts (Maturana & Varela, 1992). In the course of this interaction, we have also developed our cultural artefacts, from customs and religions, to agriculture and knowledge production systems. Western science in particular has constituted itself as one of the most powerful instruments of description and transformation of the world allowing us, for example, to become independent from seasonal phases or physical distances for example. In so doing, our lines or ways of mapping the world might be described as having become progressively more 'straight'(Ingold, 2007). In the past 30 years, the possibility of getting access to fossil energy sources has given rise to a new phase of evolutionary history. The Western model of development has successfully expanded the range of possibilities for extracting goods and services from Natural systems: a higher crops yield per year, more energy per capita. In 1997, Vitousek's comment: *'in a very real sense, the world is in our hands'* underlines at the same time the power of our techno-science and the enormous responsibility associated with its use. Decision-making processes are difficult as there is a need to grapple with novel and at times risky techno-scientific innovations which may lead to both positive and negative outcomes as well as irreversible damage (Harremoes et al., 2001). While many have identified science and technology as the most secure means for solving the global, environmental crisis (Keith et al., 2010), some have also begun to ask whether the problem lies not with the environment but with our ways of thinking (Sterling, 2009): in particular the worldview that our Western society has elaborated and translated into our current political choices, economical practices and individual behaviours. More specifically, it is argued that this worldview shapes the way in which we produce and use our knowledge of the world that we have built. From this perspective, the sustainability of human presence on the planet could be pursued by means of a radical cultural and epistemological change, rather than relying simply on increasing levels of technology.

Science, Citizenship and Sustainability: making connections

Our lives, as humans, constantly interconnect with the lives of many others. While we eat and accommodate matter accumulated by other living beings, we give some of it back transformed in a form that is useful for the sustenance of the decomposers. While we breathe and inhale oxygen molecules produced by plants, we surrender little bits of ourselves, the exhaled molecules of carbon dioxide that will be used by the photo synthesizers to build new structures. Being ecosystems ourselves, we host billions of tiny, useful creatures.

Each one of our actions is thus embedded in a web of multiple kinds of relationships, distributed both in space and in time. The Natural Sciences describe such interconnections from the point of view of the global, bio-geo-chemical cycles of important elements which are exchanged between the living and non-living components of the biosphere: for example, water is not only necessary to support the physiological functions of all living organisms, but also acts as the most important energy-broker in the biosphere, playing key roles in the regulation of the climate and the accumulation of biomass by means of plant photosynthesis. With the advancement of knowledge, we have become more conscious of the extraordinary complexity of the natural systems, which are made of multiple and interacting organisational levels. As reported by Giampietro et al. (2000), human societies and ecosystems are nested hierarchies. Their constitutive elements can be divided into smaller parts making up a whole. At the same time, each whole can be seen as a part of the larger element that embeds it. Nested hierarchical systems have a peculiar 'fuzzy' identity; their representation can change depending on whether we are looking at them as parts or as a whole.

The disciplinary approach to knowledge allows for the sophisticated exploration of specific portions of reality, but it makes it difficult to keep in mind and be aware of the interconnections among all the parts and their relationship of mutual dependency. Developing ideas already elaborated from within the field of the epistemology of science (Dupré,1993), Sarewitz (2004) concludes:

'the growth of scientific methods and bodies of knowledge results in an increasing disunity, that translates into a multitude of different yet equally legitimate scientific lenses for understanding and interpreting nature' (p. 390). And then he goes on: 'similarly, individual humans can have only the most partial of understanding of the world in which they reside and it is in the context of these always incomplete understandings that they make their decisions and judgments' (p. 390).

We are thus in danger of losing sight of a sense of limits: firstly, the limit of our knowledge, contained within self-imposed boundaries of time and space scales, methodological choices, disciplinary field etc… Secondly, and more specifically, an awareness of the biophysical and physiological limits of the planet (Wackernagel et al., 2002). Within a closed system such as our living Earth such limits correspond to the availability of resources and services. Increasing pressures in terms of waste accumulation, resource extractions, ecosystem modifications become translated into further reductions of essential supply (fertile land, clean water, humidity and so on) and increasing levels of conflict between human communities at both local and global scales.

Within this systemic perspective, it becomes apparent that science is not a neutral body of knowledge; rather it is one of the crucial elements shaping human relationships, power structures and the establishment of specific objectives and/or interests. There is, arguably, a sense of detachment between humans and nature (Zweers, 2000), largely determined by the growth of scientific knowledge, but also the product of a number of different processes.

213

The main processes are:
- cognitive features – reductionist and analytical science
- linguistic features – nominal language and the 'commodification/objectification' of nature
- ways of living – the urbanisation process, which swept away many forms of life that used to be familiar in our environment
- social practices – production and consumption of artificial goods

Any form of education for sustainability, any social-economical research, and any policy should be aiming at supporting the re-appropriation of awareness of the fact that we are living beings whose lives are sustained and made possible by a complex system of interconnections between other living beings and abiotic components. This has important implications for the regulation of public life.

Current initiatives in policy aimed at public engagement in science and technology point to the need for public participation in both formal and informal ways (Liberatore and Funtowicz, 2003). In the area of knowledge production, we are witnessing efforts to move towards interdisciplinary knowledge (Wickson et al., 2006). New areas of inquiry such as sustainability science (Clark, 2007) are emerging from an awareness of complexity and the unpredictability embedded in the evolution of the natural systems. In this scenario, it is not only individual experts reforming their traditional affiliations but more extended peer communities are being sought in which to share different forms of knowledge (i.e. from scientific to experiential), as each one provides an equally valid and valuable point of view (Gallopin et al., 2001). This has implications for decision-making processes with the need to include multiple voices and the voices of people who have been traditionally excluded from policy-making. An approach to knowledge and learning which is more respectful of the plurality of legitimate interpretations can offer the opportunity to experience the practice of inclusive and empathetic dialogue (Sen, 1999; Koerner & Singleton, 2009), an essential training for democracy. It also implies that knowledge production is dynamic, attentive to context, relevant and participatory.

Teacher education

In 2005 UNESCO published its *Guidelines and Recommendations for Reorienting Teacher Education to Address Sustainability*, stemming from a realisation that teacher-education institutions and teacher educators are key change agents for embedding principles of sustainability into education. However, while there is general agreement that the principles underlying sustainability are a good thing, Jickling (2001) maintains that many teachers and student teachers hold very diverse ideas about key concepts relevant to sustainability and suggests that there are fundamental difficulties with the language of sustainability and how it is currently used:

'it gives important glimpses at issues of environmental and educational importance, but does not reveal much about what else we must know and think about if we are to learn to live well with this planet' (p.169)..

One of the issues here concerns the image of science, with its epistemology of certainty, and teachers' practices of providing students with the simple 'foundation' of the subject (Reiss et al., 2007). In order to support all citizens in elaborating a personal reflection on the nature of the relationships between science, technology, society and the environment, and to become sensitised to the role that the non-expert can play in the elaboration of new ideas and in the participation, it is necessary to start questioning the epistemological establishment of science. In particular, we are referring to the implicit, conceptual and axiological 'frames' which underpin discourses about knowledge and development, societal practice and scientific research (Olausson, 2009).

Furthermore, Ivanitskaya et al. (2002) suggest that repeated exposure to interdisciplinary thought leads learners to develop more advanced epistemological beliefs as well as enhanced critical thinking and meta-cognitive skills and a greater understanding of the relations among different disciplinary perspectives. In practice, this calls for teacher education practices which are commensurate with such goals.

Key features of a course in Initial Teacher Education at Aberdeen University

As part of the post-graduate diploma in education course provided by the School of Education at the University of Aberdeen, students are given the option to attend an elective component designed to introduce interdisciplinary issues in science and society in such a way as to address the challenges outlined above. It is attended by circa 25 students – comprising both prospective primary and secondary teachers – and it is co-taught by four tutors respectively drawn from the natural and the social sciences.

The professional aspect of the course requires students to be assessed against the Standard for Initial Teacher Education (SITE). One of the questions we are addressing in our own teaching is that of being able to model citizenship in the learning settings offered by the course in order for students to be able to see specific aspects of SITE as being embedded in practice, rather than addressed in isolation. We also aim to bring the static and formalised knowledge that they may hold into dynamic contexts and processes of knowing, and give them the opportunity to build relationships and produce flexible, cognitive maps (Osberg and Biesta, 2008). The module is divided into six sessions of two hours each, spread over a period of 24 weeks and finished with formal peer assessed presentations. The course is rooted within an approach which aims at:

1. Promoting and encouraging the development of an 'educating community' within the class, where there will be no division between who knows and who doesn't, but many people with different competences, abilities and skills, all committed towards a shared goal. The implicit epistemology of this approach is that '*The truth resides in the very fact of the multiple viewpoints*' (Volk, 1998).
2. Activating a multiplicity of channels in interpersonal relations, from the cognitive to the emotional and promoting different forms of language communication – from the use of specialist terminology to the development of narrative abilities in the description of processes, the comparing of interpretations offered by different disciplines and the expression of creative visions and scenarios.

Strategies

In order to achieve points 1 and 2 many strategies may be implemented: moments in which the students are invited to reflect silently, the presentation of a cartoon to be commented on, small group activities, role-playing, for example. We always include a variety of situations which can provide space for experimentation and a certain degree of unpredictability within the course. However, open educational paths such as the one suggested here can be unsettling spaces to inhabit and this is particularly the case for a course which does not benefit from continuity (with the sessions distributed over 24 weeks). Each lesson needs to be designed as a self-contained unit, a state of affairs which puts the lecturers at a greater risk of wanting to 'close down' the process in favour of a summary or recap section which gives the security of having completed the session and given students something to take away with them.

To resist closure and continue to support students in their process of making connections, we make use of activities focussing on non-disciplinary features which can be used as instruments to interpret reality (as described in detail by Camino et al. 2009b).

- *Conceptual tools* can be used as connective elements between concepts apparently distant from each other, belonging to a reality determined not only by the subjects but also by the countless existing relations. For example, thinking about the concept of 'cell' we can reflect upon the cell membrane as a boundary acting at the same time as an element of continuous contact and inclusion – allowing exchanges with the surrounding context - and/or exclusion, determining the identity of the subject as opposed to what is outside.
- *The reflection on language* helps to focus on the features of the underlying epistemology: For example, talking about sustainability we can ask students to question themselves about 'who/what sustains whom/what?'

- *Being involved in first person*: each of us is both subject and object in sustainability science. Activities, such as role-plays, to deal with complex issues and conflict can be proposed to enact participatory processes of learning for the purpose of practice with various skills and self- reflection (Colucci-Gray, 2009).
- The connections between natural systems and the circumstances of our lives: for example, the actions we take every day and their consequences/interconnections with people and with socio-ecological transformations.
- Awareness of, and development of skills in, a variety of participatory decision making processes, such as those to be found in the Participatory Methods Toolkit (Slocum, 2003)

Some examples:

The glass globe activity originated from a cartoon proposed by Wackernagel and Ress (1996) shown below (Figure 1). Students were asked the question in the caption, thus engaging with the double notion of boundary as both separation and connection and raise awareness of the boundaries we put around things by means of language (i.e. labelling parts; drawing lines), geographical descriptions or mental images.

Figure 1. The glass globe. Picture taken from Wackernagel and Rees (1996).

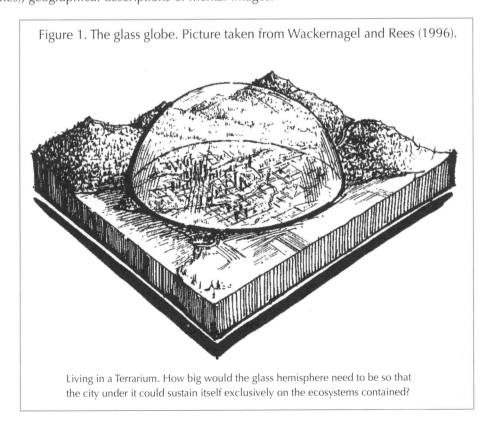

Living in a Terrarium. How big would the glass hemisphere need to be so that the city under it could sustain itself exclusively on the ecosystems contained?

Examples of students' answers include:
'To allow for indefinite survival the globe should be removed completely because any boundary would take the city to death (in more or less time)'.

'It has to be expanded until we reach equilibrium between Nature and mankind. The globe needs to include a variety of environments which are useful to the human species. A small world inside the world'.

'There should be a proportion, for example, 1/10, so for a x quantity of artificial/man made, we need 10 times the amount of nature in order to contain pollution…'

Asking questions of objects and pictures: the compass rose

A selection of everyday natural and man-made objects and pictures of various places were used to engage students with asking questions about the history of their production, use, elimination and so on. The development compass rose was given as an instrument for uncovering the connections between science, technology, culture and environment.

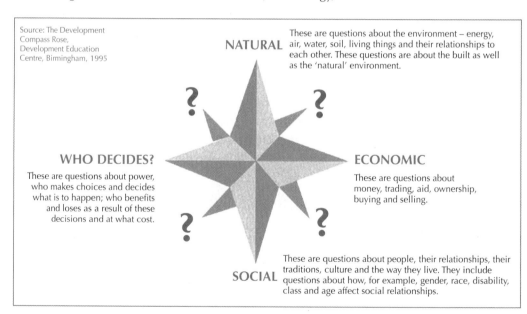

Source: The Development Compass Rose, Development Education Centre, Birmingham, 1995

NATURAL These are questions about the environment – energy, air, water, soil, living things and their relationships to each other. These questions are about the built as well as the 'natural' environment.

WHO DECIDES? These are questions about power, who makes choices and decides what is to happen; who benefits and loses as a result of these decisions and at what cost.

ECONOMIC These are questions about money, trading, aid, ownership, buying and selling.

SOCIAL These are questions about people, their relationships, their traditions, culture and the way they live. They include questions about how, for example, gender, race, disability, class and age affect social relationships.

Examples of students' comments at the end of the activity:
Uncovering complexity
'Seeing beyond the surface/object/photograph.'

'Made me really start thinking about the amount of human effect we have on the natural world, it goes much much deeper than I thought.'

Different places and environments and how issues relating to sustainability affect them.'

Working with the 'democratic classroom'

Everybody has different + a range of views depending on background, different questions arise.'

Difficult to formulate appropriate questions regarding sustainability. Conflicting interpretations within the group on what aspects may be relevant.'

Was useful to increase communication and use and respect everyone's point of view. '

Confronting limits

'It is difficult to determine what is right or wrong – there are so many grey areas'

'Challenged to think of man as part of nature rather than a separate force merely impacting on it. '

Conclusions

Working in an interdisciplinary fashion offers both opportunities and challenges. The main opportunity is that of mirroring the learning contexts anticipated by a framework of sustainability science and participatory democracy, yet drawing directly on the support provided by the new curricular framework for Scotland (Scottish Government, *Curriculum for Excellence*, 2009). The challenges include the difficulty of keeping track of 'what has been covered' in terms of curricular content in each discipline. Of necessity, there is an imbalance in the way each discipline is represented during the course, with areas that appear to be either to be dominant or overlooked. Another problem is the difficulty of locating the knowledge and understanding of the single individuals within a coherent framework. The science, citizenship, sustainability course is in fact a very small component of the programme. Next steps may involve gaining more knowledge of the potential areas of alignment between this course component as it stands and the overarching philosophy of the program that at the University of Aberdeen focuses closely on the theme of educational inclusion. There are many layers to this aim. Currently we have a means of assessing the group dimension and can gain an insight into the extent to which the participatory methodology has been embraced by the students. Students enjoy working in groups yet they are not always accustomed to open-ended, reflective activities concerned with their own reflection and learning.

Extending the opportunities for reflective writing and making a more explicit effort to draw on students' own disciplinary knowledge can be a means for enhancing participation and dialogue between disciplines. For example, proposing to look in depth at a specific topic which is non-disciplinary in nature (i.e. energy, food) can give the opportunity to see the different disciplines at work and how each one taps into a particular scale/level of the same natural reality.

There is also the need to encourage students to forge links with the assessment tasks they are required to undertake for the program in order to integrate the sustainability component within the main portfolio of professional learning. Developmental transfer (Engeström, 2004) across courses could be forged by adopting learning methodologies which are proposed elsewhere in the programme (e.g. de Bono's thinking hats) and integrating them into the specific topic of sustainability. This would also address students' ongoing, and understandable, preoccupation with acquiring specific 'techniques' for classroom practice. Investing more effort in deepening understanding of the epistemological and pedagogical basis of education for sustainability could model and eventually underpin more generic forms of educational practice. Deep and sustained dialogue between tutors who are interested in grappling with the wider aims and messages embedded in their own subjects can support natural and very feasible links between sustainability, citizenship and the core areas of the Initial Teacher Education curriculum.

We conclude by suggesting that, with the evolution of conscience and reflective thought, the relation that has always existed between natural systems and humanity can reach another level. This relationship can have a dialogical character, moving beyond both the static characterisation of early humanity as submissive to mysterious and often terrifying natural phenomena, often interpreted as signs forcing humans to undertake punitive actions (rites, purifications, etc), and the later characterisation of humanity as naively arrogant, believing itself capable of mastering a world that is perceived as being inert and shapeless. We feel that the current situation is an opportunity for developing a system of conscious knowledge derived from a view of humanity as being included in the natural systems, and at the same able to act from multiple perspectives. Education can contribute effectively by means of teaching and learning processes that are committed to promoting a complex view of socio-ecological systems and to valuing democratic and participatory approaches to problems; to perceiving ourselves as included in, rather than distinct from, natural systems; and to co-constructing our knowledge and identities at the same time.

References

Camino, E. and Dodman, M. (2009a) *Language and Science in Gray, D., Colucci-Gray, L. and Camino, E. (Eds) Science, Society and Sustainability* New York, Routledge).

Camino, E., Barbiero, G. And Marchetti, D. (2009b) Science Education for Sustainability: Teaching Learning Processes with Science Researchers and Trainee Teachers in Gray, D., Colucci-Gray, L. and Camino, E. (Eds) *Science, Society and Sustainability* (New York, Routledge).

Clark, W.C. (2007) Sustainability science: a room of its own. *Proceedings of the National Academy of Science*, 104 (6): 1737-8.

Colucci-Gray, L. (2009) Role-Play as a Tool for Learning and Participation in a Post-Normal Science Framework in Gray, D., Colucci-Gray, L. and Camino, E. (Eds) *Science, Society and Sustainability* (New York, Routledge).

Dupré, J. (1993) *The disorder of things* (Cambridge, MA, Harvard University Press).

Engeström, R. (2004) Workplace learning and developmental transfer. Online at: http://www.edu. helsinki.fi/activity/pages/research/transfer/ (accessed 20.12.2009).

Gallopin, G.C., Funtowicz, S., O'Connor, M and Ravetz, J. (2001). Science for the 21st century: from social contract to the scientific core, International Journal of Social Science, 168, 219-229.

Giampietro, M., Mayumi K., and Martinez-Alier J. (2000). Introduction to the Special Issues on Societal Metabolism: Blending New Insights from Complex System Thinking with Old Insights from Biophysical Analyses of the Economic Process, Population & Environment 22, 2, 97-108.

Harding, S. (2009) Gaia awareness: awareness of the animate qualities of the Earth, in: A. Stibbe (Ed) The handbook of sustainability literacy – skills for a changing world (Totnes, Green Books).

Harremoës, P. et al. (2001) *Late lessons from early warnings: the precautionary principle 1896-2000*, Environmental issue report n. 22 (Bruxelles, European environment Agency). Online at http://www.eea. europa.eu/publications/environmental_issue_ report_2001_22 (accessed on 20/12/09)

Ingold, T. (2007) Lines – *A brief history* (London, Routledge).

Ivanitskaya, L., Clark, D., Montgomery, G. and Primeau, R. (2002) Interdisciplinary Learning: Process and Outcomes. *Innovative Higher Education*, Vol. 27, No. 2, Winter 2002

Jickling, Bob (2001) 'Environmental Thought, the Language of Sustainability, and Digital Watches', *Environmental Education Research*, 7, 2, 167-180.

Keith, D.W., Parson E. & Morgan M.G. (2010) Research on global sun block needed now. *Nature*, 463, 28, 426-427.

Koerner, S. & Singleton, L. (2009) Revisiting Pandora's hope. Archaeologies of place and integrating difference into deliberative democracy, in D. Georgiou & G. Nash (Eds) *Archaeologies of place (Budapest*, Archaeologia).

Liberatore, A. & Funtowicz, S. (2003). Special Issue on Democratising Expertise, Expertising Democracy, *Science and Public Policy*, 3, 30.

Maturana, H. & Varela, F. (1992) *The Tree of Knowledge*, Shambala.

Olausson, U. (2009) Global warming global responsibility. Media frames of collective action and scientific certainty? *Public Understanding of Science*, 18, 421.

Osberg, D. and Biesta, G. (2008) The emergent curriculum: navigating a complex course between unguided learning and planned enculturation. *Journal of Curriculum Studies*, 40, 3, 313-328.

Reiss, M., Boulter, C. and Dale Tunnicliffe, S. (2007) Seeing the natural world: a tension between pupils' diverse conceptions as revealed by their visual representations and monolithic science lessons. *Visual communication*, 6 (1), 99-114.

Sarewitz, D. (2004) How science makes environmental controversies worse, Environmental Science & Policy 7, 385-403.

Scottish Government (2009) *A Curriculum for Excellence*. The curriculum Review Group. Victoria Quay, Edinburgh.

Sen, A. (1999) Democracy as a Universal Value, *Journal of Democracy* 3-17. Slocum, N. (2003) Participatory Methods Toolkit. A Practitioner's Manual. King Badouin Foundation and Flemish Institute for Science and Technology Assessment. www.kbs-frb.be

Sterling, S. (2009) Ecological Intelligence: viewing the world relationally, in: A. Stibbe (Ed) *The Handbook of sustainability literacy – skills for a changing world* (Totnes, Green Books).

UNESCO. (2005) Guidelines and recommendation for reorienting teacher education to address sustainability. *Education for Sustainable Development in Action Technical Paper*, no. 2. Paris: UNESCO. Online at http://unesdoc.unesco.org/images/0014/001433/143370E.pdf in 6 UN languages. (accessed on 20/12/09)

Vitousek, P.M., Mooney H.A., Lubchenco J. and Melillo J.M. (1997) Human Domination of Earth's Ecosystems, *Science*, 277, 5325, 494 – 499.

Volk ,T. (1998) *Gaia's body*. Toward a Physiology of Earth (New York, Springer Verlag).

Wackernagel, M. and Rees, W. (1996) *Our ecological footprint* (Gabriola Island B.C, New Society Publishers).

Wackernagel, M., Schulz, Niels B., Deumling, D., Callejas Linares, A., Jenkins, M., Kapos, V., Monfreda, C., Loh, J., Myers, N., Norgaard, R. and Randers, J. (2002) Tracking the ecological overshoot of the human economy, *Proceedings of the National Academy of Sciences*, 99, 14.

Wickson, F., Carew, A. L. and Russell, A. W. (2006) Transdisciplinary research: characteristics, quandaries and quality. *Futures*, 38, 1046-1059.

Zweers, W. (2000) *Participating with nature : outline for an ecologization of our world view*, Utrecht: International books.

4.10 Re-imagining Cultural Difference

John I'Anson, University of Stirling

Introduction

Within the United Kingdom, religious education is a significant subject area where global concerns and issues associated with religious and cultural difference might be engaged. For the past forty or so years, it has incorporated approaches to 'world religions' in recognition of the role that schools have in preparing young people for an increasingly pluralistic and multicultural context. Whilst differing in emphasis, each of the national contexts within the UK approaches the issue of cultural difference on the assumption that an impartial and fair account of other-than-western cultural traditions is possible. This 'rhetorics of neutrality' (I'Anson, 2010a,b) has been highly successful in stabilising how cultural difference is framed and the knowledge practices associated with this. This has become the officially mandated approach for all those wishing to teach this subject area in school and has become highly influential in many parts of the world including Australia, North America and New Zealand. Furthermore, a recent policy recommendation of the Committee of Ministers, (that comprises representatives of all 47 member states of the Council of Europe), is that all member states include the impartial study of religions within their schools (Council of Europe, 2008; Jackson, 2010).

The Rhetorics of Neutrality

The rhetorics of neutrality enables non-western cultures to have a presence within educational spaces, and encourages sympathetic attentiveness to the specific grammars of these cultures. However, the question of whose framings are deployed in this 'neutrality', and the material and socio-political effects of these framings, has been a particular focus of postcolonial critiques (e.g. Chakrabarty, 2000). So, for example, it is noticeable that many of the specific concepts that organise enquiry in religious education, such as myth, ritual, rite of passage, or experience, are all terms of western provenance and, as such, may be quite different from a culture's own distinctive idioms and assumptions (Long, 1986). Moreover, as Fitzgerald (2007) has argued, an organising concept such as 'religion' is itself quite alien to most cultural traditions, and even in the west, reveals diverse meanings through time. These critiques, along with related work in feminist and science and technology studies lead to a questioning of the various assumptions and practices that together constitute sense within the rhetorics of neutrality. The specific categories, framings and practices in and through which sense is made, perform a series of translations that surreptitiously re-frame and re-produce religious and cultural difference within recognisably western terms. The presumption that a given approach is 'neutral' deflects critical attention away from the work that is performed in the making of sense within a particular cultural context.

223

One way of surfacing the assumptions that inform claims to neutrality is to attend to the metaphors and images that inform sense-making practices. Such 'unthought elements' exercise a powerful influence upon how a given philosophical 'imaginary' (Le Doeuff, 1989) is played out in a culture's everyday notions of what passes as 'common sense'. Gatens (1996: viii) has summarised an imaginary as consisting in 'those images, symbols, metaphors and representations which help construct various forms of subjectivity'. In relation to western culture, what is immediately striking about an analysis of such metaphors, is the extent to which visual modalities are privileged. For example, it is commonplace to refer to 'world views' and 'ways of seeing' and this brings in its trail a number of characteristically western epistemological assumptions, which are far from neutral in their effects.

Sense-making practices

The Scottish philosopher John MacMurray (1969), in particular, was concerned with this visual orientation in western approaches to sense-making. In his *Gifford Lectures* he critiqued fixed standpoints that privilege a detached standpoint of observation over one based on a relational nexus. Such standpoints are premised upon a performative refusal to 'participat[e] in what [the observer] contemplates' (MacMurray, 1969: 17). This has far reaching consequences: in the first place, it installs a seer-seen binary at the beginning of the reflective process, with the primary term of the binary being privileged; secondly, it denies from the outset that the self is constituted in and through action. Its starting point, i therefore colonial, in that a fixed, disengaged standpoint is created from which judgment is given.

Such metaphors can be a hindrance to understanding cultures that foreground embodied forms of knowing, such as touch and hearing. Ingold and Kurttila's (2000) work amongst the Sami people in northernmost Finland, for example, is a case in point, where indigenous ways of inhabiting the land are more likely to acknowledge the feel of snow underfoot or the sound of reindeer bells and ice cracking. It is not accidental that visual metaphors predominate in western approaches to cultural difference, for these derive from the dominant Cartesian philosophical imaginary. This generates particular forms of 'common sense' which tend towards detachment and abstraction (Law and Mol, 2002). The concept of belief is one such abstraction. Although often assumed to be a universal category, the concept of belief is a distinctively western term that has developed within Christianity (Lopez, 1998).

A focus upon beliefs tends to orientate analysis to disembodied cognitive performances as the way to 'see' and understand the other, over a concern with embodied, action-based practices. Cognitions become the privileged mode of access to other cultures, and these are prioritised over a concern with material, affective, and political dimensions. *Apriori* beliefs, coupled with overarching categories such as 'world views' thus tend towards a two-dimensional plane of sense-making that empties events of their socio-material specificity.

Imaginaries

An analysis of some of the metaphors and terms that are routinely deployed suggests, therefore, that western 'common sense' – those assumptions that go without saying – is characterised by a visual 'world view' orientation that privileges detached judgment together with abstract and disembodied forms of sense-making. The rhetorics of neutrality can be seen as a product of this particular philosophical imaginary and this has far-reaching implications for how other cultural traditions are understood.

One example of this can be seen in Verran's (1998) work on the conflict between pastoralist and Aboriginal conceptions of land in Australia. Both cultures lay claim to the 'same' land in question, but each have very different ways of 'doing land'. The pastoralists, have a western imaginary of 'doing land', produced through quantification and measurement, with such properties being taken to inhere in the land whereas the Aboriginal imaginary is based upon reading the land in relation to significant events and kin relations. The pastoralists, on the one hand, could concede that Aboriginal ways of doing land involved different imaginaries. However, they did not see that *their* claim, through legal title, was made on the basis of another, albeit different and competing, imaginary.

A consequence of this kind of work is that *all* sense making – even as regards nature – can be seen as a complex amalgam of practices, apparatus, metaphors and concepts that diffract reality in particular ways (Barad, 2007, 2003).

Thus, questions about cultural imaginaries begin to take on renewed significance. In so far as the education project is 'under the sign of modernity' there is a tendency to recognise an imaginary in respect of other cultures, whilst remaining unaware that a distinctive imaginary informs characteristic western ways of making sense. Acknowledging cultural diversity has been possible since this is taken as a variety of *perspectives* on a singular underlying reality that is presumed independent of these particular characterisations. This would suggest that western common sense is oriented to epistemological *pluralism* to the extent that different perspectives are acknowledged, but does not extend to *multiplicity*, which acknowledges different enactments of the real. Such a recognition brings with it an acknowledgement that there is a politics involved in regard to whose conception of reality prevails (Mol, 1999, 2002).

A refusal to acknowledge this leads to the translation, and silencing, of one culture within the terms of another. A more equitable way of proceeding, therefore, demands that the specific terms of each culture's imaginary in an encounter be acknowledged. It is necessary, in other words, to attend to how each party constructs its sense of the real: 'doing ontics', in Verran's (2007) terms, is therefore vital if making sense of religious and cultural difference is to be ethical. For this to be possible, it is necessary to engage traditions of thought that can acknowledge the significance of different imaginaries.

Re-imagining cultural difference: Spinoza

Spinoza's (1985) writings offer an alternative philosophical tradition of enquiry to the Cartesian approach (Duffy, 2004, 2006). Indeed, they offer a rich resource for thinking and practicing differently, and have been engaged by a variety of contemporary theorists keen to explore other patterns of sense-making.

So what is characteristic of Spinoza's approach and how might this offer resources for thinking religious and cultural difference otherwise? Part of Spinoza's attractiveness stems from a style of philosophising that foregrounds power, desire, and imagination. And this concern with the imagination is, moreover, social, material and political in its implications. Spinoza's work offers a new means of expression for articulating a philosophy of difference (Deleuze, 1990, 1994) that is more attuned to the socio-material orientations characteristic of recent postcolonial, feminist and science and technology studies. It enables a complex reading, in which, according to Gatens and Lloyd (1999:1):

'Politics, ethics, epistemology, metaphysics and philosophy of mind are interwoven … and their interconnections raise possibilities of alternative and richer ways of conceptualising contemporary political and social issues.'

Another implication is that in place of the passions being an unwelcome distraction from the philosopher's proper task, as is traditionally the case (Le Doeuff, 1989), the imaginary and its associated affective domain becomes central to making sense at all. For according to Spinoza, the greater the power to be affected, the greater our power to act (Ethics, IV, 38). Such an understanding enables a style of thinking that can acknowledge religious and cultural difference as not being primarily philosophical in a restricted sense, but as deeply informed by the imagination and the passions (Gatens and Lloyd, 1999: 88).

Desiring Life

Spinoza's approach to the imaginary includes two distinctive concepts that are of particular relevance to making sense of religious and cultural difference. The first of these, *conatus*, is the 'striving by which each thing strives to persevere in its being' (*Ethics*, III, 7). However, as Butler (2006) argues, the self that strives to preserve itself is not necessarily a singular being, for it is in the complex interplay of relationships with others, that life is augmented or diminished. And so *conatus* is concerned with both individual and collective becomings and as such it is fundamentally affirmative. As Deleuze (1988:28) has commented:

'The ethics is necessarily an ethics of joy: only joy is worthwhile, joy remains, bringing us near to action, to the bliss of action.'

To this extent, as Anderson (2009) observes, there are affinities with the work of Jantzen (2004) who critiqued western imaginaries as being primarily oriented to violence and death. A concern with life itself and its present and future unfoldings is therefore one of the consequences of such a Spinozist orientation.

The second concept, ethology, is an approach to analysis that is radically open: the emphasis is upon trying not to foreclose in advance what may happen. In Deleuze's (1988: 125) words '…you do not know beforehand what a mind or body can do, in a given encounter, a given arrangement, a given combination' (cf. *Ethics*, III, 2). Since it is not known what kinds of sense-making will emerge in relation to a specific encounter with religious and cultural difference, this represents a fundamental departure from approaches to sense-making where the terms of understanding are given *apriori*. This involves a critique of forms of complexity reduction that produce closure in advance of engagement (I'Anson, 2010b), whilst in turn issuing in sense-making practices that are open to greater social contingency (Cope and I'Anson, 2003). In place of a grid of intelligibility that would effectively pre-order a given encounter, an ethological approach is concerned with relative speeds and intensities and how '[t]he speed or slowness of metabolisms, perceptions, actions, and reactions link together to constitute a particular individual in the world' (Deleuze, 1988: 125).

Some Pedagogical Implications: towards an uncommon sense

This chapter has critiqued existing approaches to religious and cultural difference which are informed by characteristic western common sense framings. These, it has been argued, are predicated upon a series of metaphors that produce perspectives upon diversity, but exclude alternative ways of doing the real that might disturb such a framing. The upshot of this is that a dominant western imaginary remains uncontested. An alternative philosophical lineage inaugurated by Spinoza has been traced in which different cultural imaginaries might be accorded their due significance.

One of the consequences of such a socio-material approach is that sense-making becomes empirical and experimental. There is a radical attention to how realities are assembled in a specific moment, occasion and place (Law, 2009). This attention to specific locations means that sense-making has to proceed on a case-by-case basis, since there is no 'reality in general' but only the ways in which realities are composed and understood in this place, at this time and with these effects.

This focus on performance brings about a further reorientation as regards the focus of pedagogical enquiry. In place of cultural difference being 'out there' – in some other space, which is simply and unproblematically represented – the focus of analysis becomes events and relations that take place 'here': both with respect to other persons and a variety of material practices that may include writing, drawing, engaging with digital images, narratives etc. (I'Anson, 2010b). Traditional teaching practices that are centred on the teacher and the board at the front of the class, or on a common textbook that all children must read, afford fewer opportunities for young peoples' 'coming into presence' as compared with other orderings associated with more open-ended forms of enquiry. The use of moving image and the multiple literacies that this may afford is one such example (Miller and I'Anson, 2009). Here, the use of moving image technologies refigures traditional orderings as young people seize opportunities to invent new scenarios, acknowledge different kinds of expertise whilst gaining insight into how sense is constructed through the bringing together of different modes in film making.

And so one way of exploring cultural difference is to enquire into the opportunities such practices and assemblages afford in regard to young peoples' 'coming into presence' and the new forms of expressiveness these permit. Here, there is a shift in emphasis away from world views to forms of *world making*. This is to explore how people, practices, artefacts and concepts are gathered together and ordered as a body within a particular locale, including that of a school. Such an exploration of cultural difference – as world making – also involves taking up different aspects of culture (in this instance a concept, in that, a material artefact) to see what difference this might make. This could, for example, involve exploring how a different concept re-frames an existing way of approaching a matter of concern, through placing this in a different temporal context, or through undoing familiar distinctions and orderings, and mapping the consequences of this. In each such instance the focus of attention is on the differentiating effects of engaging this difference: how, that is, reality is diffracted differently. To this extent, making sense proceeds not from a detached and neutral vantage point but from an engaged position in which 'palpating the real' might reveal how it is constructed and witnessed (May, 2005).

An orientation that engages imaginaries, in other words, gestures towards new pedagogies and forms of experimentation. In Thrift's (2004: 92) terms, it offers resources for a 'politics of imaginative generosity' within educational settings where different cultures connect. Such an approach lays claim to being educational in so far as this 'leads out' from what is known already rather than inadvertently re-inscribing existing assumptions about the real and its possibilities.

References

Anderson, P. S. (2009) 'The Urgent Wish…To Be More Life-Giving', in: E. L. Graham, ed., Grace Jantzen: Redeeming the Presence, Farnham and Burlington: Ashgate, pp. 41-53.

Barad, K. (2007) *Meeting the Universe Halfway: quantum physics and the entanglement of matter and meaning*, Durham and London: Duke University Press.

Barad, K. (2003) 'Posthumanist Performativity: Toward an Understanding of How Matter Comes to Matter', Signs: *Journal of Women in Culture and Society*, 28:3, pp. 801-831.

Butler, J. (2006) in: V. Kahn, N. Saccamano, and D. Coli, eds., *Politics and the Passions*, 1500-1850, Princeton and Oxford: Princeton University Press, pp. 111-130.

Chakrabarty, D. (2000). *Provincializing Europe: Postcolonial Thought and Historical Difference*. Princeton and Oxford: Princeton University Press.

Cope, P. and I'Anson, J. (2003) 'Forms of Exchange: education, economics and the neglect of social contingency', *British Journal of Educational Studies*, 51:3, pp. 219-232.

Council of Europe, (2008) 'Recommendation CM/Rec (2008)12 of the Committee of Ministers to member states on the dimension of religions and non-religious convictions within intercultural education'. Online at: http://tandis.odihr.pl/documents/hre-compendium/CD%20SECT%201%20laws/PARTNERS%20RESOURCES/CoE%20CMRec%202008%2012%20ENG.pdf (accessed 22/4/10).

Deleuze, G. (1994) *Difference and Repetition*, E. trans., P. Patton, London and New York: Continuum.

Deleuze, G. (1990) *Expressionism in Philosophy: Spinoza*, E. trans., M. Joughin, New York: Zone Books.

Deleuze, G. (1988) Spinoza: Practical Philosophy, E. trans, R. Hurley, San Francisco: City Light Books.

Duffy, S. (2004) 'The Logic of Expression in Deleuze'a *Expressionism in Philosophy: Spinoza: A Strategy of Engagement'*, International Journal of Philosophical Studies, 12:1, pp. 47-80.

Duffy, S. (2006) The Logic of Expression: Quality, *Quantity and Intensity in Spinoza, Hegel and Deleuze*, Aldershot and Burlington: Ashgate.

Fitzgerald, T. (2007) 'Encompassing Religion, privatized religions and the invention of modern politics', in: T. Fitzgerald, ed., *Religion and the Secular: Historical and Colonial Formations*, London and Oakville: Equinox, pp. 211-240.

Gatens, M. (1996) *Imaginary Bodies: Ethics, Power and Corporeality*, London and New York: Routledge.

Gatens, M. and Lloyd, G. (1999) *Collective Imaginings: Spinoza, Past and Present*, London and New York: Routledge.

L'Anson, J. (2010a) 'RE: Pedagogy – after neutrality?', *British Journal of Religious Education*, 32:2 pp. 105-118.

L'Anson, J. (2010b) 'After a Rhetorics of Neutrality: complexity reduction and cultural difference, in: D.C. Osberg and G.J.J. Biesta, eds., *Complexity Theory and the Politics of Education*, Sense, pp. 126-138.

Ingold, T. and Kurttila, T. (2000) 'Perceiving the Environment in Finnish Lapland', *Body and Society*, 6:3-4, pp. 183-196.

Jackson, R. (2010) 'Religious Diversity and Education for Democratic Citizenship: The Contribution of the Council of Europe', in: K. Engebretson, M. de Souza, G. Durka, and L. Gearon (Eds.) *International Handbook of Inter-religious Education, Volume 4: Religion, Citizenship and Human Rights* (Dordrecht, the Netherlands:Springer Academic Publishers).

Jantzen, G. (2004) *Foundations of Violence: Death and the Displacement of Beauty*, vol 1, London and New York: Routledge.

Law, J. (2009) 'Collateral Realities', version of 29 December 2009. Online at http://www.heterogeneities.net/publications/Law2009CollateralRealities.pdf (accessed 30/12/2009)

Law, J. and Mol, A. (2002) *Complexities: Social Studies of Knowledge Practices*, Durham: Duke University Press.

Le Doeuff, M. (1989) *The Philosophical Imaginary*, E. trans. C. Gordon, London: Athlone Press.

Long, C. H. (1986) *Significations: Signs, Symbols and Images in the Interpretation of Religion*, Philadelphia: Fortress Press.

Lopez, Jnr., D. S. (1998) 'Belief' in: M.C. Taylor, ed., *Critical Terms for Religious Studies*, Chicago and London: The University of Chicago Press, pp. 21-35.

MacMurray, J. (1969) *Persons in Relation*, London: Faber and Faber.

May, T. (2005) *Gilles Deleuze: An Introduction, Cambridge:* Cambridge University Press.

Miller, K. and I'Anson, J. (2009) 'Moving Image Technologies in and out of the Classroom', Paper given at ESRC *Centre for Research on Socio-Cultural Change*, University of Manchester, September 2009.

Mol, A.-M. (2002) T*he Body Multiple: Ontology in Medical Practice*, Durham, NC and London: Duke University Press.

Mol, A.-M. (1999) 'Ontological politics. A Word and Some Questions', in: J. Law and J. Hassard, eds. *Actor Network Theory and After*, Oxford: Blackwell, pp. 74-89.

Spinoza, B. (1985) *Complete Works*, E. trans, E. Curley, Princeton, NJ: Princeton University Press.

Thrift, N. (2004) 'Summoning Life', in: Cloke, P., Crang, P. Goodwin, M, eds., *Envisioning Human Geographies*, pp. 81-103.

Verran, H. (2007). Software for Educating Aboriginal Children about Place. In *Education and Technology: Critical Perspectives and Possible Futures*, eds. D. W. Kritt and L. T. Winegar, 101-124. Lanham, MD: Lexington Books. Online at: http://www.cdu.edu.au/centres/ik/pdf/HRV_for_Kritt_WinegarFINAL4-06.pdf.

Verran, H. (1998) Re-imagining land ownership in Australia, *Postcolonial Studies*, 1:2, pp. 237-254.

REFLECTING
ON THE GLOBAL

5. Conclusion

The Editors

DRAWING TOGETHER CONCLUSIONS from the diversity of material in a book such as this presents editors with something of a challenge. But the very diversity of the content delivers the key message that there is no single approach that can adequately attend to the complexity of our changing world. The overriding need is for a continued recognition of and engagement with the challenge so that a shared understanding of the educational and social intentions behind the concepts of global citizenship and sustainable development is achieved.

The immediate context of this volume is Scotland, but we have aimed to reveal this in an open way, relevant beyond the confines of one small education system. Teacher educators and others from different jurisdictions reading this will no doubt have felt a number of wry moments of recognition. Perennial issues highlighted in Scotland are being addressed elsewhere, as the preface indicates. That is not to say that everyone's experiences are the same. Notably, there are no educational voices in this volume from the developing world – an issue that needs to be addressed. Indeed, some of the concerns expressed here might appear to lack a sense of perspective. In contexts where the supply of teachers struggles to keep pace with the attrition rate through deaths associated with HIV/AIDS (UNESCO, 2008), our preoccupations may appear somewhat trivial. Nonetheless, it is precisely such perceptual disconnects that present a powerful rationale for global learning to be a normal component of education. They highlight a moral imperative to support the diffusion of global learning across teacher education in Scotland and elsewhere. Such stark inequities are what drives Education for Global Citizenship and Sustainable Development (GCSD).

Key Themes

In the following pages a number of issues and questions that have emerged from the contributions to this volume are identified. These are presented in terms of four key themes:

- Transformation
- Values and ethics
- Pedagogy and curriculum
- Interconnectedness.

Transformation

From the foreword to the conclusion of this volume, the need for a re-examination of how and what we teach is made clear. We can return to McKeown and Hopkins' assertion, in the Preface, that our current knowledge bases do not include the solutions for living more sustainably and equitably on this planet. As they contend, the next generation will have to learn their way to such a future and, therefore, the processes of education must be transformed. New ways of conceptualising the learning and teaching process at all levels are needed (Priestley et al, Shah and Brown, McLaren, Boyd, I 'Anson) and new ways of organising teaching are possible (Frame, Wrigley, Higgins, Curtis, Colucci-Gray). The questioning of how and what we teach is happening (Souter, McLaren, Ross, I'Anson), and a shift in the frames of reference we use when constructing knowledge is being attempted (Colucci-Gray et al., I'Anson). In Scotland, the new *Curriculum for Excellence* includes the transformative suggestion that learning goals should be negotiated between teacher and learner rather than exclusively determined by the state. This clearly demands a very different kind of teacher from the one who is required to deliver a prescriptive curriculum.

An overarching issue for global learning, however, relates to society. Transformation is required in order that the nature of the learning and teaching process more adequately represents the nature of the society we live in and more adequately prepares teachers and learners for the uncertainties and challenges of the future.

Values and ethics

Although education is essentially a matter of values, it is remarkable to note the limited extent to which specific values have been made explicit as the foundation on which learning and teaching should be based. A major challenge for initial teacher education is persuading students to unpick the values they bring to teaching, and to recognise education's value-laden structure (Priestley et al., Colucci-Gray). For the first time in Scottish education, a formal set of underpinning values for the curriculum have been enunciated; wisdom, justice, compassion and integrity (taken from the Mace of the Scottish Parliament). If these values are to offer something more than a convenient and non-controversial rhetorical glue for the curriculum, they have to be expressed and enacted in meaningful ways (Frame, McLaren, Boyd, Wrigley, Curtis). Political enthusiasm for education for global citizenship and sustainability may derive from concerns for social order and compliance, it may derive from economic motives, but the educational and ethical imperative must surely be to understand citizenship as a value-driven, active and dynamic process (Priestly et al.) which encourages critical reflection upon our lives and our societies. An important feature of effective EGCSD is engagement with controversial issues (Shah and Brown, Humes). This demands recognition of the conflicting value positions that make consideration of such issues necessary. The imperative (or not) for actions to stem from such critical reflection is another theme for development.

Pedagogy and curriculum

The introduction of changes to the curriculum in Scotland has generated heated debate, not least about the nature of curriculum and pedagogy. The proposed move from a largely subject-based structure to one in which there is much more scope for 'generative topics', cross-disciplinary planning and a premium given to 'relevance' (Boyd) has sparked heated debate (Priestley et al, Souter, Ross). Moving teachers and teacher educators from the putative certainties of well recognised subjects to something less tidy is challenging (Frame, Boyd, Ross), and while the detail of what should be taught is the focus of much of the debate the real need is to look at the what and the how in a more integrated manner (Curtis, Frame, Wrigley, Colucci-Gray).

Providing legitimacy to EGCSD in a curriculum reshaped in this way requires a strong epistemological and pedagogical base (Priestly et al), and much remains to be done on that front. Underlying the change is a fundamental move from education as transmission of a set curriculum to education as a process that gives rise to responsive and reflective practices among teachers, students, pupils, parents and communities (McNaughton, Dunn et al, Collins et al and King). Active learning (Frame, Wrigley, Curtis) is a performative activity (I'Anson) where learners demonstrate and explore their understandings and thus develop their experience. To paraphrase Dewey, education should not be a preparation for life, it should be life itself.

Throughout this volume references are made to the central importance of pedagogy as the means by which global learning can be made real to student teachers (Frame, Wrigley, Higgins, Curtis). But there is no global without the local (Curtis) and technology also has a role to play (Collins et al) as do organisational structures (Hamilton, Frame) and personal habits (Higgins). Real world outcomes (Wrigley) and controversial issues (Shah, Hume) bring the global to life. We need to draw on educators' expertise in these areas too, and develop research approaches that explore their impact. Importantly, effective and reliable means of assessing the effects of EGCSD must be developed.

Interconnectedness

This final theme recognises the contention that there is a powerful need to ensure a greater degree of connectedness across the school learning experience (Frame, Fenwick and Munro, Souter, Higgins, Colucci-Gray et al). This need is seen not only in terms of linkages and connections between and among subjects, but also in terms of connecting to a greater extent than before with the issues and events that make up our current experience. The connections between ever greater globalised economic activity and climate change and biodiversity loss as well as the disconnect between the drive for development and the existing global social and economic inequities require attention. The acceptance of and engagement with multiple perspectives (Colucci Gray et al, I'Anson) is identified as a potentially helpful way forward, as is an interrogation of the western scientific/technological model (Souter, Colucci-Gray et al). Beyond education, these issues are being engaged with and are affecting the development of subject disciplines. Formal education too often seems hermetically sealed within subject departments and classrooms but effective EGCSD needs to be understood in broader, less constrained circumstances with social and informal contexts providing opportunities for significant learning to occur (Britton and Blee) and for learners to function as 'communities of enquiry' (Boyd).

Reflections

The purpose of this volume was not to produce a template for EGCSD in initial teacher education. The aim was to provide an opportunity to develop work that can further our understanding of a set of issues that are undeniably increasing in their impact on and importance to all of us. Within each of the contributions there is an implicit or explicit recognition of the moral imperative that rests on educators. While many of the chapters place emphasis on praxis, it is perhaps worth remembering that Aristotle saw praxis as not just about the practical aspects of the craft of teaching, but as a moral disposition to act appropriately and justly in order to realise ethical values and goals. That important distinction would seem particularly apposite in the context of EGCSD which is above all else a moral endeavour. Both the practice and the disposition of the teacher are critical attributes of pedagogy. Neither offers much of educational significance without the other. We should, however, be optimistic. As the Preface states; 'every educator we know hopes that what they teach and how they teach it will lead to a better future. Given a choice between educating for a more sustainable world (e.g. characterized by social, environmental, and economic well-being) or for a less sustainable world (i.e. a place of social inequity, degraded environment, and large economic disparity) teachers choose the brighter future.'

Practical Steps for the Future

This book argues that EGCSD is an aspect of learning about which all teachers regardless of their subject qualifications must feel confident in teaching. As a relatively new field in ITE, there is a considerable research and development agenda to be addressed. It seems to the editors of this volume that the priorities for supporting the understanding and articulation of the global dimension in ITE should include:

• continued development of the conceptualisation of EGCSD and the rationale for its inclusion in ITE
• identification of teacher educator and teacher competencies aligned with the principles of EGCSD

- increased support for collaborative working practices within and across ITE and in partnership with EGCSD stakeholders outwith ITE
- capacity building within the ITE sector for devising and teaching EGCSD across the curriculum
- further research into specific aspects of pedagogy linked to EGCSD, such as participatory methods, contextualised learning, systems thinking and critical skills development, and their assessment
- improved linkages between EGCSD and other ITE agendas, particularly around Inclusion (Social Justice), Citizenship (Participation), Information Literacy (Critical Thinking) and Health and Wellbeing.
- analysis and development of research into attitudes to, and perceptions of, EGCSD
- addressing the need to challenge students to recognise the centrality of values and attitudes in the enterprise of education.

There is a lot to be addressed, but also a lot to be gained. As Jerome Bruner proposes Education must be not only a transmission of culture but also a provider of alternative views of the world and a strengthener of skills to explore them.'

References

UNESCO. 2008. Booklet 1: *Overview. Good Policy and Practice in HIV & AIDS and Education* (booklet series). Paris: UNESCO.

Notes on Contributors

Ethel Anderson is a lecturer at the University of Strathclyde, contributing to both the BEd (Honours) and the PGDE (Primary) course modules, one of which is Sustainable Development Education. She was previously a primary school class teacher, senior/principal teacher and acting headteacher.

Ian Barr is an educational consultant specialising on issues relating to culture, international development, the arts, and education and has held senior positions within the Scottish education system. Ian has an extensive consultancy network in Scotland, the UK and internationally and is a founder member of the European Educational Design Group, an international partnership with a particular focus on educational innovation.

Professor Gert Biesta is Professor of Education at the Institute of Education, University of Stirling, and Visiting Professor for Education and Democratic Citizenship at Örebro University and Mälardalen University, Sweden. He conducts theoretical and empirical research and is particularly interested in the relationships between education, democracy and democratisation.

Harry Blee is Head of Department of Curriculum Studies at the University of Glasgow. Currently Senior Lecturer in Modern Studies, he is also Director of the Global Citizenship Unit. He co-edited, with Michael Peters and Alan Britton, Global Citizenship Education: Philosophy, Pedagogy and Practice. Rotterdam,Sense Publishers, 2008.

Alan Britton is Deputy Director of the Education for Global Citizenship Unit at the University of Glasgow. He was a secondary modern studies and French Teacher before becoming the first head of the Education Service at the Scottish Parliament in 1999 and Stevenson Lecturer in Citizenship at the University of Glasgow in 2001. He has been involved in numerous research projects, funded by the Scottish and UK Governments, the European Commission and a range of NGOs.

Professor Brian Boyd is Emeritus Professor in Education at the University of Strathclyde where, until 2008, he taught and carried out research into a range of issues including learning and teaching. He was Chair of IDEAS 2005-2008. Brian has been a teacher, principal teacher, assistant headteacher and headteacher (of 2 comprehensive schools). He has been involved in Thinking Skills developments since the early 1990's.

Dr Jane Brown, Senior Research Fellow, Moray House School of Education, University of Edinburgh, is a researcher of longstanding experience. She worked on Scotland's Applied Educational Research Scheme and has been engaged in capacity building activities in education for the past 10 years. She has a particular interest in education for citizenship and the emerging field of school surveillance.

Kate Brown is Schools Programme Manager at the Development Education Association (DEA). She is a trained citizenship teacher, and has taught citizenship and humanities subjects in secondary schools in the UK and abroad. She has worked as an educational consultant for national and international NGOs, and is the author of several teaching guides.

Robert Collins is a lecturer in the Faculty of Education at the University of Strathclyde, with responsibility for managing undergraduate and postgraduate core primary science modules. He has published in various books and journals, and has recently delivered findings from his research on the use of cognitive approaches regarding the development of ITE programmes at national conferences across the UK.

Dr. Laura Colucci-Gray is a lecturer in science and sustainability education at the University of Aberdeen. With a background in natural sciences and she has taught science in ITE in Italy and in the UK. Her research focuses on the use of interactive and participatory learning methodologies, using action-research, to promote understanding of sustainability issues and introduce students to the framework of a sustainability science. She collaborates with the Centre for Interdisciplinary Research on Sustainability at the University of Turin and has authored a number of books and articles.

Elizabeth Curtis teaches social studies to primary education students at the University of Aberdeen. Her background is in archaeology and she has worked in an urban environmental education centre, following her interest in how people make sense of place and time. She has developed open-ended fieldwork designed to enable students to navigate the curriculum and learn first-hand about collaborative learning.

Brenda Dunn is a lecturer at the University of Dundee, involved in TQ (FE), Early Childhood Studies and pre-service teaching with PGCE. She is currently leading the development of the new online Childhood Practice programme as Programme Director and has research interests related to improving the isolation experienced by many distance-learning students and embedding Curriculum for Excellence into the early years curriculum

Ashley Fenwick is a lecturer at the Institute of Education, University of Stirling. She taught geography in Scottish secondary schools for eleven years before working as Geography Co-ordinator within Initial Teacher Education at the University of Strathclyde. Her research interests include early professional learning, beginning teachers, education for sustainable development and curriculum change. She is currently completing her doctorate which will examine the place of outdoor learning within the formal secondary school curriculum.

Barbara Frame is Programme Director for B.Ed (Hons) Primary at the Moray House School of Education, University of Edinburgh. She joined Moray House College as a lecturer, then senior lecturer in language studies, with responsibility for organising courses for both PGDE and B.Ed (Hons) Primary programmes. Barbara has maintained her enthusiasm for thematic work using 'Storyline', running a successful option course for her students and contributing to international conferences and publications. She has also contributed to research on gender and achievement.

Dr. Christine Fraser lectures in science education in the School of Education at the University of Aberdeen. Her background in microbiology, experience in scientific publishing and interest in education led her to specialise in communicating science to primary school children, and their teachers. Her current research interests explore teachers' engagement with topical science issues and the use of video as a tool for professional development.

Dr Donald Gray is a senior lecturer in the School of Education at the University of Aberdeen. He worked at the Scottish Council for Research in Education, at Humboldt University, Berlin and the University of Strathclyde prior to joining Aberdeen. He is co-editor, along with Laura Colucci-Gray and Elena Camino of Science, Society and Sustainability: Education and Empowerment for an Uncertain World.

Tom Hamilton is Director of Educational Policy at GTC Scotland. Qualified in both Primary and Secondary teaching, he also spent a number of years in teacher education and was Associate Dean of the University of Paisley's School of Education before joining the Council. His current post involves him in developing, promoting and implementing the Council's educational policies.

Professor Peter Higgins holds a personal chair in outdoor and environmental education at the Moray House School of Education, University of Edinburgh. He has published extensively and teaches outdoor, environmental and sustainability education on the University's MSc programmes. He is a member of national and international panels and advisory groups, has held advisory positions with the UK and Scottish Governments, and is a national representative on the UNESCO programme to 'Reorient Teacher Education Towards Sustainable Futures'.

Professor Charles Hopkins holds a UNESCO Chair on Reorienting Teacher Education to Address Sustainability at York University in Canada. Associated with this Chair is an international network of more than 200 teacher-education institutions in 70 countries collaboratively working to incorporate education for sustainable development into teacher education programmes. During his career Charles was a teacher, principal, regional superintendent, and superintendent of curriculum with the Toronto Board of Education. Charles is also a teacher educator and teaches graduate level classes in education for sustainable development.

Dr Walter Humes is Research Professor in Education at the University of the West of Scotland. He has previously held Professorships at the universities of Strathclyde and Aberdeen. His publications include work on teacher education, educational leadership and management, history of education and policy studies. He is co-editor (with Professor Tom Bryce) of Scottish Education, a 1000-page text on all sectors of the Scottish educational system. He writes a regular polemical column for The Times Educational Supplement Scotland and is a frequent contributor to the online journal Scottish Review.

Dr John I'Anson is a lecturer in education at the Institute of Education, University of Stirling and a member of the ITE programme and the proPEL initiative. His research interests include religious and cultural difference, socio-material imaginaries, professional ethics, and creative and cultural industries. He is Chair of the Research Ethics Committee and Co-Convenor of the Research in Children's Rights Network, European Conference on Educational Research.

Betsy King is Education Policy Officer for WWF Scotland based in Dunkeld, Perthshire. She has a long standing commitment to Learning for Sustainability as a geography teacher, at the Peak National Park Centre, for the University of Papua New Guinea and for a number of NGOs in the UK. She is a member of the IDEAS 'Taking a Global Approach to Initial Teacher Education' initiative Steering Group.

Dr Greg Mannion is a senior lecturer at the Institute of Education, University of Stirling. Greg has taught in primary schools and provided environmental education CPD for teachers. His doctorate focused on pupils' participation in changing outdoor places and his research has sustained a focus on how practice, learning, place and processes of identification and subjectification interrelate.

Dr Rosalyn McKeown is Secretariat to the UNESCO Chair on Reorienting Teacher Education to Address Sustainability and the associated International Network of teacher education institutions. She is a former teacher educator, professor, and secondary school teacher. She has published numerous articles and she is the primary author of the internationally popular Education for Sustainable Development Toolkit.

Susan V. McLaren, is a senior lecturer at Moray House School of Education, University of Edinburgh, specialising in design and technology (D&T) education. She is involved in curriculum development, design of support materials and research related to the development of principles, practice and values in D&T. Prior to University of Edinburgh, Susan taught at the University of Strathclyde, and in secondary and middle schools. She was also an Urban Studies Officer with Newcastle Architecture.

Dr Marie Jeanne McNaughton is a senior lecturer in the Department of Childhood and Primary Studies at the University of Strathclyde. Her main teaching and research interests are in pedagogy, sustainable development and global citizenship education, educational drama, and story as a way of learning. She has published a number of papers and articles, and has presented her work at national and international conferences.

Dr. David Miller initially trained as a primary teacher and has worked in teacher education since 1992. His responsibilities at the University of Dundee include pre-service teaching with B.Ed. and PGDE students, together with inter-disciplinary work with students from other programmes. His research interests relate to all aspects of classroom practice which impinge upon personal, social and emotional development. He leads the Dundee University Pedagogy Research Group, whose members have contributed to the publications in this volume: Teresa Moran, Peter Wakefield, Gwen Boswell, Erika Cunningham, Brenda Dunn, Paola Fallone, Brenda Keatch, Mary Knight and Loretta Mulholland.

Bob Munro was originally a geographer, teaching in secondary schools and in teacher training institutions. His research at the University of Strathclyde has concerned the educational applications of ICT, particularly with relevance to geography and history.

Moira Paterson is a lecturer in the Department of Childhood and Primary Studies at the University of Strathclyde. She teaches on post graduate and undergraduate courses and has particular interests in social studies, sciences and technologies.

Dr Mark Priestley is a senior lecturer at the Institute of Education, University of Stirling. His research interests lie in the school curriculum and the issue of curriculum change. He is also interested in the application of realist social theory to address practical issues in schooling. He was a secondary teacher, and taught history, geography, humanities and social studies in England and New Zealand. He is currently the Editor of the Scottish Educational Review.

Dr Hamish Ross is a lecturer in the Department of Curriculum Research and Development, Moray House School of Education, University of Edinburgh. His research interests are in curriculum policy and theory in the areas of outdoor learning, the environment, sustainability, citizenship and social studies.

Hetan Shah is Chief Executive of DEA (Development Education Association, England). He was previously policy director at the pressure group Compass, director of the New Economics programme at the think-tank nef (the new economics foundation) and a director of the Social Enterprise Partnership.

Jill Shimi was born in Dundee and is a Depute Lieutenant of the city. She was leader of Dundee City Council from 2003 to 2007. She is currently a lecturer at the University of Dundee working in Childhood Practice and Initial Teacher Education.

Nicky Souter is a senior lecturer at the University of Strathclyde, a Fellow of the Society of Biology and a chartered science teacher. He has many years of experience in teacher education as a secondary teacher, administrator, author, and researcher. His teaching and research has focused on biology and science pedagogical practice and he has taught on health education/ PSE programmes, and led electives on sustainable development education.

Dr. Tanya Wisely is the Coordinator of the IDEAS 'Taking a Global Approach to Initial Teacher Education' project. Her doctorate and research background are in developmental psychology. She also qualified and worked as a primary teacher and was employed by Glasgow City Council to support Eco-Schools work in secondary schools prior to taking up her current post.

Terry Wrigley recently retired from the University of Edinburgh as senior lecturer in Education. His teaching, research and writing span and connect diverse fields of interest: school development, pedagogy, curriculum reform, social justice and education for citizenship. He edits the journal Improving Schools and his publications include three books: *The Power to Learn* (2000), *Schools of Hope* (2003) and *Another School is Possible* (2006).